Motorbooks International Illustrated Bi

Illustrated
PLYMOUTH & DESOTO
BUYER'S ★ GUIDE™

Jim Benjaminson

First published in 1996 by Motorbooks International Publishers & Wholesalers, 729 Prospect Avenue, PO Box 1, Osceola, WI 54020-0001 USA

Motorbooks International books are also available at discounts in bulk quantity for industrial or sales-promotional use. For details write to Special Sales Manager at the Publisher's address

Library of Congress Cataloging-in-Publication Data

Benjaminson, Jim,
    Illustrated Plymouth & DeSoto buyer's guide / Jim Benjaminson.
       p. cm. -- (Motorbooks International illustrated buyer's guide series)
    Includes index.
    ISBN 0-7603-0107 (pbk. : alk. paper)
    1. Plymouth automoblie--Purchasing. 2. Plymouth automobile-Collectors and collecting. 3. DeSoto automobile--Purchasing.4. DeSoto automobile--Collectors and collecting. I. Title. II. Series.
TL 215.P65B43   1996
629.222--dc20   96-35797

On the front cover: Two cars that epitomize power and innovation. The 1958 Plymouth Fury, owned by Bill Craffey, symbolizes the company's early years of manufacturing factory hot rods. Jim and Paula Lightfoot's 1934 DeSoto Airflow defines what automotive streamlining is all about. *David Gooley*

On the back cover: A pair of beautiful muscle cars: Pete Maccarone's 1968 Plymouth GTX and Brent Walker's 1959 DeSoto Adventurer.

Printed and bound in the United States of America

Contents

Acknowledgments

There were several individuals that literally "came to my rescue" in preparing this book. First and foremost of these was Lanny Knutson. Lanny followed in my footsteps as editor of the *Plymouth Bulletin*, a position he has more than adequately filled for the past 10 years. His work on the *Plymouth Bulletin* has been rewarded by receiving the "Golden Quill" Award on eight consecutive occasions. On rather short notice, Lanny wrote the text covering the full-size Plymouths from 1969 through 1974 in addition to the Valiant's and Barracuda's for this Buyers Guide. Lanny's photos also appear throughout the book.

As an oft-overlooked orphan make, members of the National DeSoto Club were more than happy to help in the search for photos to illustrate the book. John Gnorski and D. David Duricy, Jr., co-editors of *DeSoto Adventures*, along with Greg Walters, provided many of the photos; other photos were loaned by individual members of the organization. Richard Bowman, president of the WPC Club and himself owner of a '29 DeSoto, dug into that group's archives for photos. Likewise, members of the Plymouth Owners Club also loaned photos of their cars. My longtime friend, Alvin Janzen, kindly loaned me his collection of DeSoto sales catalogs for use as reference.

Last, but certainly not least, was the cooperation of Mitch Frumkin and Frank Peiler of *Collectible Automobile* magazine in loaning photos from their library. To each and everyone involved in this project, thank you.

Jim Benjaminson
May 1996

Introduction

When Motorbooks International asked me to write a Buyer's Guide that includes both Plymouth and DeSoto, I accepted the assignment with some trepidation. Plymouth would be easy, as its been the subject of my research for some 30 years. My area of "expertise" lies mostly with the early cars, and they asked me to include Plymouth through model year 1996. Perhaps most significant was their decision to include DeSoto, on which I had done little research. To combine the two marques was a logical choice. Plymouth and DeSoto shared much of their early heritage, both being introduced in 1928 as 1929 models, and both for a time shared the same production facilities to the point where a lot of the cars major components were interchangeable. Then they went their separate ways. DeSoto's path would lead it to oblivion, a point many would argue was the path Plymouth was also headed in recent years.

Neither marque has proven to be a "high dollar" collector car; both fall into the category of limited market appeal, but that is an appeal that makes both Plymouth and DeSoto an affordable alternative to the old-car enthusiast on a limited budget. Restoring either make is a challenge. Unlike Ford or Chevrolet, where cars can literally be built using a telephone and credit card, restoration parts for both Plymouth and DeSoto are hard to come buy. Mechanical parts are no problem, as Chrysler's penchant for interchangeability and longevity have provided today's collectors with an abundance of these parts. It is items such as body panels, interior fabrics, trim, and accessories that can drive one to distraction in restoring these cars. The result can be a car with more invested in it than may be realized upon sale of the car.

Of course, certain models do, and will, command premium prices. Included in this list are early open cars, coupes of the 1933-34 era which have proven to be so popular with the hot rod crowd, and muscle cars of the late 1950s and early 1960s. It is these later-cars that have generated most of the "hobby press" where both marques are concerned, yet it is these cars that were built in the lowest of production numbers.

Output of the Plymouth Fury between 1956 and 1958 amounted to no more than 17,226 cars, the Golden Adventurer DeSotos built between 1956 and 1959 amounted to fewer than 4,100 units, while the fabled Hemi-powered Plymouth came to around 5,500 units.

Plymouth's bread-and-butter car was the plain-Jane four-door sedan and it is these cars that have survived in the greatest numbers, ditto for DeSoto. Early models, such as the wood-body station wagon, are rare as hen's teeth but other models, even rarer, such as the seven-passenger sedan and limousine have drawn little hobby interest. Only in recent years has the DeSoto Suburban become a genuine collectible.

In preparing this Buyer's Guide, no production figure lists have been included as these have been published in other Motorbooks reference books and are readily available. In rating these cars as to their collectibility, a five-star rating has been employed.

Five stars indicate a car that has established a solid collector following, those cars that will bring top dollar. Four-star ratings include more-common but still-desirable body types. Cars with one, two, or three stars indicate a decreasing collector value. This is not meant to indicate these are not good cars, but reflect the fact these cars are more commonly available. It should also be noted that *any* car, regardless of body type, will be worth more if it is in good to excellent original condition. The typical "little old lady" '47 Plymouth four-door sedan that looks as if it just rolled off the showroom floor will command a higher price than a ratty business coupe, for instance.

One word of caution to the potential collector seeking an early Chrysler product: Interchangeability was a by-word at Chrysler Corporation. It was a common practice for newer engines, or engines from another Chrysler line, to be swapped into the engine bay of an older Chrysler product. Originality brings the highest dollar in collector markets, so make sure you know what you are buying as it's not uncommon to find a '53 Plymouth six residing under the hood of that '36 Plymouth coupe.

Likewise the Chrysler and DeSoto six, although larger in overall physical dimensions, was a common swap both in Plymouth and DeSotos. Plymouth never built a Hemi-powered car prior to the Street Hemi of 1966, but these engines would fit and they were swapped into these cars by early racers.

A similar word of caution about the later Street Hemi cars. The Street Hemi was a special car from the bottom up. These cars have in recent years brought astronomical prices but it is strictly "buyer beware." Know what you are buying before writing the check. Again, authenticity makes the difference between a good or a poor investment.

Chapter 1

1928-1974 Plymouth Full-Size Cars

Walter P. Chrysler had retired in 1919. It had been a voluntary retirement—of sorts. He was barely 44 years old but he had come a long way since his birth in the sleepy little Kansas town of Wamego. His childhood had been spent in western Kansas, at Ellis, where his father was an engineer with the railroad. His first job, in fact, had been with the railroad, sweeping floors for 10 cents an hour. From there he moved through the ranks until he had become the youngest man to hold the position of Superintendent of Motive Power for the Chicago & Great Western Railroad.

His jobs had taken him and his beloved wife, Della, across the face of the nation. When the superintendent's job no longer held a fascination for him, he moved the family to Pittsburgh, where he took the reigns of the ailing American Locomotive Company (ALCO), transforming the locomotive builder into a financially solid organization. It was at ALCO that Chrysler came to the notice of James J. Storrow, an ALCO director and former president of General Motors (GM). At Storrow's urging, Chrysler visited Flint, where General Motors' huge Buick plant was struggling. GM's boss, Charles Nash, offered Chrysler a position with Buick—at half his ALCO salary. Chrysler accepted the job, and within weeks the Buick plant was turning out 200 cars a day rather than the paltry 45 they had been building earlier.

By 1912 Chrysler was president of the Buick Division. GM's flamboyant founder, William C. Durant, entered the picture and Chrysler's life began a series of "hills and valleys." By 1915 Chrysler was being paid half a million dollars a year in cash and stock—but Durant's reckless business style clashed steadily with Chrysler's

Mrs. Ethel Miller of Turlock, California, claimed to have purchased the first Plymouth ever sold. In 1934 she traded the car back to Chrysler to purchase the one-millionth Plymouth built. Later she would trade that car for the two-millionth Plymouth in 1937. Chrysler Corporation still retains and owns Mrs. Miller's Model Q Deluxe Coupe. *Joe Suminski*

no-nonsense approach until Chrysler decided he'd had enough and walked out in 1919.

Retirement, of course, did not suit the likes of Walter Chrysler. It was welcome relief when friends in the banking industry approached Chrysler in 1920 to ask if he would consider taking over the reigns of the ailing Willys Corporation. Willys was one of the oldest U.S. automobile manufacturers, but John North Willys ran the business in the same reckless abandon that continued to get Billy Durant in trouble. Willys was rich in assets and the offer to Chrysler was sweet—a million bucks a year, with a two-year contract. To the relief of Della, Walter accepted the job and she could get him and his cigar-smoking pals out of her living room!

The author at the wheel of Loyd Groshong's Model Q Sport Roadster. While no production figures exist for the early cars, open models were among the rarer body styles. This roadster sports accessory fender-mounted spare tires and wires wheels. *Plymouth Owners Club*

During his stay at Willys, Walter Chrysler meet the three engineers who would influence the rest of his life—Fred Zeder, Owen Skelton, and Carl Breer. While still at Willys, they collaborated on building a car under the Chrysler banner. Their plans—and their car—were whisked out from under their feet when Durant, who had once again been ousted from General Motors, bought the plant and plans for the car at auction. The Chrysler name had already been affixed to the plant roof, but Durant put the car on the market as the Flint.

It wasn't long before bankers were once again seeking Walter Chrysler's help. This time it was for Maxwell-Chalmers Corporation. Unlike Willys, which had an abundance of liquid assets, Maxwell was nearly broke, saddled with a huge inventory of cars that were not salable. This time Chrysler took his salary in stock, a move that would eventually put him in full control of Maxwell-Chalmers. He moved quickly to unload the inventory, repairing problems that had plagued the cars (fixing cars already in the field at gratis) and selling the remaining cars at $5 over cost. They were sold as the "Good Maxwell," to regain the buying public's confidence.

Once again, Zeder, Skelton, and Breer designed a new car and once again the Chrysler nameplate was attached to it. When they attempted to display it at the 1924 New York Auto Show, Chrysler was refused entry because the car was, technically, not available to the public. Undaunted, Chrysler rented the lobby of the nearby Commodore Hotel, where most of the industry bigwigs were staying! It was a marketing coup of gigantic proportions. On June 6, 1924, Maxwell-Chalmers became Chrysler Corporation, the ailing Chalmers had been discontinued, and Maxwell would be phased out the next year. Within four years, Walter Chrysler introduced three new vehicle lines—the four-cylinder Plymouth, the six-cylinder DeSoto, and the Fargo commercial car line. Furthermore, in a move that rocked the industry, he purchased the huge Dodge Brothers complex from the banking firm of Dillon, Reed, and Company. And if that weren't enough to keep him busy, workmen at the corner of 45th and Lexington in New York City began construction on what would briefly be the tallest building in the world, the 1,046 foot-tall, 77-story Chrysler

Building. For someone who had "retired" in 1919, Walter P. Chrysler was a busy man!

Model Q
Roadster, phaeton, rumble seat coupe ★★★★★
Business coupe ★★★★
Deluxe Sedan ★★★
Two- and four-door sedan ★★

1929—The Model Q
"We have named it the Plymouth because this new product of Chrysler engineering and craftsmanship so accurately typifies the endurance and strength, the rugged honesty, the enterprise, the determination of achievement and the freedom from old limitations of that Pilgrim band who were the first American colonists," read the press release signed by Walter P. Chrysler.

First shown to the public at New York's Madison Square Garden on July 7, 1928, Chrysler's entry into the low-priced field was a conventionally styled automobile, designed by purpose to emulate its larger Chrysler brethren. Like the big Chryslers, the "thin line" radiator design, exposing only the outer lip of the radiator, gave the visual effect of greater car length than was actually incorporated. Sitting atop the radiator was a delicate, winged "Viking" hat radiator cap. Called a "daring and refreshing change in motor car design," the thin shell radiator design would be discarded for more conventional designs within two model years. "Airwing" fenders swept gracefully, accenting the length of the car, with full rear fender aprons and the gas tank shield helping form a neat, unbroken appearance. Arched windows on closed models, with cloth-roof covering stretched down over the side of the car, resulted in a slightly lower look, although interior headroom was generous. The louvered hood panels were embossed with the same arched design found on the side windows.

Bumpers were of the two-piece type, each bar carrying two horizontal grooves running the length of the bumper. Standard equipment on all models included an automatic vacuum-powered windshield wiper, motor-driven horn, semispark advance controlled from the dash with hand throttle, light controls, and horn button located on the steering column.

History
As production began early in 1928, the Model Q was considered by the factory to be a 1929 model—some states, however, demanded that the car be registered for the year in which it was built, causing much confusion today as to whether there actually was a "1928" Plymouth.

Plymouth's bread-and-butter car was always the four-door sedan. This model Q can be easily identified by the grooved bumper bars and small hubcaps. The radiator emblem on these early cars reads "Chrysler Plymouth." *Jim Benjaminson*

Chrysler's model year policy had been adopted from Dodge's policy established in 1922: "All cars manufactured after June 30th are known as of the series of the next calendar year." Following this policy, approximately the first 3,500 Model Q Plymouths built should be considered as 1928 models. Production had begun June 14, 1928, at the Highland Park complex, which Plymouth would share briefly with Chrysler and DeSoto.

Built on a 109 3/4-inch wheelbase, the new Plymouth was powered by a Chrysler-built

Most of the changes to the Model U were under the hood. External differences include rounded bumper bars, larger hubcaps, and the radiator medallion which now read only "Plymouth." *Jim Benjaminson*

four-cylinder engine. That Plymouth could trace its heritage back to Maxwell was obvious, yet there were few similarities in the cars outside of wheelbase and the four-cylinder engine. The last Maxwell, the 25-C, had ridden a 109-inch wheelbase, its four-cylinder engine developing 38 horsepower. Its replacement, the Chrysler F58, had exactly the same specifications. The succeeding Chrysler Fours, the "50" and "52" had a wheelbase that was 3-inches shorter, with horsepower edging up to 45—same as the new Plymouth.

With a bore and stroke of 3 5/8x4 1/8 inches, the Plymouth Four bore little resemblance to the Maxwell four. The Maxwell four had been built with separate intake valve ports for each cylinder and siamesed exhaust ports. Cooling problems with this engine caused the Maxwell Four to overheat and warp the valves. This problem was cured by Chrysler Engineers while still in the Maxwell chassis—simply revamping the camshaft and manifolds, swapping the location of the intake and exhaust valves. When used in the Chrysler "50," the engine was converted from two to three main bearings.

Improvements in the Plymouth engine over the Chrysler "52" included: full force-feed lubrication, larger-diameter chrome nickel intake valves, crankcase ventilation, aluminum alloy-ventilated bridge-type pistons, silchrome steel exhaust valves, frictional-type impulse neutralizer for dampening vibration, and an oil filter and air cleaner as standard equipment.

Of the low-priced cars, Plymouth was the only one to feature internally expanding four-wheel hydraulic brakes. An independent parking brake was mounted on the front flange of the forward universal joint. Transmitting power to the rear wheels was a three-speed, spur-gear transmission operating through a single, dry clutch plate. Wood wheels were standard on all models, while wire wheels were optional.

Offered in six body styles, including two- and four-door sedans, roadster, phaeton, business coupe, and Deluxe coupe with rumble seat. The Deluxe coupe, although fitted with a cloth top and landau irons, was fixed in position and did not retract. Early roadsters were built without rumble seats, a feature soon added to the line-up. The Model Q—and it successor, the Model U— would be the only Plymouths to use composite metal over wood framing construction. Bodies were supplied to Plymouth by both Briggs and, for some four-door sedans, Hayes. Two-door sedan bodies were built by Budd and acquired through the Dodge Division, as were some Kercheval bodies—which was a Chrysler-owned subsidiary. Briggs, also, would become a wholly

The Model 30-U Plymouth switched to a wide radiator shell, mounting the horn midway between the headlamps. Hood louvers were divided into two distinct groups, as shown on this example formerly owned by the Harrah Automobile Collection.

owned Chrysler holding in December of 1953. At $725, the car was considerably more expensive than the rivals it hoped to take on—the $595 Ford Model A and $495 Chevrolet. Model Q production totaled 60,270 U.S.-built and 5,827 Canadian-built cars—good enough to put Plymouth in 15th place for calendar year 1928.

Model U
Roadster, phaeton, rumble seat coupe ★★★★★
Business coupe ★★★★
Deluxe Sedan ★★★
Two- and four-door sedan ★★

1929-1930 Model U

Model year changeover occurred January 7, 1929, with car number RR120P. An additional 4,000 Model Q's would continue to roll off the line during this same period. The Q quite literally became a U by the use of a changed engine, minor mechanical revisions, and an almost imperceptible change in appearance.

It took a sharp eye to detect the external changes between the Q and U. Bumpers, which were still of the double-bar type, were now rounded, rather than flat, missing the two horizontal grooves of the Model Q. Headlamps looked the same, but the supplier had been changed from Depress Beam to TwoLite. The radiator medallion, which previously read "Chrysler Plymouth," now read simply "Plymouth." Hubcaps were larger, with the "hex" for the hubcap wrench located behind the face of the cap rather than on the leading edge.

The Model Q and early Us rode on 4.75x20-inch wheels until after car number Y076LE, which

Midway through the production year, 30-U Plymouths received an oval-shaped rear window, a styling mark that would last through the PA series. Early cars had a normal rectangular-shaped rear window. *Allen McFall*

switched to 19-inch rims. Wooden wheels remained standard with wire wheels—in both 5- and 6-bolt pattern—optional.

Revamping the engine again: manifolds were revised so exhaust gases exited at the front of the engine to eliminate heat build-up near the passenger compartment. The distributor drive housing, which sat vertically on Model Q's, was changed to an angle position (these distributor housings which had a tendency to crack over the years, are now being reproduced).

Front and rear main bearings were increased in size, with a quarter-inch increase in stroke, raising displacement to 175.4 cubic inches (ci). Despite these changes, horsepower remained at 45.

Offered in the same six body styles as the Model Q, an October addition to the U line was the Deluxe Sedan, which, for $20 more, netted the buyer cowl lamps with chrome cowl band and plusher upholstery. The Model U remained in production through April 5, 1930, although cars built after July 18, 1929, were considered to be 1930 models (somewhere around car number Y020W).

To meet demand for the new car, Chrysler

Among the rarest of the PA series cars is the phaeton or touring car. Only five are known to exist worldwide. President Franklin Roosevelt was often photographed in his PA phaeton, which was kept at the Little White House in Warm Springs, Georgia. *Ross McLean*

PA series Plymouths introduced Floating Power engine mounts, which eliminated vibration between the engine and passenger compartment. Fender-mounted spare tires continued to be an option available on all models. *Robert McMulkin*

built what would for many years be the largest assembly plant under one roof. Work began on the Lynch Road plant during the winter of 1928-29. At nearly a half-mile in length, construction crews began work at four locations—two teams at the center of the plant, working out to the ends, and two additional crews beginning at the ends of the building, working their way toward the center. A steam railroad locomotive, parked on a siding, provided steam heat for the workmen!

Approximately 13,157 Model U's were built in the old Highland Park plant before production switched to the newly completed Lynch Road complex. Production of 99,178 U.S.-built and 9,167 Canadian-built Model U's moved Plymouth into 10th place in sales for calendar year 1929.

Model 30U
Roadster, phaeton, rumble seat coupe ★★★★★
Business coupe ★★★★
Deluxe Sedan ★★★
Two- and four-door sedan ★★
Convertible ★★★★★
Commercial sedan ★★★

1930-1931 Model 30U
Production of the slightly revamped Model 30U began April 5, 1930. The first cars were again considered 1930 models, until car number 1530245 rolled out the door on July 1st as a 1931 model. Despite March price cuts of $65-75 per car and a fourteen-month production run, the Model 30U did not see the success of the earlier models. The 30U, in its original form, was still very much like its predecessors, the most visible difference being the wide radiator shell which replaced the thin line design. Fenders looked the same, but were in fact heavier than previous models (open models retained the same rear fenders as before). Also retained was the 109 3/4-inch wheelbase, although the frame of the car had been lengthened by 2 inches. And for the first time, Plymouth could offer customers the safety of an all-steel body. Like earlier models, the 30U shared a great deal of sheet metal with the smaller Chryslers and the DeSoto.

For its first two years, Plymouth had been the exclusive property of Chrysler franchise holders. As the Great Depression began its stranglehold on the world economy, Walter Chrysler

Plymouth's PB series of 1932 would be the last year for open touring cars (except for some Australian-built cars). The rarest body style for 1932, this PB phaeton was found in Katmandu, Nepal. When delivered new, it had to be hand-carried over the Himalayan Mountains! *Les Leather*

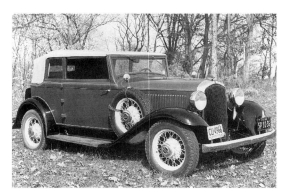

Making a one-year-only debut for 1932 was the PB Convertible Victoria. Standard equipment included fender-mounted spare tires and a trunk at the rear of the body. Only 690 were built. *Earl Buton, Jr.*

made a move designed to protect not only his Chrysler-Plymouth dealers, but the Dodge and DeSoto dealer network as well. Each car line would be paired with Plymouth, a move that would place Plymouth in over 7,000 dealerships. Those dealers selling only the higher-price lines would have an "economical" car to sell.

Six body types were offered during new model introduction—a four-door sedan, sport roadster with rumble seat, business coupe, rumble seat coupe, phaeton, and convertible coupe. The convertible coupe, with roll-up windows and a fixed windshield post, would soon spell the end for drafty, side-curtained roadsters. A short-lived business roadster (fixed windshield posts and no rumble seat) and "Commercial Sedan" were also built but were soon discontinued for lack of sales. A two-door sedan made its appearance later in the model run.

Retaining the "arched window" design of previous years, the most obvious change in the car was the wide radiator shell and Klaxon Model 16 horn mounted on the headlamp bar. Arched hood panels were discontinued, with hood louvers being split into two groups—15 louvers in the forward panel, 14 at the rear. Bumpers were still of the double-bar variety. At midyear the rectangular rear window was replaced by an oval window, which became a Plymouth trademark for the next several years. Headlamps were now painted on all models.

The venerable old four was again completely revamped, starting with a 1/4-inch increase in bore, raising displacement to 196 ci and horsepower to 48. The crankshaft and camshaft were both beefed up, and after engine number U276061, pistons were fitted with four, rather than three, piston rings. Early

engines relied on thermo-siphon cooling with fuel supplied by vacuum tank. July changes saw the addition of water and fuel pumps.

Some 75,510 Model 30U Plymouths were built, and by calendar year 1930, Plymouth had climbed two more notches, to eighth place in industry sales.

Model PA
Roadster, phaeton, rumble seat coupe ★★★★★
Business coupe ★★★★
Deluxe Sedan ★★★
Two- and four-door sedan ★★

The PB Sport Roadster is among the most sought-after of the early four-cylinder Plymouths. For those preferring a closed car, the rumble seat coupe offered the best of both worlds. Examples of both styles are shown here. *Jim Benjaminson*

Two- and four-door Thrift Sedan ★★★
Deluxe Sedan ★★★★

1932 Model PA

Despite the ever souring economy, Chrysler Corporation sank $2.5 million into the car that would replace the Model 30U. Coded as the PA series, the first car came off the line May 1, 1931. Regardless of its previous policies, Chrysler considered every PA built to be a 1932 model. Reducing prices on most models, Plymouth was at the same price level as Chevrolet but still considerably higher-priced than Ford's Model A.

The PA Plymouth again shared many of its major body components with the DeSoto SA and Chrysler CM. Styling took on a gentler, more-rounded appearance—the radiator shell was gently sloped, with a built-in radiator grille, flanked by bright, bowl-shaped headlamps mounted on a cross bar between the fenders. The elongated hood gave the car a more massive appearance, the radiator topped by a graceful, highly detailed Flying Lady cap.

Buyers' choices included a business roadster (which would soon be discontinued), rumble seat coupe, sport roadster with rumble seat, convertible coupe, phaeton, business coupe, and two- and four-door sedans. A special taxi cab model was also cataloged. As in earlier years, open cars were fitted with leather upholstery while closed cars received pile or broadcloth, with leather optional.

Added in the fall of 1931 was the Deluxe Sedan. It sold for $55 more than the regular sedan and the buyer again got chrome cowl band and cowl lamps, side-mounted tires with tread and sidewall covers, chrome windshield frame, and solid one-piece rear bumper. In addition, there was more-luxurious upholstery featuring broadcloth without pleats, three-window pull-down shades, rope-type robe rail, two assist-pull straps, and two rear-seat ashtrays.

January 1, 1932, saw addition of the PA Thrift. Built in just two body styles—two- and four-door sedan—the Thrift was initially available only in black (including the radiator shell, grille, and headlamps) with wood spoke wheels. There was no shock absorbers, dome light, or instrument-panel temperature gauge. It did have a gas gauge, found on the gas tank at the rear, and a two-piece rear bumper. Free-wheeling transmissions, found on all other PA cars, was also not available on the Thrift series. By April, wire

The PB four-door sedan was still the biggest seller for the year. Full leather interiors were optional on all closed body styles but standard on open cars. *Dr. Jose Menendez*

The PA Thrift continued in production after the regular PA series had been discontinued and was offered as a lower-priced alternative to the PB series. PA Thrifts were bare-bones models, with wood wheels and solid black paint (other colors and wire wheels later became available). PA Thrifts had the gas gauge mounted at the rear on the gas tank. *Jim Benjaminson*

wheels, free-wheeling, and colors other than black were also available on the Thrift.

Mechanically, the PA was little-changed from before. Engine displacement remained at 196 ci, with horsepower raised to 56 through the use of higher compression ratios. New for 1932 was a fully automatic mechanical spark advance, with vacuum-controlled spark retarder. The crankshaft was statically and dynamically balanced with each piston and rod set being matched in weight to within .02 pounds.

The biggest news of the year was "Floating Power," a unique method of mounting the engine in rubber along the axis of its own center of gravity. Mounting the engine high at the front and low at the rear allowed the motor to rock and vibrate without transmitting these motions into the passenger compartment.

The wheelbase remained the same, although the frame was of the "double drop" type with kick-ups over the front and rear axles to lower the car for both better looks and better handling by lowering the center of gravity. Tire sizes remained at 4.75x19-inch on adjustable spoke wire wheels.

As calendar year 1931 came to a close, over 105,000 PAs had come off the line. And Plymouth had managed to slip past Buick to become America's number three selling automobile—a position it would occupy for the next quarter-century.

Model PB

Roadster, Sport Roadster, phaeton, rumble seat coupe, convertible sedan ★★★★★
Seven-passenger sedan, business coupe ★★★★
Two- and four-door sedan ★★

1932—Model PB

"Look At All Three" Walter Chrysler boldly challenged, as he was pictured standing with one foot on the front bumper of the new PB series—his hand wrapped around the Flying Lady. The PB series, despite having one of the shortest production runs in Plymouth history, is the zenith of the four-cylinder Plymouths. Style had come to Plymouth—and in a big way. New body styling featured forward-opening "suicide" style doors. Hoods stretched from the forward reaches of the radiator back over the cowl to the smartly raked windshield posts. The slant of the rear edge of the hood approximated that of the front door line, as did the hood louvers. One-piece bumpers—along with one-piece fenders, added to the clean, luxurious look. Free-standing headlamps replaced the headlamp tie bar while a bolder grille, convex in shape, sloped forward near the bottom of the radiator shell. Simply put, this car did not look like a four-cylinder automobile! Sales quickly proved that Plymouth was on the right track—it would be the only make of automobile to increase its sales, selling more cars in 1932 than 1931, fully 119 percent over the previous year (Chevrolet sales were 55 percent of its 1931 sales, and Ford's were only 49 percent of the previous year's mark.)

Ten body styles were cataloged, including the largest offering of open cars ever in Plymouth's history. Buyers could choose between a business coupe, rumble seat coupe, convertible coupe, two-door sedan, four-door sedan, business roadster, sport roadster, phaeton, a seven-passenger sedan on a special 121-inch wheelbase, and a two-door convertible Victoria.

Roadsters, with their rakish "chopped top" look (the roadster windshield measuring just

Plymouth's PC series introduced the first six-cylinder engine for 1933. It could be identified by its broad chrome-plated radiator shell and pancake style headlamps; the PC was discontinued in favor of the restyled PD and PCXX in midyear. *Ed Lausch*

Introduced for the spring selling season, the redesigned PD series for 1933 featured a longer wheelbase than the PC it replaced, painted radiator shell, stainless bul-let-shaped headlamps, and a dip-center front bumper. Options seen on this model include external trumpet horns and the flying lady radiator cap. *Jim Benjaminson*

7-inches high at the center) took on an especially pleasing appearance. Wire wheels (wood optional) and twin Klaxon horns below the headlamps added to the look of richness.

The PB series would be the end of the line for the drafty roadster and phaeton models, which would be discontinued at year's end (although limited production of these body style continued outside the United States).

Closed car interiors were offered in taupe broadcloth with a faint stripe or Bedford cord or leather as options, while all open cars received full leather. As would be Plymouth's practice for years to come, front floors were covered with rubber mat while rear passenger compartments were carpeted. An expensive-looking "engine turned" panel housed the instruments.

A stronger X-braced frame carried the 65-horsepower four-cylinder engine. Bore and stroke had remained the same as the PA series, with the horsepower increase achieved by employing a larger carburetor incorporating an acceleration pump, changes to the spark curve,

enlarging the exhaust ports, and increasing the diameter of the exhaust manifold, pipe, and muffler. A beefed-up 55-pound crankshaft utilized the same bearings as earlier models.

Buyers could also choose vacuum clutch controls combined with the free-wheeling transmission. With the extra horsepower, Plymouth's brakes were improved by the addition of Centrifuse brake drums, combining cast-iron linings fused to an inner lining of steel.

Hoping to expand its foreign markets, an export version (identical except for a smaller 3 7/64-inch engine bore) known as the PBX was announced in April. Of the low-priced three, only Plymouth offered buyers a choice of wood or wire wheels—standard tire size being 5.25x18-inches; an extremely rare option was special 7.50x15-inch Airwheels, which required factory engineering changes.

There were 81,010 PB's built between February and September of 1932, when the four-cylinder engine was phased out of production—it would be decades before Plymouth would build another four.

15

Model PC, PCXX, PD

Convertible, rumble seat coupe ★★★★★
Business coupe ★★★★
Two- and four-door sedan ★★

1933—Models PC, PD, and PCXX

Forty-five days and $9 million after the last PB was manufactured, Chrysler Corporation introduced its new 1933 six-cylinder model PC to the world. There had never been another new car announcement like it. For two and a half hours on November 2, 1932, Chrysler Corporation took over the Columbia Broadcasting Company (CBS) radio network to introduce its new model line to the public and 75,000 Plymouth dealers and employees around the nation. Narrated by popular commentator Lowell Thomas, the program featured Walter P. Chrysler, B. E. Hutchinson, Fred Zeder, Harry Moock, and race drivers Billy Arnold and Barney Oldfield. Simultaneous dealer meetings in 25 cities around the country were staged to unveil the new six-cylinder Plymouth.

Three-hundred pounds lighter and on a 107-inch wheelbase, (5 inches shorter than the PB),

All 1933 Plymouths shared the same body shell. As shown on this car, the PD's extra length was forward of the cowl, requiring a longer hood and fenders. *Lindy Willis*

Replacing the PC was the restyled PCXX. The PCXX featured a painted radiator shell like the PD with painted headlamps and straight bumper bars. Hood louvers were redesigned as well. *Jim Benjaminson*

Nineteen thirty-four PE Plymouths, such as this one, featured a unique three-way front window. Those positions included the "normal" position seen here, with the vent window in place, and with window rolled down. By flipping a lever, the entire unit could be locked together and rolled as one piece into the door. *Jim Benjaminson*

the PC Plymouth came in just four body styles— four-door sedan, business coupe, rumble seat coupe, and convertible coupe, starting at prices as low as $495. A two-door sedan would be added in February. A broad, chrome-plated radiator shell; thin, pancake headlamps; and an odd relationship between the angle of the hood, windshield, door lines, and hood louvers made the car look short and stubby—more like a four-cylinder car than a six. The wheelbase was too short to mount fender-mounted spare tires, still a popular option, causing customers to complain bitterly.

Sales surged briefly—then fell like a rock. Styling wasn't entirely to blame—a short-lived economic panic caused by the closure of Detroit-area banks, which led to further closings around the country, had not helped—but clearly something had to be done. A stop-gap measure was increasing the wheelbase of the PC by 1 inch—just enough so side-mount spares could be mounted, although they sat higher than the hood level when so equipped.

Immediate plans were put into place to alleviate the problem for the spring selling season. A search of corporate parts bins found Plymouth raiding Dodge for its 111-inch wheelbase chassis from its DP series—then extending that wheelbase an extra inch to 112 inches, same as the PB's had been. (Dodge, in turn, revamped its DP to a 115-inch wheelbase).

A crash program in styling set about to correct the PC's problems. A longer hood, with louvers matching the cut of the door and windshield, along with longer front fenders were designed to fit the existing body structure. The upright radiator shell would be painted, with just a small chrome bead around the grille opening. Bullet-shaped stainless headlamps would add to the illusion of length—and side-mount spare tires would fit properly in the fenders. Even the bumpers received attention, the front one getting a 1 1/4-inch dip in the center. Interiors were upgraded as well—the redesigned car got an oval instrument cluster in the center of the dashboard along with a real glove compartment, replacing the individual gauges of the PC.

The new car, coded the PD Deluxe, began rolling off the lines March 17—and Plymouth couldn't build them fast enough. The PD offered the same five body types as the PC—leaving Plymouth with a marketing decision to make—should they retain the PC—or trash-can it?

In reality, it did a little bit of both. The PC, as such, would be discarded. Needing to market a car with an advertised selling price of $495, the short-wheelbase chassis—now called the PCXX—would remain. It would be redesigned through the use of a new hood, radiator, and headlamps, to look like the PD. PC body styles would be continued, except the convertible would be discontinued. For the first time in its history, Plymouth would offer two series on different wheelbases.

While the six-cylinder engine was new to Plymouth, it was actually in corporate use two years earlier. Displacing 189 ci, the six had less displacement than the four-cylinder it replaced, although its horsepower rating of 70 with the standard head was greater. An optional aluminum cylinder head raised compression—and horsepower to 76. The engine would become a familiar sight, serving with only minor refinements through the 1959 models (and even later in truck and industrial uses).

Like all Chrysler engines, it was a valve-in-block design with insert rod and main bearings, insert valve seats, full-pressure lubrication, manifold heat control, a redesigned water pump which eliminated the need for a packing nut, oil filter, and down-draft carburetion. Pistons were aluminum with four rings per piston. A redesigned 12-cam free-wheeling unit saw use in the PC and PD, but not the PCXX.

Chassis changes were not limited to just wheelbase increases—the PD and PC both shared a tubular front axle, the PCXX utilized an "I" beam-type axle. Centrifuse brake drums, free-wheeling, an automatic clutch control, manifold heat control, and an engine impulse neutralizer did not see use on the PCXX. Even the transmission—which used helical cut gears on the PC and PD—was of the earlier "silent second" type of years past. The gas tank on the PC carried 11 gallons, the PCXX 11 1/2 gallons, and the PD 15 gallons.

There were no changes to the body itself between the PC, PCXX, and PD (save for dashboards), but each had its own unique set of front fenders—rear fenders interchanged between similar body types.

By end of the model run, Plymouth managed to drop the price of the PCXX business coupe

A rare and unusual option for any 1934 Plymouth two- or four-door sedan was the Form Fit trunk, a $37.50 option. As seen on this car, the spare tire could still be mounted at the rear, requiring extended bumper brackets. *Jim Benjaminson*

down to $445. With year-end sales of 298,557 cars, one out of every four low-priced cars being sold was a Plymouth.

Model PE, PF, PFXX, PG
Convertible, rumble seat coupe, wood-body station wagon ★★★★★
Business coupe, Town Sedan, seven-passenger sedan ★★★★
Two- and four-door sedan ★★

1934—Model Series PE, PF, PFXX, and PG
Following the lead set in 1933, Plymouth entered the 1934 model year with two series. The price leader was the "New Plymouth Six" PF, built on a 108-inch wheelbase in business coupe, rumble seat coupe, and the two- or four-door sedan form. At the top of the scale sat the Deluxe Plymouth PE, with the same body line-up plus a convertible coupe.

As the year progressed, the PE series would be expanded by two body types—the Westchester Semi-Sedan Suburban wood-body station wagon (Plymouth's first "official" station wagon), and a close-coupled, blind quarter-window Town Sedan with built-in trunk.

Before year's end, Plymouth would build its one millionth car, a Deluxe PE four-door that was sold to Mrs. Ethel Miller of Turlock, California, who claimed to be the purchaser of the first Plymouth sold in 1928. Mrs. Miller's car was shipped to the Chicago World's Fair for display, where Mrs. Miller took delivery of the car, trading in her Model Q Deluxe Coupe, which was then displayed at the Fair.

Sales continued to climb but competition was stiff, so two additional series were added to the sales line-up. The price leader PG "Standard Six" came on line in March, in business coupe and two-door (62 four-door PG sedans were built, probably as a fleet order for the military).

The "Special Six" series PFXX debuted for the spring selling season. Differing from the regular PF, the PFXX featured chrome-plated grille, chrome windshield frame, twin trumpet horns, twin tail-lamps, chrome headlamp shells, interior sun visor, ashtray, and glove compartment on the dashboard. A PFXX Town Sedan joined the body line-up as well.

Deluxe PE Plymouths rode a longer wheel-base, stretched to 114 inches. The PF, PFXX, and PG all shared a 108-inch wheelbase. Joining the trend to independent front suspension, all models except the PG featured upper and lower "A" arms with coil-spring suspension, the PG sitting atop an "I" beam axle. Wheels on the PE were 6:00x16-inch steel artillery (early cars were fitted with 16-inch wire wheels). Wires were standard on the PG and PF, and the PFXX rode for a time on 17-inch artillery wheels before switching to 16s.

The engine was stroked 1/4-inch to a displacement of 201 ci, where it remained through 1941. Horsepower was now rated at 77 (82 with the optional aluminum cylinder head). A small-bore (2 7/8-inch) engine was built for export use only. PE engines all featured automatic manifold heat control and crankshaft impulse neutralizer. The optional automatic clutch and free-wheeling were also exclusive to the PE series.

At first glance the 1934 Plymouth appeared to be little more than a redesign of the '33 bodies, even though major changes had taken place in the upper body structure. Sharply raked windshields and low rooflines gave the closed cars, especially coupes, a "chopped top" look. Setting the PE apart from the other series was an extra-long hood featuring both louvers and doors for ventilation.

Sitting atop the radiator was a delicate (and fragile) sailing ship ornament—the radiator cap could be found under the hood!

Perfected ventilation, which featured both vent wing windows and normal windows, could be locked together to roll the entire unit into the door—this again, was an exclusive to the Deluxe series. And for the first time, a radio could be mounted into the dash panel on PE and PFXX cars. Bedford cord with optional mohair was found in closed PE and PF cars, with full leather optional (standard in the convertible and station wagon), while the PG featured "hard-weave cord."

At year's end, a record 321,171 cars had been built. The '34 Plymouth was voted "The Most

A midyear 1934 introduction was the Town Sedan in both the PE and PFXX series. Featuring blind rear quarters, close-coupled passenger compartment, and special taillamps, the Town Sedan featured a built-in trunk (the Form Fit trunk was an "add on"). The most expensive body type for 1934, the Town Sedan saw only 7,049 units built. *Ken Bauldry*

Beautiful Plymouth" ever built by members of the Plymouth Owners Club in 1987.

Model PJ
Convertible, rumble seat coupe,
wood-body station wagon ★★★★★
Commercial sedan, Traveler Sedan,
seven-passenger sedan ★★★★
Two- and four-door sedan ★★

1935—Model PJ

Chrysler's radical Airflow of 1934 had proven to be too much for the motoring public. When first shown at the New York Auto Show in January, the cars, which were basically prototype cars, had taken the show by storm. Unfortunately, Chrysler wasn't able to deliver until later in the year, by which time the competition had done a number on the car. People were shying away from the controversial styling of the car in droves. Although the Airflow was never a sales success, the concepts of automobile engineering it pioneered have been carried into the industry to this very day. Plymouth's 1935 models moved from the square box school of design to a more acceptable, rounded look, but never included a car as radical as the Airflow.

Fenders took on a teardrop shape, flowing toward the rear of the car. A softly rounded, more massive radiator shell flowed back to a gracefully sloped hood, which melded neatly into the body. Running boards melded into the front fenders, matching a slight bulge at the trailing edge of the

Plymouth for 1935 took on a more streamlined look. The Deluxe PJ series was easily identified by the hood trim consisting of three horizontal trim strips over five circles. Rumble seat coupes were losing their favor with buyers, making them among the rarest body types. *Jim Benjaminson*

fender where the two came together. The windshield frame carried the theme, with no sharp angles anywhere around its circumference, sloped at a steeper angle but still curved gently into the roofline. At the rear of the car, the roofline sloped downward at an angle tapering out toward the bottom of the car. Compared to earlier models, the cars simply looked more massive—deceiving since the wheelbase had actually been decreased to 113 inches.

Sold in two series, each known as the PJ model, the bottom line was the "Business Six" that included flatback two- and four-door sedans without trunks, a business coupe, commercial sedan, and Westchester Suburban station wagon.

Deluxe Six models included flatback two- and four-door sedans; two- and four-door "Touring" sedans, so called because of their built-in humpback-style trunks; a business coupe; rumble seat coupe; and convertible coupe with rumble seat. Two April editions included a 128-inch wheelbase five-passenger "Traveler Sedan" with built-in trunk and a seven-passenger trunk-less sedan.

A short-lived (just 837 built) "PJ Six" appeared on the Canadian market.

Deluxe PJ's were identified by their bullet-shaped chrome headlamps, chrome windshield frame, and hood design that included three long stainless strips over five circular "port" holes. The PJ Six models featured the Deluxe's hood trim but with painted headlamps, while the Business PJ had painted headlamps with just three horizontal hood trim pieces, sans portholes. Atop

the radiator sat a slightly redesigned Mayflower sailing ship.

Sitting on a completely revised double-drop "X" frame, all PJ series reverted back to a tubular front axle, abandoning independent suspension that was pioneered the previous year. Frame rails were ballooned out to form a perimeter matching the contours of the body, and the body mounted down over the frame rather than on top of it, secured both vertically and horizontally by 46 bolts in what was called "Unit Frame & Body" construction.

Under the hood, major changes had taken place to the engine. A completely redesigned water jacket with the addition of a water distribution tube was employed to prevent hot spots around the two rear cylinders. The block was recast to form a full water jacket on the left side of the engine—overall dimensions of the engine remained the same—and only the starter motor had to be moved outward on its axis from the bell housing by about 1/4 inch. An increased compression ratio raised horsepower to 82. Vacuum control of the distributor automatically eliminated spark knock. The small-bore export engine was used in cars sent overseas, and for the first time, an economy engine package with 1-inch bore carburetor and 5.2:1 compression ratio rated at 65 horsepower was offered.

There would be no further changes to the external dimensions of the Plymouth six-cylinder engine throughout its lifetime, a factor that kept many an old Plymouth on the road when its original engine expired. Newer engines, up through Plymouth's last flathead six of 1959—and even later truck engines—were a bolt-for-bolt swap. For a 1935 or later engine to be used in a 1933 or 1934, the bellhousing had to be modified to move the starter outboard of the water jacket. Even when Chrysler Canada began putting 2-inch-longer engines into its Canadian-built products in midyear 1938, engines continued to be interchangeable—this time by merely swapping the radiator support from front to back.

Some 350,880 PJ Plymouths broke all existing production records, keeping the Mayflower solidly in third place in industry sales.

Model P1-P2

Convertible, rumble seat coupe,
wood-body station wagon ★★★★★
Business coupe, Commercial sedan,
seven-passenger sedan ★★★★
Two- and four-door Touring sedan ★★★
Two- and four-door sedan ★★

1936—Models P1 and P2

With an improving economy and a slimmer, trimmer looking car, Plymouth was well on its way

Among the biggest changes for 1936 were painted headlamps and a body color stripe down the center of the grille. Deluxe models could be easily identified by the three chrome chevrons on the headlamp stands.
Jim Benjaminson

to setting an all-time sales record. To many, the '36 Models, coded P1 for the Business Six and P2 for Deluxe, didn't look all that different from the previous year's car. As in 1934, the changes were deeper than most people realized. The X-braced frame had again been redesigned, body structuring had been slimmed down yet made stronger, and exterior sheet metal changes were evolutionary.

Popular as dress-up accessories today, it's doubtful whether many 1936 Plymouths were delivered with whitewall tires. Dual windshield wipers and dual taillamps were optional, even on Deluxe models.
Andy Lippa

Business Six customers had their choice of trunk-less two- and four-door sedans, a business coupe, and a sedan delivery for the commercial buyer. Small quantities of Business Six touring sedans, in both two- and four-door form, were built only for export markets. Those considering a Deluxe model had the choice of regular or touring sedans in two- or four-door, business coupe, rumble seat coupe, convertible coupe, and seven-passenger sedan styles. The wheelbase remained at 113 inches with the lone seven-passenger offering on a 128-inch chassis. Unit Body & Frame construction was carried over—the major change in the frame being at the front cross-member, although the center "X" was moved further forward.

A new three-section grille—consisting of two outer chrome-plated grilles separated down the center by a grille painted body color, gave the cars a slimmer look. A sturdier sailing ship rode atop the radiator shell. Body color, bullet-shaped headlamps replaced the bright metal lamps of 1935—still mounted on stanchions bolted to the catwalk between the radiator shell and fender. Deluxe models had the stanchions decorated with three bright metal chevron stripes.

Hood trim consisted of a teardrop-shaped stainless strip (mimicking the headlamp shape) followed by three "speed streaks" running the length of the hood. A redesigned roofline melded nicely into the bustleline of the touring sedan trunk. Front and rear fenders received beaded edges around the wheel openings, and on touring sedans, taillamps were attached directly to the body rather than on the fender.

Nineteen hundred and thirty-six would be the last year side-mounted spare tires would be offered on a Plymouth passenger car. The wheels rode rather high and restricted front door opening—outside-mounted spare tires were becoming a thing of the past—only the convertible coupe and trunk-less sedans would continue to carry the spare at the rear of the body; the spare was moved behind the front seat on all coupe models and into the trunk on touring sedans.

Unusual options first cataloged in 1936 included a removable pickup box for use in the trunk of the business coupe, and the $40 hearse-ambulance conversion, which allowed a gurney to be inserted through the deck lid until the patient's head and torso were in the passenger compartment. A split rear seat, which hinged to the roof, allowed the gurney into the rear compartment while allowing the attendant to be seated next to the patient. The pickup box would last as an option through 1939, the ambulance conversion through 1941.

Engines remained virtually unchanged from 1935; the small-bore export and economy engine continued to be available. Standard tire size on he the Business was 17 inches, 1 inch more than Deluxe cars.

In the best sales year Plymouth would see until 1950, the 1937 models took on a heavier, "fat fender" look. This would be the last year for opening windshields for ventilation. *Richard Legg*

For the first time in its history, Plymouth production passed the half-million mark, reaching 520,025 units, more than enough to guarantee a third-place finish in sales.

Model P3-P4
Convertible, rumble seat coupe,
wood-body station wagon, limousine ★★★★★
Business coupe, seven-passenger sedan ★★★★
Two- and four-door Touring sedan ★★★
Two- and four-door sedan ★★

1937—Models P3 and P4

1937 was quite a year for Chrysler. The last payments were made on the debt incurred when Chrysler Corporation purchased Dodge Brothers in 1928, the corporation was sitting solidly in second place behind General Motors, and it was the first year the Corporation would build over one million cars in a single year. Also, the two-millionth Plymouth—a 1937 model—came off the line after new model changeover in the fall of 1936.

Although outsold by the four-door sedan, this Deluxe two-door touring sedan made a perfect car for the family man with small children. *Robert Semichy*

Marred by a severe recession, sales of the 1938 Plymouths were cut nearly in half. Photographed at a Plymouth Owners Club Spring Meet were these five different body types, including a P6 four-door, P6 business coupe, P5 two-door, P6 convertible, and P5 four-door. *Frank Chillemi*

By model year's end, a record 551,994 Plymouth passenger cars had been built. Offered in two series, the P3 "Business" Six and P4 Deluxe six, the cars had found a ready market in a much-improved economy. The 1937 Plymouth would set an all-time record in sales of Deluxe versus business models when the P4 captured fully 86 percent of sales.

While the chassis and drivetrain were little changed, the 1937 models received all-new bodies. "Impressive, artistic massiveness in design" the brochures called it—the hot rodders' term of "Fat Fender" fits even better.

The car was swept clean from end to end of every projecting ornament or accessory while every line or contour was softly rounded and smooth flowing. Despite its massive appearance, the wheelbase was again reduced—this time to 112 inches, where it had been in 1933.

The grille was fuller, with a slender painted vertical section surrounded by right and left halves of bright chrome, rounded to curve from side to side. Headlamps were mounted directly to the radiator shell and painted to match body color. The redesigned Mayflower ship spilled over the top of the shell, in a smoother-flowing line— long horizontal stainless strips adorned the hood

sides, accentuating the speed bulge running back to the cowl. Fenders were crowned and dipped lower in front—and at long last, the cloth-roof insert had been replaced by a solid steel stamping.

Prospective customers had the choice of a business coupe or flatback two- and four-door sedans in the Business line; Deluxe buyers could choose between a business coupe, rumble seat coupe, two- or four-door sedans with or without trunks, and convertible coupe with rumble seat. This time three long-wheelbase models made their debut—on an even longer 132-inch wheelbase including a seven-passenger sedan, seven-passenger limousine with a divider window, and a seven-passenger taxi package for the taxi trade.

Safety became a big issue with the 1937 models—all interior knobs were located under the dashboard (both push-pull and drawer-pull types used) while door and window handles were curved inward to prevent passengers from catching their clothing, front seat backs were heavily padded, and the dome light was moved from the center of the roof to directly over the rear window—even exterior door handles were redesigned.

Changes to the engine were nearly nonexistent—the 201-ci, 82-horsepower six was the only engine with the exception of the 65-horsepower economy engine and 170-ci export engine. Chassis changes included "airplane" type shock absorbers, a kick shackle on the left front spring, and hypoid rear axle replacing the spiral bevel-type used in previous years. Interesting options included 20-inch-high clearance wheels (which had been available for rural mail carriers since 1933) and a sliding package tray for the trunk of business coupes.

As the year drew to a close, dealers were counting record profits and looking forward to another record setting year—they would have to wait 13 years.

Model P5-P6
Convertible, rumble seat coupe,
wood-body station wagon, limousine ★★★★★
Business coupe, seven-passenger sedan ★★★★
Two- and four-door Touring sedan ★★★
Two- and four-door sedan ★★

1938—Models P5 and P6

Slightly restyled for 1938, the Jubilee models were graced with a shortened grille, not really any wider than the previous year but enough to visually give the car a rather pug-nosed appearance. Not helping any were the larger headlamps, made purposely larger to increase nighttime illumination (so big that generator capacity had been increased to handle the extra load). Adding to the cars' heavy look was a massive winged medallion below the waterfall grille. Marking its tenth anniversary, the Mayflower grille medallion was finished in red and white cloisonné rather than the familiar white on black. Adding insult to injury—prices had increased by 12 percent across the board.

The less-expensive "Business" models, series P5, were available in business coupe or two- or four-door fastback sedans. The flatback sedans were proving so unpopular that a line of P5 touring sedans with built-in trunks were added, the four-door in February, a two-door in March. Export buyers could also choose a P5 rumble seat coupe, a choice U.S. buyers couldn't make. Sales resistance to the term "Business" six was so great that at midyear the P5 officially became the "Roadking" series.

P6 Deluxes came in business coupe, rumble seat coupe, two-door and four-door flatback sedans, two- and four-door touring sedans, convertible coupe with rumble seat, and Westchester Suburban station wagon, marking the first year the wagon was built on the Deluxe chassis. Two long-wheelbase seven-passenger chassis, in sedan and limousine form, were also cataloged.

Plymouth never built open cars in great numbers, making this Deluxe convertible coupe with rumble seat extremely rare. Early convertibles had fixed vent windows, which was later changed to externally mounted wind wings such as seen as this car. *Jim Benjaminson*

As dealers and customers alike complained about the car's "bug-eyed" look, Chrysler responded by casting a new headlamp-mounting bracket which moved the headlamps 2 inches lower and 4 inches further back—just enough to take the edge off the original design.

Upholstery continued in the same vein as years before—cloth was standard in all but the wagon and convertible, and leather was extra in all closed models—with the exception of sedans fitted with Accessory Group C, which

Plymouth offered its first "factory" station wagon in 1934. Never built in great numbers, bodies were supplied by U.S. Body & Forging. This 1938 Deluxe Westchester Suburban is one of only two such wagons known to still exist. *Lawrence Dirksen*

Most people did not realize the 1939 Plymouth still carried the same body as the 1937-38 models. A completely redesigned front end with integral headlamps, two-piece vee'd windshield, and prominent nose helped disguise the car. This would be the last year for the "Touring Sedan" hump-back-style trunk. *Jim Benjaminson*

received "pillow-type" upholstery, special door design, chrome trim, carpet strips on bottom door panels, special seat-back trim, lighter wood grain, contrasting colors on the instrument panel, colored escutcheon plates, two front door armrests, special color steering wheel with chrome horn ring, special gearshift knob, chrome windshield wipers, front grille guard, wheel trim rings, glove-box lock, and chrome trim on the running boards—all for $35 extra.

Mechanically there were few changes, the engine remained an 82-horsepower 201-ci six. An optional aluminum head which would have raised compression and horsepower to 86 was cataloged but dropped before it ever saw production. The small-bore export engine was still in use but the economy engine was available in two versions—the first with small-bore carburetor and manifold, the second adding a throttle stop to hold speeds to 45 miles per hour or less. Canadian buyers did see a distinct change under the hood, as the Windsor engine foundry came on line at midyear. Chrysler

Canada, because of its lower production requirements, could justify casting just one block size. In the United States, Dodge and Plymouth shared a 23-inch "small block" while Chrysler and DeSoto shared a 25-inch "long block." If one block had to be chosen by Chrysler Canada for use in all its production, it was natural it would choose the long-block—Plymouth and Dodge, while having a smaller displacement, would still be fitted with the 25-inch-long-block. The Canadian block (identified by the letter C in its serial number) would displace 201 ci, same as its U.S. cousin—only the dimensions would be different, derived from a 1/4-inch larger bore (3 3/8 inches) and 5/8-inch shorter stroke (3 3/4 inches). The Canadian "long" block would remain in production until replaced by the Slant Six in 1960.

Caught with higher prices in the midst of a brief economic recession, and with car lots filled with good used trade-ins from the previous year, industry wide sales fell by nearly half, to 285,704.

A one-year-only offering on a special 117-inch wheel-base was Plymouth's only four-door convertible sedan. Built by Murray Body, the convertible sedan shared many components with the 1937-38 Chrysler and DeSoto convertible sedans. Only 387 were built. At $1,150, they were the most expensive Plymouths built to that time. *Mearl Ziegler*

Model P7-P8

Convertible, convertible sedan,
rumble seat coupe, wood-body station
wagon, limousine ★★★★★
Business coupe, Utility sedan,
panel delivery, seven-passenger sedan ★★★★
Two- and four-door Touring sedan ★★★
Two- and four-door sedan ★★

1939—Models P7 and P8

Plymouth for 1939 was lower—in both price and height—longer and wider, with a deeply prowed front end, vee'd two-piece windshield, and streamlined features such as headlamps and taillamps mounted flush into the fenders. Underneath it all was the same body structure that had graced both the '37 and '38 Plymouths. By cleverly juggling sheet metal and utilizing a new roof stamping, the car had taken on an entirely different look. The hood alone was 10 inches longer and the vee'd windshield added another 6 3/4 inch of room to the passenger compartment.

Full-length bodyside chrome (a first for Plymouth—on Deluxe models only) and multi-piece horizontal grille bars aided the illusion of extra length and width. The return to independent front suspension meant a 2-inch increase in wheelbase to 114 inches. It was only when viewed in profile—and from the doors back—that one got a hint to the '39's origins.

The Roadking (P7) was available with two- or four-doors, as either flatback or touring sedans, business coupe, utility sedan, or panel delivery (see commercial chapter). A handful of

rumble seat coupes and station wagons were built for export markets. Deluxe body styles also cataloged two- and four-door trunk-less and touring sedans, convertible coupe with rumble seat, station wagon with side curtains or full glass enclosure, business coupe, rumble seat coupe, Westchester station wagon, seven-passenger sedan, limousine, and taxi.

New for the year was Plymouth's first and only four-door convertible sedan. Built on a special 117-inch wheelbase chassis, the convertible sedan shared the same body (aft of the cowl) as the '37-'38 Chrysler and DeSoto convertible sedans, supplied not by Briggs but by Murray. Only 387 were built, at the premium price of $1,150, making it the most expensive Plymouth built prior to World War II.

A year of transition, 1939 found Plymouth with the only open models in the entire Chrysler line-up (even rival Chevrolet did not offer a convertible). It also marked the last year for the rumble seat and introduced the industry's first power-operated convertible top. Another first was the addition of an optional black convertible top, on both open models.

Mechanically, the car was much the same as before. An optional aluminum cylinder head raised horsepower to 86. The small-bore export engine was in its last year of production as European demand dried up for the duration of the war. Canadian-built Plymouths continued to use their own long-block engine.

Station wagon buyers in 1939 had two choices, with or without real glass in the rear windows. When ordered without, these openings were covered with removable side curtains. Most wagons carried the spare tire in the front fender. *Harold Fick*

Deluxe 1940 Plymouths carried full-length chrome trim on all body types, whereas Roadking trim stopped midway along the hood. Three-passenger business coupes (shown here) were joined by an "extended cab" auxiliary seat coupe when rumble seats were discontinued. *Jim Benjaminson*

The return to independent front suspension came as no surprise, as the other Chrysler lines had been adopting it in previous years; Roadkings would be the only Chrysler-built cars to still retain floor-shifted transmissions. Deluxe P8s featured "Perfected Remote Control Shifting," placing the shift lever on the steering column, using cables and levers while retaining the old transmission by fitting a special plate to convert it from top to side shifting. "Power Shift," a vacuum-controlled aide to shifting, was a seldom seen $9.50 option.

The unique "Safety Signal" Speedometer cleverly incorporated a small round "eye" attached to the speedometer needle. Run over a colored band underneath, the "eye" glowed green from zero to 30 miles per hour, amber from 30 to 50, and red at any speed over 50. Versions of the Safety Signal speedometer would still be in use as late as 1959!

Production totals for the year were up, although not to the record level of 1937. Included among the 423,850 cars built was the three-millionth Plymouth.

Model P9-P10
Convertible, wood-body station wagon, limousine ★★★★★
Business and auxiliary seat coupe, utility sedan, panel delivery, seven-passenger sedan ★★★★
Two- and four-door sedan ★★

1940—Models P9 and P10

When the "Low-priced Beauty With The Luxury Ride" made its showroom arrival September 21st, little did anyone realize this same basic body would still be in production nine and a half years later. Carrying the basic theme set down in 1939, nothing interchanged between the two. The body was all new, carried on a 117-inch wheelbase chassis for all body styles. This longer chassis allowed the engine to be moved 4-inches forward and the rear axle pushed back 7 1/2-inches, providing 10 cubic feet more passenger space and 18 1/2 cubic feet of trunk space—even with a 1-inch lower roofline, headroom remained the same as 1939. Increased glass area (18 percent front windshield, 23 percent rear window), and a new one-piece rear window gave the driver

Plymouth convertibles and station wagons shared the same cowl and windshield, but that's where the similarity ended. Wagon production grew steadily each year but their survival rates have been minimal. Nearly all wagons were built on the Deluxe chassis although a handful were built on the Roadking chassis, for export markets. *Larry Fator*

better visibility. Flatter, squared-off fenders carried "speed lines" from forward of the wheels up over the wheel cutout. Deluxe models could be easily identified by their bright windshield moldings and full-length body molding.

The number of body styles was reduced considerably with the demise of the flatback trunk sedans. The familiar humpback-style trunk was now smoothly integrated in all sedan body types. Both P9 Roadking and P10 Deluxes included a business coupe and auxiliary seat coupe (although the P9 auxiliary seat coupe was built only for export), two-door and four-door sedans—the Deluxe offered a convertible coupe with fold-away auxiliary seats in place of the rumble seat, station wagon with full glass enclosure, and seven-passenger sedan and limousine on a 137 1/2-inch wheelbase. Two Roadking commercial vehicles, a utility sedan and panel delivery, along with an export-only station wagon were also built.

Oftentimes referred to as an "Opera" coupe—or club coupe—the Auxiliary Seat Coupe was fitted with two small folding cushions behind the main seat that could be folded against the body sidewall when not in use.

Minor engine changes brought horsepower up to 84, and the optional aluminum high-compression head raised it to 87. Other engines included the economy packages, small-bore 70-horsepower export engine (records indicate just one Roadking was shipped with this engine!), and the Canadian long-block-powered cars.

A new transmission, incorporating a blocker-type synchronizer, was standard on all models. Identified by its side-mounted cover, an extension case at the rear enabled the shorter 1939 driveshaft to be used despite the car's increased wheelbase—and years later allowed easy conversion to overdrive after Plymouth finally made it available in midyear 1952.

Rotary safety door latches, Safety Signal speedometer, concealed door hinges (on all except sedan rear doors and a few P9 business coupe deck lid hinges), along with an across-the-board switch to sealed-beam headlights helped Plymouth garner its second Eastern Conference Safety Award.

Production increased slightly, to 430,208 vehicles. Market penetration was at a near-all-time high with sales projections for the next year showing Plymouth could well surpass Ford as the number-two automobile in industry sales. It took an all-out blitz by Ford, with a much-improved product, to stave off Plymouth's advances.

Model P11, P11D, P12
Convertible, wood-body station wagon, limousine ★★★★★
Business and auxiliary seat coupe, utility sedan, panel delivery, seven-passenger sedan ★★★★
Two- and four-door sedan ★★

1941—Models P11, P11D, and P12
Advertised as the "One For '41" Plymouth again marketed three distinct series, something it hadn't done since 1935. At the bottom of the totem

This 1940 Deluxe two-door was purchased by the author's father in 1948, and it's been in the family ever since. *Jim Benjaminson*

A pair of 1941 Special Deluxe Plymouths in sedan and business coupe form display the bumper wing tips and center "Super" guard that were special to that model. Plymouth built two special orders of four-door sedans for military use as army staff cars. *Plymouth Owners Club*

pole was the P11 "Plymouth," followed by the upgraded P11D, which now took the name of Deluxe, the Roadking name having been discontinued. At the top of the line was the P12 Special Deluxe.

Unlike 1934, when the PF and PFXX shared different serial number sequences, the P11 and P11D had a common group of numbers assigned to them, yet the factory kept separate production records. P11s came in two- or four-door sedans or a business coupe. A handful of auxiliary seat coupes were built, mostly in Canada, although a handful came from U.S. plants, of which all but 20 were exported. Slightly more than 200 P11 station wagons were also built; the commercial car line included a sedan delivery and utility sedan. Total P11 production came to 97,130 units.

P11D "Deluxe" production included the same body line-up, again with all auxiliary seat coupes sold in export markets. A single utility sedan and single panel delivery were also built as P11Ds—total production amounting to 94,542 vehicles.

With a booming economy, sales of the P12 Special Deluxe easily outstripped the combined P11 total, amounting to 354,139 vehicles. With a price difference of just $60 between the P11 and P12 four-door—and only $20 over the P11D its

easy to understand why buyers opted for the top-of-the-line model. Special Deluxes came in two- or four-door sedan, business coupe, auxiliary seat coupe, convertible coupe with full rear seat (but the passengers had better have been friendly!), station wagon, and two long-wheelbase sedans, in seven-passenger and limousine form.

To the casual observer, the '41 was a mildly restyled '40—"with a chrome-plated bib." Underneath, there was little mechanical difference with exception of a regeared transmission; automatic shifting was still light years away, although "PowerMatic" vacuum-assisted shifting was a seldom-seen option still offered. The wheelbase remained at 117 inches, and the only change was the adoption of Safety Rim Wheels, designed to hold the tire on the rim in case of a flat or blowout. Without proper tools, the tires were miserable to get off the rim (a special tire tool was shipped with each car), but it was a feature it would take some of the rest of the industry decades to catch up to. Eighteen-inch high-clearance wheels (2 inches less diameter than previous years) could also be ordered.

Nineteen hundred and forty-one would mark the last year for the 201 ci six. Horsepower

I bet there isn't anyone who wouldn't like Santa's little helper to deliver a 1941 Special Deluxe convertible coupe under their Christmas tree! *Art Ubbens, Sr.*

had increased slightly, up 3 from the previous year to 87, with 92 possible with the optional high-compression aluminum cylinder head. Buyers could still opt for the economy engine; the small-bore export engine was not cataloged. Canadian-built Plymouths continued to use the long-block engine.

A front-opening, alligator-type hood replaced the butterfly type of years past, and at long last the battery was moved underneath the hood from its position

Sporting extremely rare accessory fender skirts, this 1942 Deluxe business coupe is back on the road again after being rear-ended while on the way home from the Iola, Wisconsin, old car show a few years ago. Restoration proved difficult because of the lack of replacement parts. These cars were rare even when new! *Jim Benjaminson*

under the driver's seat. A counter-balanced deck lid was a much-appreciated change for the better.

Continuing the design theme of '39-40, horizontal grille bars were employed, this year surrounded by a stainless "heart." Additional body side trim provided a break line for two-tone paint schemes, a $10 option on two- and four-door sedans only. Interiors now featured two-tone upholstery—even the wood body station wagon could be two-toned, with buyers choosing between Honduras mahogany or white maple side panels. Front and rear fenders again had the speed line differing in the addition of three smaller speed lines embossed at the trailing edge of the fender. Nineteen hundred and fourty-one marked the first use of stainless steel fender beading between the fenders and the body. Like 1940, running boards remained a "delete" option.

Cars built early in the year were fitted with a flush, 1940-style headlamp door replaced by the more commonly seen "bug eye" parking lamp—the change made to apparently appease some state law. The early flush-type headlamp door was used exclusively on cars built to order for the U.S. military, of which Plymouth delivered better than 2,000 units. Predating Federal law by 46 years, Plymouth pioneered a center-mounted stop light in its own housing on the deck lid—unlike 1987, there were no stop-lamp bulbs in the regular taillamps. The four-millionth Plymouth, a Special Deluxe convertible, was built at the Los Angeles plant during the year.

Sales surpassed the half-million mark again, to 522,080 units—shy some 75,000 units of overtaking Ford for second place.

Model P14
Convertible, Town Sedan, wood-body
station wagon ★★★★★
Utility sedan, business and auxiliary
seat coupe ★★★★
Two- and four-door sedan ★★

1942—Models P14C and P14S

Even though Plymouth began early production of the 1942 models (on July 25, 1941), it was becoming evident that automobile production would be taking a back seat to military orders. Although the country was not yet at war, military build-up was beginning. Customers and dealers alike were advised "under Government allotment, Plymouth is building a reduced number of cars to serve the public's needs for automotive transportation." Wise indeed, was the consumer who "read between the lines" and took early delivery of a new car—of any brand!

Only two series were offered—retaining the same model names as '41—Deluxe (P14S) for the

In use when new by the U.S. military, this 1942 Plymouth Town Sedan was wrecked while still in service. After sitting for decades, the car was restored to its prewar glory. The

1942 Town Sedan was a one-year Plymouth offering, featuring normal-opening rear doors and blind rear quarters. Only a handful of this body type still survive. *Lloyd White*

less-expensive models, Special Deluxe (P14C) for the top of the line. The Deluxe line included a three-passenger coupe, five-passenger "club" coupe, and two- and four-door sedans. The utility sedan was still cataloged but would be discontinued at the end of the model run after only 82 had been built.

The Special Deluxe line included a three-passenger coupe, five-passenger club coupe, convertible coupe for five, two-door and four-door sedan, station wagon, and, new for the year, four-door Town Sedan. (Town Sedans had been added to the other Chrysler lines in '41.) Differing from regular sedans, the Town Sedan had rear doors that opened in the normal fashion (rather than "suicide" style), with rear vent windows built into the door frame. The rear quarter-panel was scooped out for the extra width of the door. As a premium model it also had stainless moldings around the exterior windows and a fully carpeted trunk. Selling for just $45 more than the regular sedan, fewer than 6,000 were built, regular sedans outselling it by a 13 to 1 ratio.

Built on the same body as 1940, the '42 Plymouths took on a more massive look. Running

boards were concealed by the lower portion of the door, which flared out to cover them. Grille bars were still horizontal but reduced to just five heavy bars—the top bar containing the parking lamps at the outer edge, inboard of the headlamps. A more massive bumper with two large over-riders protected the front license plate. Under the bumper was a sheet metal "air scoop" to provide "race track cooling."

The familiar sailing ship took on a different look as well, with the ship outline molded into a plastic insert.

At long last, major changes had taken place both under the car and under the hood. A new perimeter frame replaced the "X" brace frame of previous years, although the wheelbase remained at 117 inches.

Motive power now came from a 95-horse-power 217 ci six (formerly used by Dodge) with a bore and stroke of 3 1/4x4 3/8-inches (Canadian buyers got a 218 ci, with bore and stroke of 3 3/8x4 1/16 inches). As demand for war material continued to siphon supplies of aluminum, cooper, chromium, steel, and tungsten,

Plymouth's postwar car was the P15 series. For three years there would be no discernible change in the appearance of the cars. Wood bodies for station wagons was still supplied by U.S. Body & Forging. *Lawrence Abbott*

Plymouth's familiar aluminum pistons were replaced by cast-iron—as were war-year replacement pistons. Prior to shutdown of assembly plants—dictated by the government—stainless steel moldings and grilles were replaced by steel moldings and painted gray in color. Known now as "black out" models, these cars have become highly collectible.

Only 152,427 1942 Plymouths were built prior to shut down of the assembly line on January 31, 1942. New car sales had been frozen January 1st, awaiting regulations of a rationing program to be announced by January 15th—the rationing program was postponed until February—an amendment to the sales freeze came on January 10th, when sales of new cars were permitted to the military and those holding an A-1 preference rating. Cars shipped after January 15th were ordered into government "stockpiles." Sales to doctors, nurses, veterinarians, law enforcement officers, and mail carriers were allowed under a January 29th amendment to the original sales freeze order. On Valentine's Day, 1942, all new cars in stock were put into long-term storage—dealers were ordered to make the vehicle's tires and tubes available to the military when requested—and owners were required by law to certify to the government they had only five tires and tubes for each vehicle they owned. Spare parts became nearly non-existent. Gasoline rationing (three gallons per week) and a 35 mile-per-hour "Victory" speed limit insured that most vehicles saw only minimum use "for the duration."

It would be four long years before new cars of any kind would be available again.

Model P15
Convertible, wood-body station wagon ★★★★★
Business and auxiliary seat coupe ★★★★
Two- and four-door sedan ★★

1945 Through 1949—Models P15C and P15S

As the war in Europe came to an end and with the defeat of Japan imminent, the government began letting the auto industry return to production of automobiles. Chrysler Corporation was late getting back into building automobiles (although production of civilian Dodge trucks had begun earlier), with the first new cars not coming off the line until October of 1945. Chrysler's total production for 1945 amounted to just 1,880 cars—420 Dodges, 368 DeSotos, 322 Chrysler Sixes, and 770 Plymouths. Plymouth production was so minuscule that Nash ranked third in industry sales!

Before production could begin, 18,000 prewar machines had to be rebuilt and 20,000 machine tools had to be set in place, along with 70 miles of conveyors, 3,100 linear feet of spray booths, and half a mile of drying ovens, before assembly could begin.

Pent-up demand, along with material shortages, would see the new postwar Plymouth built virtually unchanged until being replaced early in 1949. The 770 cars built in 1945 (684 Deluxe P14S and 86 P15C Special Deluxe) were considered to be 1946 models. Cars built after January 1, 1947, became '47s as those built after January 1, 1948, became 48s. Cars built after December 1, 1948, were considered "first series" 1949 models.

The P15 Plymouth convertible was one of only three U.S. convertibles that did not have rear quarter windows in its postwar models. Tops were powered-operated by two vacuum cylinders mounted behind the rear seat. *Jim Benjaminson*

Bodies for the P15 series were virtually the same as '42, with minor trim differences. The grille followed the same design motif used since '39, only now the bars were no longer divided across the front of the car, but fell in an alternating wide and narrow pattern. Parking lamps moved below the headlamps, incorporated in the third wide bar. A heavy metal casting now contained the Mayflower ship, cloisonné emblems going by the wayside. The front bumper wrapped around the fender to the wheel opening and most cars were fitted with a pair of bumper over-riders.

Bodyside trim was wider and smooth—eliminating the groove found on '42s. At the rear, only the taillamps and stop lamp were changed—with the Mayflower emblem embedded into the stop light glass.

Few mechanical changes had taken place, the engine remaining a 95-horsepower, 217 ci six. Compression ratio was reduced to 6.6:1 from 6.8:1 (export cars boasting only 5.6:1). The economy engine package of years past was also continued. Material shortages found Stromberg supplying carburetors in place of Carter, Auburn clutches replacing Borg & Beck, and some engines built in 1948 had to be fitted with steel camshafts (these engines carried the letter "S" in their serial number).

Tires sizes remained at 6:00x16-inches on cars built through October of 1947, when a gradual phase in of 6.70x15-inch tires began. Whitewall tires were not available from the factory at any time during this period and early production cars were shipped with five wheels but only four tires.

Visual changes were non-existent although running changes were made—interior robe rails and engine splash pans were discontinued during 1946—externally only the cover on the door lock changed!

Prices, although controlled by the Office of Price Administration, continued to escalate to the point where the most-expensive model of '46 would not have purchased the least-expensive model of 1948! Individual model year production totals were not kept—1,059,489 P15s were built during this time period, with Plymouth solidly holding its traditional third place in industry sales.

Model P17 & P18
Three-passenger business coupe,
convertible, wood-body station wagon ★★★★★
All-metal Suburban station wagon,
fastback two-door ★★★
(add ★ for Savoy or Deluxe Suburban)
Club coupe ★★★
Four-door ★★

It wouldn't be until March of 1949 that Plymouth would introduce its first all-new postwar car. The 1949's ribbed bumpers (like those of the '37 DeSoto) would prove to be extremely popular with customizers. Conservatively styled four-door sedans would again be the most popular model with consumers. *Lanny Knutson*

Although built on the longest wheelbase ever for Plymouth, the 1949 models were criticized for being too boxy looking. Even the sporty convertible coupe appeared short and stubby when the top was up. *David Kruger*

1949—Models P17 and P18
In 1939, Plymouth had been the first of the low-priced three to unveil its new models. For 1949, it would be the last. Entering its Silver Anniversary year, Chrysler spent $90 million bringing its first all-new postwar designs on the market. True to its heritage, Plymouth was conservatively styled—in what would later become

Also relegated to the short-wheelbase, low-line model was the fastback two-door sedan, which like the busi- ness coupe, is enjoying a resurgence in popularity with collectors. *Jim Benjaminson*

known as the "Keller three-box school of styling"—one box piled on top of two boxes laid end-to-end.

Riding on a longer 118 1/2-inch wheelbase, the new cars were 4 3/16-inches shorter than the P15 they replaced. The concept of "larger on the inside, smaller on the outside" is again blamed on Chrysler President K. T. Keller—and it would haunt the corporation for years to come.

Introduced to the public in March, the cars were referred to as the "second series" 1949 Plymouths. Plymouth again returned to offering three distinct series. At the bottom of the ladder was the P17 Deluxe, built on a 111-inch wheelbase. Austere in terms of trim, brightwork, and upholstery, it came in just three body styles—single-seat three-passenger businessman's coupe, five-passenger fastback two-door sedan, and a revolutionary two-door, all-steel-body "Suburban" station wagon.

A second Deluxe series, this on the longer 118 1/2-inch wheelbase, was also devoid of extra brightwork but featured slightly better interior appointments. It was built in just two body styles—two-door notchback "club" coupe and four-door sedan. Why it and the P17 both bore the designation "Deluxe" was never explained.

At the top of the line was the P18 Special Deluxe, also on the long-wheelbase chassis. Enjoying more external brightwork and sumptuous interior appointments, the Special Deluxe was available in club coupe; four-door, convertible club coupe; or four-door, wood-body station wagon.

From the cowl forward, all three cars shared the same sheet metal, grille, and bumper. Sedan doors were all hinged at the front and for the first time since the Town Sedan of '42, rear quarter-windows were placed in the door frame rather than the body. Not one single piece of sheet metal, glass, or trim was retained from previous years. New "Bulls-Eye" headlamps sat higher and further apart, above a wider grille that was easily recognizable in terms of family resemblance. Three wide and two narrow grille bars alternated down the face of the car, with parking lamps set under the headlamps, surrounded by the edges of the widest middle and lower grille bar. The unique bumpers carried three horizontal ribs, giving a delicate but expensive look (they would prove to be popular with the custom car set!).

Hood and deck lids sat lower, yet still rose above the fenders; a heavy belt molding

34

Nineteen fifty would be the last year for Plymouth wood body station wagons. Since 1949, the wood wagon had been built with an all-steel roof panel. Higher initial cost and high-maintenance costs spelled doom for the woody in favor of the all-steel wagon. Less than 2,100 were built in its final year. *Patricia Murphy*

separated the rectangular greenhouse from the lower body. More glass area (a 37 percent increase in windshield glass area, and 35 percent increase in the rear window glass area) and blind rear quarters all contributed to a formal look. Fenders blended neatly into the doors—detachable rear fenders remained a Plymouth hallmark.

All series were treated to one of the most beautiful instrument panels ever placed in a low-priced automobile. Three circular white-on-black gauges sat on a rich, dark wood-grain panel, and near the center sat chrome-plated heater-defroster controls. Equally new was a key-start ignition switch replacing the key and push-button of previous models.

Four-door sedans, in Deluxe and Special Deluxe trim, continued to be the most popular Plymouths in 1950. Special Deluxe models can be easily identified by bright windshield trim. *Charles Park*

Mechanical changes for the second series '49s were few. The box perimeter frame and double-wheel cylinder front brakes continued from the P15. Engine displacement remained unchanged, although horsepower was increased to 97 by raising compression to 7.0:1. A most-welcome upgrade was replacement of fuses with a circuit breaker electrical system.

The all-steel station wagon was an industry first (true, Jeep—a "commercial" vehicle—had an all-steel wagon earlier), and was literally the run-away hit of the year. Although expensive (exceeded only by the convertible and four-door woody wagon), it accounted for 3.7 percent of all '49 Plymouths sold—and its sales would only continue to climb. Years later, Dell's Car Buyer's Guide would call it "probably the most functional automobile built after the Model T." Its popularity would spell doom for all wood-body wagons.

Not getting as early a start because of its delayed introduction, sales of 520,385 "second series" 1949 Plymouths was slightly lower than those of 1941. To help meet postwar new car demands, an assembly plant at San Leandro, California, went on line, joining those at Windsor, Ontario, Canada; Detroit's Lynch Road; Los Angeles, California; and Evansville, Indiana.

Model P19 & P20
Three-passenger business coupe,
convertible, wood-body station wagon ★★★★★
All-metal Suburban station wagon,
fastback two-door ★★★
(add ★ for Savoy or Deluxe Suburban)
Club coupe ★★★
Four-door ★★

1950—Models P19 and P20
First glances can be deceiving. In the case of the 1950 Plymouth, the first assumption would be that the car was little more than a restyled '49; although the two were definite siblings, a host of changes had taken place, so much so that only the doors and deck lid were bolt-for-bolt interchanges. As in 1949, three distinct series, on two wheelbases, carrying the same model names but different engineering codes were built.

The short-wheelbase P19 Deluxe included a fastback two-door sedan, three-passenger business coupe, and all-metal two-door Suburban station wagon. Long-wheelbase P20 Deluxes offered only a two-door club coupe and four-door sedan. The Special Deluxe, also coded P20, included the club coupe, four-door sedan, convertible club coupe, and wood-body four-door station wagon.

Spelling doom for the wood wagon was the introduction of the all-steel "Suburban" in 1949. For 1950, a deluxe version was added to the option list. Although built on the short-wheelbase chassis, the all-steel wagon was relatively expensive but it still outsold the wood body wagon by a wide margin. *William Bell*

A simplified three-bar grille and plain bumper face plate distinguished the 1950 from its predecessor. Changes at the rear included wrap-around taillamps incorporating the stop lamps—gone was the center-mounted stop light. A "T" type trunk lid handle and repositioned license plate light marked the remaining changes.

Sitting on a wider stance, the front tread was increased 7/16-inch by moving the centerline of the wheel rim outward. A wider rear axle pushed the rear tread out 2 inches. Gear ratios remained the same, and the center carrier was interchangeable with earlier years. Engine displacement and horsepower remained the same as '49.

Sales of the all-metal Suburban wagon continued to soar, despite grumbling from consumers the vehicle was "too plain." This demand was met by the addition of the Special Suburban. Extra equipment on this wagon included armrests on both

Known as the Concord series for 1951, the three-passenger business coupe on the short-wheelbase chassis shows off its charm in this profile view. Many owners prefer to dress them up with trim from the Cranbrook series. *Frank Matteo*

A bolder three-tooth grille and sloping hood marked the 1951 models. The Cranbrook four-door sedan, as pictured here, was again the top seller. *Chris George*

doors, assist straps and armrests in the rear compartment, glovebox lock, dual horns, horn ring, chrome radio grille, exterior beltline moldings, front bumper guards, chrome-plated tailgate hinges, and chrome rear window divider. Upgraded upholstery in the Special Suburban included rear sidewalls and wheelwells upholstered in pleated brown vinyl resin fabric, a headliner in brown checked woven fiber, and two-tone door panels of brown vinyl and brown checked fabric.

Sales of the wood-body, four-door wagon had continued to slide, dwindling to just 2,057 units. Although beautiful to look at, the wood wagon required constant upkeep—the factory recommended refinishing the woodwork every six months or "more often if needed," a chore usually ignored. Without much fanfare the woody wagon slipped into oblivion at the end of the model run.

Sales of 610,954 cars broke 1937's record for Plymouth, helping it retain its traditional third place in industry sales.

Model P22 & P23
Three-passenger business coupe,
convertible, wood-body station wagon ★★★★★
All-metal Suburban station wagon,
fastback two-door ★★★
(add ★ for Savoy or Deluxe Suburban)
Belvedere hardtop (1951-52) ★★★★
Club coupe ★★★
Four-door ★★

1951—Models P22, P23S, and P23C
Plymouth entered the 1951 market with, if not three completely new models, at least three new model names. Abandoning the term "Deluxe" (used since 1933) and "Special Deluxe"

(since 1941), the new models were named Concord, Cambridge, and Cranbrook. Engineering codes attempted to alleviate some of the identify problems of the 1949 and 1950 long- and short-wheelbase Deluxe. The Concord, built on the 111-inch wheelbase chassis, became the P22. In turn, the Cambridge was coded P23S, while the other long-wheelbase Cranbrook became the P23C.

The names were new, but body styles remained the same as before—Concords were built in fastback two-door, business coupe, and Suburban station wagon forms. Last year's Special Suburban upgrade continued, and was now known as the Savoy Suburban.

The Cambridge continued to offer only a club coupe and four-door sedan while the Cranbrook offered both of those plus a convertible club coupe—and for the first time in Plymouth's history, a sporty two-door "hardtop convertible" called the Cranbrook Belvedere. Unlike the real convertible with a folding top, the "hardtop" convertible had a fixed roof with pillar-less side windows. Although Chrysler had originated the hardtop idea back in '46 with a handful of Town & Country hardtops, it dropped the ball, leaving the door open for GM to popularize the body type. The Cranbrook Belvedere was a "catch-up" model to match Chevrolet's Bel Air, which was introduced the previous year.

With a new front end marked by a sloping hood and new lower and wider grille, the car took on a heavier look, effectively hiding its '49 origins. A heavy center bar floated across the grille cavity, carrying three massive vertical teeth—the outer two of which were nearly hidden by the similarly shaped bumper over-rides.

The once-familiar Mayflower ship ornament continued to grow more abstract each year, now sprouting "speed waves" that looked more like wings. Wheel cutouts were squared off, side trim was revised, but from the rear the car had changed little—the deck lid, in fact, would interchange with the '49.

With the addition of the Cranbrook Belvedere, two-tone paint returned to Plymouth for the first time since 1941. The Belvedere was available in any of eight solid colors or four two-tone combinations. Seldom seen was two-tone paint on the Cranbrook club coupe or four-door, a late-year addition to the option list.

Under the hood the '51 Plymouth was boringly the same—a 217-ci six developing 97 horsepower. The Korean War continued to siphon off badly needed raw materials, placing restrictions on the auto industry's use of chromium and copper; many "chrome"-plated trim pieces such as parking light bezels, taillight bezels, headlamp rims, name plates, and license plate housings were coated with a colorless enamel protectant. Unless cared for properly, the "chrome" would soon begin to look dingy. Cars built after mid-April began using steel asbestos cylinder head gaskets in place of copper gaskets and engines which had traditionally been painted silver aluminum were painted gray. Eventually the lack of copper affected the availability of radios and heaters. Unlike the post-World War II era, all cars were still shipped with five tires, although whitewalls were unavailable.

For a time it appeared rationing of automobiles was a likely possibility, with curtailment of production all together possible if the industry was called back into service. This time consumers heeded the warnings and didn't delay taking delivery of new cars.

1952—Models P22, P23S, and P23C

Despite continued shortages and threats of nationwide steel strikes, cars built to 1952 specifications began coming off the lines in November, although they wouldn't officially be announced until January.

Plymouth boasted "46 advances"—but the casual observer commented "no change!" What changes were made were hardly perceptible. The hood medallion, now round instead of shield-shaped, was most obvious at the front. The Mayflower ship sat lower and regained some its "ship" shape, as the "bow waves" of '51 were washed away. The grille, headlamps, parking lamps, bumpers, and over-riders were identical. From the side, the fender script, for those who cared enough to notice, was in script, rather than block letters, and at the rear the nameplate was moved down with the letters becoming part of the license plate light. Taillights, rear bumper, and over-riders were unchanged.

The changes were so minimal Plymouth chose to carry over the same engineering codes and model names. Serial number sequences were not consecutive as they had been with the P15 from 1945 through 1949; the numbers bumped just enough to provide positive model-year identification.

Body styles remained the same: the Concord in business coupe, fastback two-door sedan, Suburban, and Savoy Suburban form on the same 111-inch wheelbase; the Cambridge club coupe and four-door sedan; Cranbrook club coupe, four-door sedan, convertible club coupe, and Cranbrook Belvedere convertible hardtop on the 118 1/2-inch wheelbase.

Only the Cranbrook Belvedere could easily be identified as a '52 by virtue of its new roof and paint treatment. The side window drip molding, rather than stopping at the beltline, swept down behind the quarter-window, crossed over the beltline, and flowed down the fender-body seam (rear fenders were still detachable) to the rear

Because of Korean War restrictions, changes were kept to a minimum for 1952. Most notable are the round hood medallion, different hood ornament, and different-style lettering on the side of the car. *Alf Munthe*

bumper. When two-toned, the color of the top cascaded across the deck lid, the moldings serving as the dividing line between colors. Available in one standard color—Belmont Blue—three two-tone combinations were optional. The rarely seen two-tone was still offered on the Cranbrook club coupe and four-door sedan.

A new cylinder head changed combustion chamber design, with no gain in horsepower. Of the low-priced three, Plymouth was the only one to offer only a three-speed manual transmission. Chevrolet gave buyers a choice with the addition of Power Glide in 1950 while Ford offered both overdrive and Ford-o-Matic in '51. Having

A one-piece windshield and integral rear fenders marked the significant changes to Plymouth for 1953. Chrome trim was kept to a minimum even on the Cranbrook series. *Norman Townsend*

First introduced in 1951, the Cranbrook Belvedere hardtop convertible was the most changed of any of the 1952 models, as evidenced by the two-tone paint treatment, which cascaded off the roof panel, over the rear quarter, and onto the trunk lid. *Dale Reinke*

pioneered overdrive in 1934, Chrysler made little use of it over the years, and it would be midyear before Chrysler saw fit to make it available on both Plymouths and Dodges (and reintroduce it to DeSoto). By year's end, 17 percent of production had been fitted with it.

Separate production totals were not kept for the years 1951-1952. Twenty-two months and 1,007,662 cars later, the P22-P23 series ceased production on October 2, 1952.

Model P24
Convertible ★★★★★
Suburban, club coupe, business coupe ★★★
Four-door ★★

1953—Models P24-1 and P24-2
Nineteen hundred and fifty-three marked both Plymouth's and DeSoto's Silver Anniversary—the company chose not to even mention it (perhaps in light of both Ford and Buick's fiftieth anniversaries?). The 1949-1952 cars had been big

cars that looked small. For 1953, overall length was decreased just 1 inch—but the cars looked considerably smaller. Keller's dictates of smaller on the outside, larger on the inside were at work once again.

The 1953 Plymouth was caught in a time warp—at a time when bigger was better, it had grown smaller. As other makes plastered on chrome trim, Plymouth took it off. As the horsepower race began to heat up, Plymouth's only powerplant was a 20-year-old flathead six. Plymouth was one of only seven makes not to offer power steering, and of the low-priced three, the only one not to offer an automatic transmission.

Built under the engineering code P24, models were pared to just two: the Cambridge (P24-1) and the Cranbrook (P24-2). Deleted from the lineup was the short-wheelbase Concord; from now on, just one wheelbase would have to do—114 inches—3 inches longer than the Concords had been, but 4 1/2-inches shorter than before.

Among the rarest accessories for 1953 are the real wire wheels which were available either painted or chrome-plated. Other rare accessories include the continental spare tire carrier and fender skirts, all of which were available through Plymouth dealers. *Jim Benjaminson*

Body styles in the Cambridge series included a four-door sedan, club sedan (two-door sedan to most), business coupe, and Suburban station wagon. The club sedan and business coupe shared the same general body details, the club sedan having a rear quarter-window while the business coupe had a solidly fixed rear side window. Business coupes came without a rear seat and the option of carrying the spare tire in the trunk or rear compartment. An optional rear seat cushion could be ordered to turn the vehicle into a family car on weekends while still retaining its business capabilities during the week.

Cranbrook body styles included a four-door sedan, club coupe, convertible club coupe, Cranbrook Belvedere hardtop convertible, and the Savoy Suburban station wagon.

Modern touches included a one-piece windshield and non-detachable rear fenders. And they were plain—Cambridges were especially devoid of chrome trim. Headlamps sat higher

Nearly devoid of chrome trim was the bottom-line Plaza series for 1954, an example of which is shown here. *Jim Benjaminson*

The Belvedere name, which had originally been applied only to the hardtop convertible, was now used across the board for the top car line. Nineteen fifty-four would mark the only year a customer could order a factory-installed continental kit on any body type except station wagon. The hardtop convertible, now known as the Sport Coupe, featured special below-beltline trim across the top of the doors and rear quarters. *Darrel Davis*

and wider, with parking lamps directly beneath them at the extreme outer ends of the grille bar, which flowed across the grille cavity into a similarly shaped body crease wrapping around the side of the car to form a rub rail contour on the front fender. The rub rail ran back to the leading edge of the front door, while a similar rub rail began on the lower rear door to flow across the rear fender to a point just beneath the taillamps. The grille was a simple horizontal bar, chromed only across the center one-third—provided the buyer had opted for the option which included a chrome hood molding. Chrome trim on the front and rear fender rub rails was also optional.

Plymouth for 1953 sat on a fully boxed, four-cross-member-perimeter frame that was 6 inches wider than before. The rear axle was moved 4 1/2-inches ahead of center on the springs, with a higher kickup for the axle, resulting in a lower frame allowing a flatter floor and more leg room in the rear seat.

Under the hood sat the same engine used since '42, still at 217 ci, now rated at 100 horsepower by virtue of a .1 increase in compression. Transmission choices at the beginning of the model run included a regular three-speed manual or three-speed with overdrive. Added to the option list in April was a semi-automatic called Hy-Drive.

In its simplest form, Hy-Drive placed a torque converter ahead of the standard clutch and transmission in place of the flywheel; it consisted of four major parts: impeller, turbine, primary stator, and secondary stator. The converter was a welded, self-contained assembly with a replaceable ring gear. Hy-Drive received its oil supply from the engine oil pump through passages in an adapter plate and the converter housing. Oil changes required 11 quarts of oil, but were called for only semi-yearly.

Tire size remained at 6.70x15 inches. Despite its otherwise Plain Jane appearance, the addition

The Belvedere series added its own station wagon model for the year featuring deluxe trim and upholstery. *Darrel Davis*

All Belvedere models for 1955 could be two-toned using the bodyside trim as the dividing line for what was called Sport Tone trim. While some Chrysler lines offered three-tone paint, Plymouth did not. *William Brisbane*

It was unusual to see the Belvedere convertible painted a solid color but that's the way this owner preferred his car. *Merv Afflerbach, Jr.*

Taking Plymouth out of the old maid class was the high-performance Fury sport coupe introduced midyear 1956. It was powered by a 303-ci V-8, and featured egg shell white paint with gold anodized side trim, grille, and hubcaps. *Jim Benjaminson*

of real wire wheels—in either painted or chrome finish—was a welcome albeit expensive option. Supplied by Motor Wheel, painted wire wheels upped the price of the car by nearly $95; chrome wires increased it by nearly $250.

As the model run came to a close, Plymouth looked back on the best year it had ever had. Record sales of 650,451 cars helped Plymouth maintain its traditional third place by a substantial margin over a hard charging Buick... but then came 1954...

Model P25

Convertible ★★★★★
Suburban, club coupe, business coupe ★★★
Four-door ★★

1954—Model P25

Once again Plymouth would field only a slightly warmed-over redesign, as it had done in 1952. Only a new grille, taillamps, and additional body trim would set the car apart from its '53 stablemate. This time, there would again be three models, each pirating the model name from individual body styles of the past. Leading the pack was the Belvedere (P25-3)—now a complete line consisting of four-door sedan, sport coupe (formerly the Cranbrook Belvedere), convertible coupe, and two-door Suburban station wagon. Next in line was the Savoy (P25-2)—the name pirated from the deluxe station wagon. Savoys came in four-door sedan, club sedan (two-door), or club coupe forms. At the bottom end of the pricing ladder sat the Plaza (P25-1) in four-door, club sedan, business coupe, or Suburban wagon form.

A restyled grille bar, now chrome-plated across the width of the car, again acted as a beveled cap running to the rub rail on the fender. The center of the bar featured the Plymouth name spelled out in red block letters against a gold plastic background.

Belvederes were treated to a full-length chrome sill molding and full-length side moldings, while a rear fender molding gave just the slightest hint of a tail fin. Longer by 3 5/8-inch than the '53s, (except station wagons) the extra length was accomplished by moving the bumpers outward.

Two-tone upholstery helped spruce up the interior, and for the first time, front-seat floors were covered with carpet rather than rubber mats.

Added to the sales line-up for 1956 was the four-door Sport Sedan hardtop. A special two-piece rear side window folded into itself to allow a completely open window area. *Arthur Hoock*

Commonly referred to as a "two-door post" by most enthusiasts, Plymouth preferred to call this model a "club sedan." Later in the model run, a special blue-and-white Savoy club sedan (opposite to the way this car is painted) was built and sold as the "St. Louis Blues Special" to honor outstanding sales by Plymouth dealers in the St. Louis district. The car, which sold for $1,776, came with two-tone paint, Sportone trim (as seen on this car), and whitewall tires as standard equipment. *Jim Benjaminson*

At the start of production Plymouth retained the same mechanical features as in 1953. In April, PowerFlite was introduced, and it was a fully automatic transmission. More expensive ($189 vs. $146 for the Hy-Drive), PowerFlite was a two-speed using essentially the same torque converter as Hy-Drive; unlike Hy-Drive, PowerFlite relied on its own oil supply. With PowerFlite came a more powerful engine as well, a 110-horsepower 230-ci six "borrowed" from Dodge. Built under the same engineering code (P25) as the 217, the 230 could be identified by the diamond stamped on top of the cylinder head and in the engine serial number.

In spite of these upgrades, Plymouth soon found itself in trouble—by December of 1953 sales began to tumble; February sales were down 40 percent from 1953 with the factory building only cars already ordered and sold. When the smoke cleared, Plymouth had fallen from third to fifth place, behind both Buick and Oldsmobile, with production of only 463,148 cars.

1955 All Models
Convertible, Sport Coupe ★★★★★
Club sedan, station wagon ★★★
Four-door ★★

1955—Models P26 and P27

Ninteen hundred and fifty-five was a year of magic for the automobile industry. Chevrolet, Ford, and Plymouth introduced all-new cars for the season, the economy was booming, and automobile sales set all-time records. Chevrolet hit the boards on October 28, Ford on November 12. The new Plymouth made its debut five days later. If ever an automobile had come full circle in its thinking, the 1955 Plymouth was proof of the turn-around.

Truly a "clean sheet of paper" design, these were the first cars that Virgil Exner and his design teams were able to influence from start to finish. From the outset, Exner dictated form and function be correlated in every step of the design—a car designed with motion as its basic styling theme. It had no sooner hit the streets than the automotive press began writing it "could well become a classic." Gone forever was the bigger on the inside, smaller on the outside concept K. T. Keller so dearly loved. Everything that could be done to make the car look long and low was done. Rooflines were lowered by 1.35 inches, the wheelbase was increased to 115 inches, but it was the addition of 10.3 inches to the overall length that made the car most noticeable. Even the front tread was increased by 2.56 inches so the front wheels tracked the same as the rear.

Sharply canted front fenders nosed into the air, forming a clean, sweeping line to the rear,

Torsion bar suspension, smaller wheels, and radical new styling gave Plymouth its sleekest look ever for 1957. Accenting the "Forward Look" best were the hardtop and convertible models. Especially pleasing was the Belvedere Sport Sedan, such as this one owned by Dennis Cutshall. *Jim Benjaminson*

where a reverse cant undercut the taillamps. The grille was a simple bar, only bolder, running from side to side before forming a box over the parking lamps. A massive front bumper with slight prow swept from wheel opening to wheel opening. On the hood rode an abstract form of the good ship Mayflower. Taillamps were hooded by the reverse cant of the rear fender. A lip along the trailing edge of the deck lid rode above a pronounced cove running across the rear of the car. Rooflines were accentuated by a wrap-around "Full View" windshield that curved up into the roof and around the A-pillars.

But there was more to the car than just looks. Engineering had been busy and underneath the hood sat a real, live V-8 engine. With the introduction of a V-8 Plymouth found it necessary to code cars according to engine type—either six-cylinder or V-8. Six-cylinder cars all became the P26 series, and V-8s were coded P27. About the only things carried over from 1954 were the model names, Belvedere, Savoy, and Plaza, each again assigned its own code number. A six-cylinder Plaza was a P26-1; a V-8 Plaza was a P27-1. The Belvedere was coded as 2, the Savoy as 3.

Plazas were sold in five body types, including business coupe (no rear seat and fixed rear quarter-windows), club sedan (two-door), four-door sedan, two-door station wagon–and for the first time since the last woody wagon of 1950 a four-door wagon. The Savoy was available in just two body types, club sedan or four-door, while the Belvedere came in club sedan, four-door sedan, sport coupe (two-door hardtop),

Continuing the tradition set in 1956, the high-performance Fury Sport Coupe was continued for 1957. Available only in white with gold trim and special interior, the Fury was a top-dollar car for the enthusiast who demanded the best regardless of cost. *Bill Burge*

convertible coupe–available only with V-8 power–and a four-door station wagon.

The new body rode on a longer, boxed frame fitted with two additional body mounts, located both inside and outside the frame rails. Front suspension changes included non-parallel "A" arms, Oriflow shocks inside coil springs, splay-mounted rear springs widened to 2.5 inches, and "sea-leg" mounted rear shock absorbers. Standard equipment on all models was a one-piece, spring-steel, torsion-type sway eliminator. V-8 cars had idler-arm steering with equal-length tie rods. Safety Rim wheels, introduced back in 1941, were standard and all cars received larger brakes.

Fleet buyers and old maid school teachers could still order the 230-ci 117-horsepower PowerFlow six, coupled to any of Plymouth's three transmission offerings, manual, overdrive, or PowerFlite (Hy-Drive had been discontinued).

For those who demanded change, the choice to make was one of the Hy-Fire V-8s. First offered in 241-ci, 157-horsepower or 260-ci, 167-horsepower form, it wasn't long before a 177-horsepower 260 equipped with a four-barrel carburetor was available. While new to Plymouth, the engine was supplied by Dodge and had been used in its B series truck line earlier. Unlike the other Chrysler V-8s, Hy-Fire was of a polyspherical design, rather than hemispherical such as was used in Chrysler, Dodge, or DeSoto engines. Like the six, any of Plymouth's three transmissions could be coupled to the new V-8.

And at long last, Plymouth owners could order power steering as a $96.50 option, power brakes (released as a service package to be retrofitted on all cars back to 1951), two-way power front seat, power windows on all models, and AirTemp air conditioning.

Sales of the '55 took off like a rocket. Demand far outstripped supply of V-8, PowerFlite-equipped cars, with dealers being told to steer customers to sixes with straight sticks! Sales jumped 40 percent as the factory began working three shifts to keep up. At the close of the model run, Plymouth had broken its 1950 production record, delivering 705,455 cars—still not quite enough to dislodge Buick from third place. Which had been most important—the new

Although station wagons would be a big part of Plymouth sales, models such as this Savoy four-door continued to be Plymouth's sales leader. *Donald Sprayberry*

styling or the new V-8—is hard to say, but V-8 sales accounted for 48 percent of all cars sold.

1956 All Models

Convertible, Sport Coupe ★★★★★
Club sedan, station wagon ★★★
Four-door ★★
Fury Sport Coupe ★★★★★

1956—Models P28 and P29

For 1956, Ford and Chevrolet were content to offer minor restyling of their product. Of the low-priced three, Plymouth changed the most radically with the addition of new rear quarter-panels, giving a hint of what would come in the future. Exner called it "airfoil" styling.

Longer—by only an inch—slimmer, and taller, the airfoil fenders trailed off into space, "leaving no question that the car is racing forward." Slashed at a steep angle, the fenders gave a "flying away" look when viewed in profile. Airfin taillights, slim and tapered to emphasize height over a "jet-tube" back-up lamp housing all emphasized the flight-sweep styling of the car.

With this emphasis on the rear of the car, the front was little changed—a slightly revised grille bar featured a grid pattern in the center of the bar, adorned with a gold "V" if the car was V-8 equipped. What had once been the Mayflower ship on the hood had now sprouted wings and became a jet plane.

Model designations again remained the same—Belvedere, Savoy, and Plaza—with engi-

neering codes bumped one number to differentiate over the previous years. Six-cylinder cars were coded P28, V-8s were P29. Plazas carried the additional code of 1, but this time the Savoy and Belvedere swapped numbers, Savoy becoming 2 and Belvedere becoming 3.

Leading the charge was the Belvedere, available in four-door, club sedan (two-door), sport coupe, or convertible coupe (the convertible again required V-8 power). New to the line-up this year was Plymouth's first "Sport Sedan," a true four-door hardtop. Stressing it was a full-size

Changes were kept to a minimum for the 1958 Plymouth. Most noticeable from the rear were the round taillamps. A single back-up lamp resided in the center of the rear bumper as well. *Michael Morelli*

The 1958 Fury, called the "Star of the Forward Look," now sported Buckskin Beige as its only color. The grille, hubcaps, and side trim continued the theme of gold accents. Two engines were available, both sporting dual four-barrel carburetors. *Jim Benjaminson*

four-door, engineering had devised a clever—but complicated—method of rolling the entire side window into the rear door. Two window glasses were employed, the rear-most window moving forward and down alongside the forward window, which moved slightly rearward and down, all controlled by a single handle.

The Savoy line gained a sport coupe in addition to the club sedan and four-door. Plazas came in four-door, club sedan, or business coupe.

Station wagons continued to grow in popularity (14 percent of 1956 production), and were given their own model designations. Corresponding to the Belvedere was the Sport Suburban four-door wagon. What would have been a Savoy became the Custom Suburban, in either two- or four-door, with the Deluxe Suburban, corresponding to the Plaza, available only as a two-door. All wagons were available with buyer's choice of six-cylinder or V-8 power.

Chassis changes were minimal but there was a new V-8 under the hood. Looking much like its predecessor, the new V-8 was Plymouth's own version, slightly longer in block length, with more "meat" between the cylinder bores and larger bearings on the crankshaft. Enlarged valve ports helped the new engine breathe better. At 277 ci producing 187 horsepower, it was found exclusively in Belvederes and Sport Suburbans. The "old" Hy-Fire 270 was carried over in Plazas and Savoys. A four-barrel carb brought the new V-8's horsepower up to an even 200. Fully 60 percent of '56 production would be built with V-8 power.

For the 40 percent staying with the PowerFlow six, horsepower was bumped up slightly, to 125. For the first time, an optional Power Pack utilizing a dual-throat Stromberg carburetor, special intake manifold, larger air cleaner, and higher rear axle ratio could be ordered, raising horsepower of the six to 131.

Other engineering changes included a switch to 12-volt electrics and push-button shifting, which was mechanically controlled and virtually trouble-free. Plymouth drivers had to learn to use their left hand as the shift buttons were located in a pod to the driver's left, where it would be out of reach of curious children. "Typewriter" shifting would be a Chrysler Corporation hallmark through 1964.

If the image of an old maid's car had tarnished in '55, it went completely out the window with the introduction of the hairy-chested Fury announced in January. Based on the Belvedere Sport Coupe, the similarities between the two cars ended there! Just days before introduction, a Fury running on the sands at Daytona Beach, Florida, set a record at 143.598 miles per hour. This was no old maid's car.

Under the hood sat a Canadian-sourced 303-ci V-8 pumping out 240 horsepower. It had a bore and stroke of 3 13/16x3 5/16-inches, 9.25:1 compression, a single Carter four-barrel, reinforced dome-type pistons, high-performance camshaft, high-load valve springs, balanced connecting rods, and a high-speed distributor. The Fury used a heavy duty Borg & Beck 10-inch clutch, and ran on 7.10x15-inch high-speed nylon cord blackwall tires fitted to 5 1/2-inch rims. With all of this and its heavy duty springs and 11-inch brakes, the Fury was not a car for the timid.

Topping the sales ladder for 1959 was the Sport Fury, in either hardtop or convertible form. The Fury name was degraded to include an entire line of models, including four-door sedans. The fake spare tire imprint on the deck lid was a favorite styling gimmick of Virgil Exner. *Robert Hinds, Sr.*

Built only overseas for export markets was this 24-inch stretch seven-passenger sedan. Buyers were given the choice between V-8 or six-cylinder power, or manual or automatic transmission. *Johan Veltmans*

If that wasn't enough go power, a $746.90—install it yourself—package was available with dual four-barrel carbs, special air cleaners, an aluminum intake manifold, high-performance camshaft and tappets, and hand choke—raising the Fury's horsepower to 270. (The same kit could be installed on the 277 V-8, raising its horsepower to 230).

Looks, as well as "go," were also part of the package. Finished only in Eggshell white, with gold anodized side trim, gold grille, nameplates, and hubcaps, even a gold-and-white interior, there was no mistaking the Fury.

In an industry wide downturn, Plymouth production was off 37 percent, as sales dropped to just 571,634 for the year—and Buick was still third.

1957 All Models
Convertible, Sport Coupe ★★★★★
Club sedan, station wagon ★★★
Four-door ★★
Fury Sport Coupe ★★★★★

Plymouth for 1957
At the hallowed halls of General Motors styling, a bombshell called Flight Sweep Styling had scored a direct hit. The only problem was, Chrysler had it and GM wasn't happy! How unhappy were they? Unhappy enough to spend millions scrapping a one-year-only body in an attempt to catch up.

In an unprecedented move, Chrysler Corporation had completely redesigned all five of its car lines after just two years (normal industry practice was a three-year cycle). Rubbing its nose into GM Styling's face, Plymouth ads cooed "Suddenly—It's 1960!" And this was only 1957...

Nowhere was the Forward Look of Motion more evident than in the wedge-shaped silhouette of Plymouth. Low front fenders and a hooded, gently sloped windshield, a "razor thin" roof with a tapered rear window, and rising fins created the wedge effect. Convertibles and hardtops naturally complimented the style best. Station wagons, which usually adapted worst to a design, came off looking even sleeker than sedans. From the eyebrowed headlamps to the unobstructed greenhouse, to the smooth, clean, sculptured sides, the effect of an earth-bound space vehicle was everywhere.

Its redesign from the frame up (the frame was flatter, lower, and wider), along with a switch to 14-inch wheels helped lower the '57

Buyers could choose between two convertibles in 1959: the Belvedere or the Sport Fury, shown. This would be the last year the familiar sailing ship emblem would appear on a Plymouth until introduction of the Breeze in 1996. *Gary Behling*

Plymouth 5 inches from comparable '56 models. A longer wheelbase—118-inches on sedans, 122-inches on wagons—was still half an inch shorter than the 1949 through 1952 Plymouths, but who would have believed it? And the '57 was 1 inch shorter than the '56! Looks could be deceiving.

Designed with dual headlamps in mind, final approval of all 48 states for such a setup had fallen short by eight states. Placing the parking lamp alongside the headlamp gave the illusion of dual lamps (some Cadillac and Mercury models, as well as Imperial, actually got by using duals in 1957). A massive front bumper split the grille in two, the bumper bar rising as it crossed the middle of the car, giving a "barbell" shape to the grille. Above the bumper sat the regular grille of thin horizontal bars adorned with an abstract version of the Mayflower ship. Under the bumper the grille took on an ungainly appearance with vertical slots breaking up the wide expanse of the upper grille. By mid-January the lower pan had been modified, dividing the vertical slots with thin vertical stainless trim strips.

Standard equipment on the 1959 Sport Fury and optional on most other models were swivel front seats, an option that never really caught on. One such seat is shown on this car. Early seats had to be swung out manually but this was later changed to an automatic operation when the door was opened. *George Dalinis*

Unusual headlight eyebrows that swooped behind the front wheels and seemingly outrageous tail fins marked Plymouth for 1960. At the low end of the sales chart was this Savoy club sedan. *Hugh Biggers*

In back, a taillamp lens completely filled the slightly canted rear fin. Between the lamps only an unbroken expense of deck lid appeared. As on the hood, the name Plymouth appeared in separate letters stretching across the deck lid. Round back-up lamps sat below the taillamps. A grooved center bumper section with a chrome extension cascaded down over the rear body pan. Side trim was restrained, model names appeared on rear fenders, and a gold V was on the front fender if the car was V-8- equipped.

Engineering had been just as busy as styling. Gone was the "old" style independent front suspension of years past, trash-canned in favor of torsion bars and ball joints. Called "Torsion-Aire Ride" (there was no air to the system at all, unlike GM's experiments with air suspensions), the suspension would garner Plymouth the title of best handling car by *Motor Trend* magazine. Eventually the entire Chrysler Corporation would receive *Motor Trend*'s "Car Of The Year" Award based on "superior handling and roadability qualities."

Torsion-Aire was more than just torsion bars, as everything had been re-engineered, including the frame, wheels, tires, and suspension and steering linkage. The center of gravity had been lowered and the car sat on a wider stance. Torsion-Aire incorporated two chrome steel bars mounted parallel to the inner front frame rails, the front portion of the bar mounted to the lower control arm with the opposite end anchored to the frame. The twisting motion of the bars, rather than the compression of springs, provided the cars with soft but stable suspension. Even the rear springs had been redesigned to work in concert with the torsion bars up front. Plymouth brakes, always a high spot, were increased in size.

With all the design and engineering changes, there was little need to change model names. Buyers had their choice of a Belvedere club sedan, four-door sedan, Sport Coupe, Sport Sedan, and convertible—the ragtop again commanding eight-cylinder power. Six-cylinder cars were coded P30, and V-8s were P31.

Savoys came in club sedan, four-door sedan, Sport Coupe, and a newly introduced four-door hardtop Sport Sedan. Plaza soldiered on with a four-door, club sedan, and business coupe.

Wagon buyers could choose between the six- or nine-passenger four-door Sport Suburban, Custom Suburban six- or nine-passenger four-door, and six-passenger two-door wagon, or the six-passenger two-door Deluxe Suburban.

The Fury didn't make its debut until December. Like the first Fury, it was designed as a high-performance, personal luxury car, again available only in Eggshell white with gold anodized side trim. Under the hood sat the most potent Plymouth engine ever, a 290-horsepower 9.25:1 compression ratio 318 engine fed by dual Carter

A top-of-the-line model was the Fury Sport Sedan. All Fury models had stainless trim along the rear quarter panels. This would be the last year for tail fins. *Gerald Klinger*

Below
Shorn of its tail fins, the 1961 Plymouth featured Virgil Exner's straight-line styling with hairpin swoop around the headlamps. Although many had sought the demise of tail fins, the finless 1961 has gained a dubious honor in consistently being named one of the ugliest automobiles ever built. *Harris Stone*

carburetors. Heavy-duty everything best describes its mechanical equipment. Drivers got a firsthand view of its 150 mile-per-hour speedometer—and many of them easily reached that mark.

Added to the option list was a second automatic transmission, the three-speed TorqueFlite. Aptly named, the transmission was up to its name, easily handling even the awesome Street Hemi of the next decade. TorqueFlite was optional on all V-8-equipped Belvederes, and was available on V-8 Plazas and Savoys equipped with the V-800 engine option. Having been a late-comer in offering automatic transmissions, Plymouth was now in the forefront, selling more automatic-equipped cars than either Ford or Chevrolet. Plymouth would sell a higher percentage of V-8 powered cars as well.

Engine options for 1957 included the tried-and-true 132-horsepower PowerFlow six (no longer offering the power pack); the 197-horsepower 277 (available only in the Plaza); or the one-year-only 215-horsepower Fury 301 as the standard V-8 in Savoy or Belvedere (optional in the Plaza). A second "Fury" engine, the Fury V-800 was a $245 option in any model. Unlike most "power pack" options, the Fury V-800 included heavy-duty transmission—either manual or TorqueFlite—heavy-duty torsion bars, springs, shocks, and 14x6-inch wheels.

With sales of 726,009 cars, 1957 proved to be Plymouth's best year ever, bettering the record set in 1955 by more than 20,000 units. In the process, Plymouth marched smartly ahead of Buick, reclaiming its traditional third place in sales. The ten-millionth Plymouth came off the line January 24, 1957, and Plymouth sales accounted for over half of Chrysler Corporation's 1957 sales.

But it all came at a terrible price. Without doubt they were the best-styled Plymouths turned out by Virgil Exner's stylists. But in the rush to production, with breakneck schedules to meet demand, quality control rode straight into the sewer. The cars leaked dust and rain water vociferously. Paint faded and flaked in chunks while upholstery materials disintegrated in the sun. Torsion bars, deprived of rubber boots during early production, rusted and snapped like match sticks—thankfully usually only at slow speeds. Despite its killer good looks, the '57 Plymouth—and its stablemates—gave Chrysler a long-standing reputation for poor quality, an image still haunting the Corporation as late as 1980, when Lee Iacocca went before the U.S. Congress to plead for a billion-dollar loan guarantee to save Chrysler from extinction.

1958 All Models
Convertible, Sport Coupe ★★★★★
Club sedan, station wagon ★★★
Four-door ★★
Fury Sport Coupe ★★★★★

Station wagons continued to grow in popularity but few have been rescued by collectors, who favor hardtops and convertibles instead. *Steve Wright*

Plymouth for 1958

In an era when change for the sake of change was prevalent, some complained the '58 Plymouth hadn't changed enough. What few changes had been made were mostly for the better. Again, it would take a perceptible passer-by to notice the differences. Most evident was the front grille—the much-maligned lower pan on the '57s gave way to a grille matching the upper grille and looking somewhat like that of the Chrysler 300. Real dual headlamps replaced the headlamp-park lamp of the previous year, with park lamps cleverly hidden above and between the lamps. A new winged hood ornament replaced the individual letters used to spell Plymouth on the '57s. And for the first time since 1928, the good ship Mayflower was nowhere to be found.

At the rear, simple round taillamps capped by a "Reflecting Tower" blade replaced last year's fin-filling lens. A single back-up lamp was centered in the rear bumper (except on station wagons).

Belvederes all sported a Fury-like side trim, using silver anodized aluminum rather than the Fury's familiar gold. Body choices remained the same as '57 in all three lines—except for the addition of a four-door wagon to the Deluxe Suburban line—and all were available with a choice of six-cylinder or V-8 power, with the exception of the Fury and Belvedere convertible, which mandated the V-8.

Engine options included the 132-horsepower PowerFlow six, or the base Fury V-800 225-horsepower 318-ci two-barrel. The Dual Fury V-800 was exclusive to the Fury but for those wanting more power, there was the one-year-only Golden Commando 350. Based on the Chrysler "B" block, it was optional on all models, including the Fury. Last—

Very rare is the 1961 Fury convertible. This example was purchased new and kept in mint condition by its owner, Hubert Roark.

and in this case, least—was the cataloged but rarely seen Golden Commando with fuel injection.

Designed and built by Bendix, the "Electrojector" fuel-injection system, which was to have been optional in all models except station wagons, offered 315 horsepower. Touted as a "limited-production, optional engine designed for and offered to a select group of high-performance enthusiasts who demand an engine that's truly out of the ordinary, mating fuel injection with the most advanced high-performance engine available in the field," the Electrojector was installed on a handful of cars before being withdrawn from the market. Unreliable sources claim just two Plymouths were sold with the option along with a dozen or so Chrysler 300s, and even fewer DeSotos.

As the "Star of The Forward Look," Plymouth's factory hot-rod Fury made its final appearance, this time with the choice of two V-8 engines, the standard 290-horsepower Dual-Fury

Plymouth offered its first police package in 1957. It was a market Plymouth would come to dominate in later years. Here, a North Dakota state trooper renders assistance to a damsel in distress.

V-800 318, or the new 305-horsepower Golden Commando 350. Both sported dual four-barrel carburetors and heavy duty everything. Unlike earlier Furys, this one came only in Buckskin Beige.

In the midst of a deep economic recession, Plymouth found itself in need of a "price leader." Enter the "Silver Special," a specially equipped Plaza in either two- or four-doors. It consisted of Sportone trim with anodized aluminum inserts, front fender and door moldings, special metallic silver roof paint, full wheel covers, whitewall tires, directional signals, electric wipers, and "Forward Look" emblems pirated from the '56 Plymouth. With a choice of six-cylinder or V-8 power, the Silver Special was to retail for $1,958 in 1958.

Despite sharply curtailed sales of 443,799 units, Plymouth still managed to maintain its hard-won third-place standings.

1959 All Models
Convertible, Sport Coupe ★★★★★
Club sedan, station wagon ★★★
Four-door ★★
Fury Sport Coupe ★★★★★
Sport Fury Convertible ★★★★★
Sport Fury Hardtop ★★★★

Plymouth for 1959

Both Chevrolet and Ford entered the year with completely new automobiles. Chrysler Corporation was at a disadvantage, being forced to rely one more year on its current body shell. GM's answer to Chrysler's 1957 styling coup was a wild, bat-wing affair, while Ford took on a more traditional and formal look. The '58 Plymouth had been less than a mild restyle of the trend setting '57—this time Exner would be called on to do a major revamping, to the tune of $150 million, most of it directed at Plymouth.

The restyle included a new anodized aluminum egg-crate grille with wrap-around park-turn signal lamps, with the grille split by a black screen center where the Mayflower ship once again made its appearance—albeit shared with a rocket ship. For the first time in its life, the ship was seen from the forward profile. It wouldn't be seen again on a Plymouth until the 1996 Breeze!

Double-barreled fenders drew attention to the sculpted eyebrows and dual floating headlamps. An under-bumper "jet intake" filled the space above the lower body pan. Fins began to rise at the C-pillar in a smoother upsweep than previous years, making the car look longer than it really was. The hood and deck lid were sculpted, with the hood having a center wind split.

Reacting to a rumor that Chevrolet was going to down-size its cars for 1962, Plymouth did a chop job on its full-size models. Although rather attractive today, the cars were considered too radical, and sales fell through the floor. It was a costly mistake that would haunt Plymouth for years to come. *Plymouth Owners Club*

Back-up lamps moved back to the taillamp cluster, now found in an oval beneath the deck lid.

Gone from the model line-up was the Plaza, and the Savoy slipped down to take its place. Next in line came the Belvedere, it too lowered one notch in rank. Taking the Belvedere's place was the Fury line, with the Fury name now being a series, rather than a high-performance specialty vehicle. At the top of the line rode the Sport Furys.

Body styles remained the same as years past, with the Savoy coming in club sedan, four-door, or business coupe. Belvederes came in club sedan, four-door, sport coupe, sport sedan, and convertible form. Fury offerings included a four-door, Sport Sedan, and Sport Coupe. Sport Fury buyers could choose between sport coupe or convertible, marking the first time Plymouth offered two convertibles at the same time. Station wagon choices were unchanged.

An era had ended with the loss of the Fury. Sport Furys were powered by the Fury V-800 with Super Pack, a 260-horsepower 318, with a single high-performance carburetor, high-performance cam and intake manifold, and low-restriction exhaust. It was an engine available on everything else Plymouth built except the Savoy business coupe.

The standard V-8 was the 230-horsepower 318 with a two-barrel carb (not available on the Sport Fury or Savoy business coupe). Optional was the Golden Commando 395 "B" block, now bored out to 361 ci and rated at 305 horsepower. It took its name from its stump-pulling torque rating of 395 foot-pounds of torque at 3,000 rpm.

For the fleet buyer, the 132-horsepower PowerFlow six soldiered on for its final year.

Chassis changes were non-existent except for the addition of "Constant Level" Torsion-Aire employing an under-hood air compressor supplying high-pressure air to a reserve tank distributing air to rubberized nylon air springs mounted between the body and rear leaf springs.

The eleven-millionth Plymouth was built in March, but the Corporation was in the midst of a shake-up—trying hard to keep Plymouth in third place and not quite knowing how to do it. Year-end sales were up slightly, to 458,261 units.

Originally designed with just two taillamps, a third lamp was added shortly after production began, as was a full-length chrome strip added to the beltline (not seen on this car), to make the 1962 Plymouths look longer than they really were. *M. J. Hertog*

Plymouth had managed to remain in third, despite the fact half the new cars sold in '59 had been Fords or Chevrolets. It would be 11 years before Plymouth would again see third place.

Model 1960

Belvedere & Fury hardtop coupe ★★★★
Fury hardtop sedan ★★★★
Fury convertible ★★★★★
Sedans & wagons, all series ★
361 or 383 cross ramV-8
regardless of body type ★★★★★

Plymouth for 1960

Three years earlier it had seemed so simple to say "Suddenly, it's 1960!" Suddenly, it *was* 1960. The '57s had been both a styling and engineering coup of no small proportions. Nineteen hundred and fifty-eight and 1959 had been lackluster years in comparison. The question was, could Plymouth stage another coup that it so badly needed? Or would it find itself "out-finned" by its own excesses? In the long run, it was a little bit of both.

Cadillac had shown everyone what fins were all about with its '59 models, even though Chrysler Corporation now called them "stabilizers," supposedly serving a useful purpose at keeping the car straight at high speeds—a claim that was highly suspicious.

Underneath it all was a totally new car—powered by, in the case of the sixes, a completely new engine. The only problem was, it just didn't *look* like a new car. To many, it was too much—too late. Virgil Exner had been praised for his designs of the 1955 through 1958

Plymouths. The '59's restyle had not been not very well received but for 1960, Exner's renderings were beginning to turn sour—with worse yet to come when he would receive outright blame for his designs.

As rumored for several years, Chrysler Corporation unveiled Unibody construction across the board (save Imperial). Chrysler had originated the idea of unibody construction with its Airflows of the mid-1930s. Unibody was more technically advanced, framed much like a bridge truss. The body was made up of box-section rails that extended upward from the sills, outlining windows alongside the roof before descending to a foundation near the rear wheel openings. Some 5,400 welds held the frameless vehicle together. Plymouth claimed 100 percent greater body rigidity and 40 percent greater beam strength, with the "girders" which provided that strength touted as being 75 percent heavier than those used in conventional construction. Stronger, still lighter in weight, was the claim. There was a frame, of sorts; a subframe bearing the engine; and "Torsion-Aire" suspension that bolted to the otherwise unitized body.

Before the body panels were welded together, the seams were shot with a special welding sealer designed to expand under the heat of drying ovens after painting. A drawback of any unitized construction was that no sound-insulating material could isolate the body from frame and road noise. To counter this, Plymouth developed extra-large rear spring bushings, a new exhaust system hanger, and a drive shaft redesigned to reduce high-speed hum. Special sound-deadening fiber matting and liquid-applied coatings contributed to making sure the car was quiet on the road.

Six chemical sprays and seven chemical dips plus four coats of paint ensured rust would not be a problem in the frameless vehicle. And the cars were advertised as "Solid." Barely any piece of literature failed to mention the word "Solid"—with the cars invariably photographed against backgrounds of steel girders, bridges, or other examples of engineered strength. Rust was a word Plymouth didn't want to hear, especially in light of the fact that the fabulous '57s, which garnered so much good publicity, were now ill-thought-of buckets of rust.

Revolutionary construction—evolutionary styling. Sticking with the tried-and-true finned silhouette, the '60 Plymouth relied on other gimmicks such as the hooded headlamps whose brow wrapped around the corner of the fender and swept back behind the front-wheel cutout. The same general wheel cutout shape was carried over the rear wheel, but in a more subdued manner. Fury models continued the eyebrow stainless trim around the front wheel, along the bottom of the car to the rear wheel, where the trailing edge was fitted with a stainless panel, ala the '59 Ford Galaxie 500. Belvederes and Savoys had to settle for broad expanses of otherwise plain sheet metal. And then there were the fins—towering higher, or so it seemed—then ever before and looking for all the world like last-minute add-ons. Many people wondered aloud what the car would look like without them. They would have to wait one year to find out.

The "razor-thin" roofline that gave GM stylists such fits in 1957 continued, only now with a heavy C-pillar that cut forward, emulating the wheel cutouts. Optional on the two-door hardtop was a Sky-Hi rear window that rose to give back seat passengers a virtual sun roof—or baking! Costing only $23, it should have been mandatory to include the $43 tinted glass option.

The 1960 Plymouth returned to a three-model line-up, with the Sport Fury disappearing from the catalog. At the bottom of the list was the Savoy in two- or four-door sedan form. In the middle was the Belvedere in two- or four-door sedan style or two-door hardtop. The top-of-the-line Fury came in a four-door sedan, four-door hardtop, two-door hardtop, and convertible. Station wagons carried their own names, corresponding in trim levels to the passenger car as the Deluxe, Custom, and Sport Suburban.

A fourth line of cars, known as Fleet Specials, were offered specifically for taxi and high-use commercial applications. Police packages (the first had come in 1957) included the Patroller Six, Patroller Special V-8, and for highway patrol use, the Pursuit Special V-8. In years to come, Chrysler would dominate the police car market, supplying fully 80 percent of the nation's police vehicles. During the halcyon muscle car days, no finer compliment was paid police cars than calling them "Four-door Road Runners."

Passenger cars all rode on a 118-inch wheelbase (still a half-inch shorter than the 1949 through 1952 Plymouth!), and the wagons were

In what could best be described as a crash program, Plymouth for 1963 added 3 inches to the length of the car and redesigned sheet metal to make the cars look longer and more conventionally styled. The results, as seen in this Sport Fury coupe, were highly successful. *Marvin Raguse, Jr.*

A heavy C-pillar, vertical, widely spaced parking lamps, and horizontal quad headlamps helped hide the fact the 1963 Plymouth was a redesign of the poorly received 1962 model. The 1962 body shell, despite all its bad press, would serve for many years as the basis of Plymouth's intermediate Belvedere line. *Lanny Knutson*

built on a 122-inch chassis shared with the other corporate wagons.

At long last, a new, up-to-date overhead-valve six replaced the tired 27-year-old flathead. Displacing 225 ci, the engine sat at a 30-degree angle to the right (a move necessitated to allow lower hood heights), and thus it soon affectionately became known as the Slant Six. This layout necessitated a long intake manifold with individual tubes running back to each cylinder, an unusual and unique sight in 1960. Actually there were two versions of the Slant Six: a smaller 170-ci engine with 2-inch-lower block-deck height for use in the new Valiant economy car introduced for 1960, and the larger 225 for use in Dodge and Plymouth full-size cars and Dodge commercial vehicles.

Other engine choices included the Fury V-800, the base two-barrel 318-ci; Fury V-800 with Super Pak (four-barrel, 260-horsepower); and the Golden Commando 395, the 361-ci "B" block pumping out 305 horses. For the performance enthusiast something new had been added: the SonoRamic Golden Commando, a 383-ci 330-horsepower dual-quad-carbureted cross-ram manifold monster.

Popping the hood of a SonoRamic Golden Commando-powered car was an experience few would forget. Long aluminum castings rising up and over the valve covers pumped fuel from two Carter four-barrel carbs to the engine. The carb on the right side fed the left bank of cylinders, the carb on the left fed the right bank. Each ram manifold measured 30 inches from carburetor venturi to intake valve. At 2,800 rpm, the manifold would reach its maximum effect as the speed-of-sound waves gave a mild supercharging effect. The engine was awesome to look at and words can't describe its actual performance. It was an expensive engine to produce and a challenge to keep in tune—and it would only last two years. (A modified shorter ram would be available to drag racers for years to come.)

Transmission choices continued as in previous years, although a heavy-duty manual transmission was coupled to higher-horsepower engines. Both the two-speed PowerFlite and three-speed TorqueFlite were continued as well.

When the first two Volkswagen "beetles" were imported into the United States in 1949, most people laughed. By the late 1950s the Big Three had begun to take the small car market seriously, rushing into production for the 1960 model year. Chevrolet spewed forth the radical, rear-engined, air-cooled, opposed-six Corvair. Ford chose the moderate path of the Falcon. Chrysler Corporation's answer was the "Corporate" Valiant, an Exner-designed car—in the European look—of unusual proportions, featuring an odd assortment of curves and angles.

Valiants began coming off Dodge's Hamtramck assembly line in September of 1959. Ads boasted Valiant was "Nobody's Kid Brother," which it truly wasn't. No single division of the

Don't let the plain-Jane appearance of this 1963 Belvedere fool you—that's no Slant Six under the hood. Cars such as this one, with a potent 426-ci Super Stock V-8, soon dominated the nation's dragstrips. *Jim Benjaminson*

A sight to make any enthusiast's heart pound faster, a 426-ci Super Stock V-8. *Jim Benjaminson*

corporation would lay claim to the new car, causing a franchising problem of no small proportions. By January 1, 1960, less than half of Plymouth's 4,100 dealers were franchised to sell the car. It wouldn't be until 1961 that Valiant would become a Plymouth exclusive (in Canada it would remain a Chrysler Valiant). Unfortunately for Plymouth, Valiant, along with Dodge's restyled Dart, would both provide "internal" competition, stealing sales away from the big Plymouths. Technically, Valiant production of 194,292 cars should not have been counted with Plymouth's total of 447,724—a combined total still only good enough for fourth place on the sales charts. Had Plymouth been left to stand alone, it would have been recorded as a ninth-place finish, a far cry from Chevrolet and Ford, who recorded sales of nearly 1.5 million cars apiece. The Valiant will be covered later in its own chapter.

Model 1961

Belvedere & Fury hardtop coupe ★★★★
Fury hardtop sedan ★★★★
Fury convertible ★★★★★
Sedans & wagons, all series ★
413 V-8 regardless of body type ★★★★★

Plymouth for 1961

For those who had wondered what the '60 Plymouth would look like without fins, '61 was the answer. And they didn't like the answer. The automotive press hailed the car, calling it a much-needed improvement and sleek. Consumers saw it otherwise, voting with their pocketbooks—for a new Ford or Chevrolet. To make matters worse, the '61 Plymouth has consistently been voted to the top of every list of the "ugliest automobile ever built." Even members of the Plymouth Owners Club voted it number one of the "Worst Five

Plymouths," making comments such as "Exner gone berserk," and "remember laughing at this one in the showroom." How bad was it? Sales slid to a dismal 350,285—putting Plymouth in seventh place for the year.

The first of the Chrysler brands to forsake flying tail fins, the car was designed around the concept of smoothly integrated curves sweeping from front to back. A single band of chrome originating inboard of the headlamps swept up and over the fender, along the length of the car, wrapping around the deck lid and continuing forward to the opposite side of the car. Exner loved heavily eyebrowed lights but this treatment gave them an odd look. The grille sloped inward as it fell to bumper height—the bumper smooth except for a series of raised ridges matching grille width.

At the rear, taillamps tacked to the body side in their own little rocket pods looked for all the world like last minute add-ons. The pod was chromed on the Fury, body color on everything else. The car may have looked worlds different from the '60 but it was nothing more than a clever restyling. The rooflines and doorlines were unchanged, although new fenders and quarter-panels hid this fact.

The model line-up continued as per the previous year: Savoys in two- or four-door sedan form; Belvederes in two- or four-door sedan style, or two-door hardtop form; and Furys in four-door sedan, four-door hardtop, two-door hardtop, and convertible coupe form. Wagon offerings again followed the familiar Deluxe, Custom, and Sport Suburban names.

Swivel front seats, which had been a novel item in the 1959 and 1960 Plymouths, had disappeared, replaced by the "Command Seat," which provided the driver with a higher backrest.

Engine choices ran the gamut from the 145-horsepower 225-ci Slant Six to the base Fury V-800 230-horsepower 318, or the four-barrel Super Fury V-800 318 pumping out 260 horses. Both Golden Commandos, the 361-ci 305-horsepower "395," and 383-ci 330-horsepower ram-induction SonoRamic Commando, also returned.

Transmission choices were unchanged, although a new "Heavy-Duty Synchro-Silent" manual transmission was mandatory with the big Commando V-8s. Adoption of an alternator, in place of generator, was the only major mechanical change for the year (the alternator had made its first appearance the year before on Valiants).

Plymouth's dismal sales record was laid solely at the feet of one man—Virgil Exner. He had been praised to the heavens for his work just a few years earlier, and now he was stripped of his vice-presidency and booted out the door in the fall of '61. Adding insult to injury was his replacement,

Elwood Engle, brought over from Ford's conservative styling staff.

Sales had continued to tumble with just 356,257 units built—a figure that was barely more than Plymouth's 1935 production total. Plymouth's sale slide tumbled to seventh place, with worse yet to come.

Model 1962
Belvedere, Fury and Sport Fury
hardtop coupe ★★★★
Fury hardtop sedan ★★★★
Fury & Sport Fury convertible ★★★★★
Sedans & wagons, all series ★
383 or 413 cross ram V-8 regardless
of body type ★★★★★

Plymouth for 1962
Exner's "Forward Look" cars had set automotive styling on its ear and brought competitors scrambling to catch up. True, his finned cars had stuck around a little too long, and his finless '61 had become a laughing stock. Consumers had already gotten a taste of his latest innovation: the Valiant with its "Forward Flair" long hood, short deck, flush C-pillar with no beltline, close-coupled passenger compartment, and "speedboat" windshield. But when those designs were applied to a full-size car, what would happen?

A series of events beyond Exner's control would soon answer that question. Chrysler President William Newberg had barely taken office when he was caught in a "hand-in-the-cookie-jar" scenario and forced to step down in favor of Lynn Townsend. But it was a cocktail party rumor that would spell doom for Exner at Chrysler. "The Rumor" was that Chevrolet was going to downsize its cars. Clearly Chrysler couldn't be caught with its pants down and not downsize, too. The rumor was only partially true. Both Chevrolet and Ford were planning downsized models, in this case the intermediate Fairlane and Chevy II, not their full-size cars.

Exner's proposed full-size car designs were heavily oriented to the asymmetrical look Exner had used on his XNR show car. Word from on high reached Exner that the full-size Plymouth and Dodge were to be downsized. Townsend took one look at these designs and ordered that everything be more conventional. Had Townsend not done so, the new Plymouth would have been more radical than they turned out to be, with an asymmetrical wind split in front of the driver, only one taillight on the left, and two on the right. (It must be remembered these cars were on the drawing boards three years before they saw production; Exner was long gone when the '62 made its debut.)

What followed was plenty of midnight oil by Chrysler stylists, attempting to rework designs for a 116-inch wheelbase car, and do it at minimum expense. Much was lost in the translation, with many people perceiving the car to be nothing more than an overgrown Valiant. Nearly devoid of chrome trim and with an odd "big light—little light" split dual-headlamp arrangement, the cars were so unusual looking as to be controversial.

When the car hits the street, the press hailed it as "unique" and "sophisticated." Bill Burge, a longtime South Dakota dealer came home from the dealer preview and told his wife, "We're going to have to sit this year out. I can't sell that car." In a 100 car-per-year dealership, Burge sold just 11 cars! Buyers voted with their pocketbooks. Ford sales increased 16 percent, but most of the gain went to Chevrolet, whose sales rose 35 percent. Solidly rejected on a full-size car in 1962, the long hood, short deck—when applied to Ford's sporty Mustang just two years later—would soon become common throughout the industry.

Savoys, Belvederes, and Furys came in the usual line-up of models, available with either six-cylinder or V-8 power. (Fury four-door hardtop and convertible, and Sport Furys mandated the V-8.) Station wagons dropped their separate titles and joined their respective series according to trim level. Trying to make the best of a bad situation, the Sport Fury, both coupe and convertible, returned to the line-up in January featuring a special interior with bucket seats and console, partially blacked-out grille, and two extra taillamps.

Engines for 1962 included the 225 slant six (which was built briefly with an aluminum block but was soon replaced by conventional cast-iron after about 55,000 had been built); both two- and four-barrel 318s; and a four-barrel 361. Gone was the long-ram 383, replaced at midyear by a short-ram 413-ci monster (in 365, 380, and 410 horsepower) that would establish Plymouth as a force for years to come on the drag racing circuits.

Unseen—and unappreciated—was the elimination of the sub-frame used since 1960, a move that reduced car weight by 200 pounds and provided as much interior room as before, although exterior dimensions had been shorted by 7 1/2 inches from 1960-61. A new aluminum-case TorqueFlite also aided interior space, while reducing overall weight by 60 pounds (total weight reduction came to over 400 pounds). Gone forever was the old two-speed PowerFlite. A new reduction-gear starting motor gave all Chrysler products a distinct sound, if not better starting, and dash wiring now used "printed" circuit boards.

Sales of full-size cars came to just 182,520 units, which was only slightly better than the war-shortened year of 1942. Worse yet, year-end sales slid Plymouth back another notch to eighth, a position Plymouth last held in 1930.

Model 1963
Belvedere, Fury and Sport Fury
hardtop coupe ★★★★
Fury hardtop sedan ★★★★
Fury & Sport Fury convertible ★★★★★
Sedans & wagons, all series ★
383 or 426 cross ram V-8 regardless
of body type ★★★★★

Plymouth for 1963

With sales at an all-time low and 1963 just around the corner, there was little time to design—nor any money to build—an all-new car. The only solution would be to redesign as much sheet metal using the basic '62 body as possible. A new front end design had already been done to be mated to the 1962 body (which reached production pretty much intact). Additional money was appropriated to change the entire exterior appearance. Everything that could be done to make the car look longer was done. Three of the four series featured full-length front-to-rear bodyside moldings—in bright metal on the Belvedere, paint-filled on Fury, and with an engine-turned insert on the Sport Fury.

Actual length was increased by 3 inches, although the wheelbase remained 116 inches. The beltline kickup was eliminated, again to aide the look of length. Front end design featured vertical park and turn lights at the widest edge of the fender, slightly canted inward from the top. Inside of this sat dual headlamps against a full-width grille. At the rear, shield-shaped taillights with "gun-sight" trim sat on either side as far apart as possible. All models had a horizontal stainless molding across the deck lid, with Furys and Sport Furys featuring an additional ribbed horizontal stainless steel panel between the taillamps. Widely spaced letters on both the hood and deck lid aided the horizontal illusion, yet the cars were still nearly 4 1/2 inches narrower than 1961. Sedans and hardtops shared a vertical backlight with wide C-pillar. The cowl, one of the most expensive items on any car, had to be retained, and Exner's "speedboat" windshield was the only obvious clue to the '63s' origins.

Engine choices remained pretty much the same as 1962: the Slant Six, 318, 361, and 383 unchanged—until one reached into Plymouth's racing parts bins. New for the year was a 426 cubic-wedge engine available in 370, 375, 415, or 425 horsepower configurations. The 370 featured

Once redesigned for 1964, Plymouth lost its "high-speed boat cowl." That, along with a new roof on hardtops, completely obliterated any traces of the cars' 1962 origins. *Lanny Knutson*

a single four-barrel carburetor and 11:1 compression; the 375 had a 13.5:1 ratio. Both the 415- and 425-horse versions used two four-barrels on a short-ram manifold, the difference in horsepower coming through 11:1 or 13.5:1 compression ratios. While most racers preferred TorqueFlite, a four-speed, Hurst-shifted manual transmission built by Borg-Warner entered the option list.

Buyers again had the choice of the bottom-of-the-line Savoy, in two-door, four-door, or six- or nine-passenger wagon form; and the Belvedere, adding a two-door hardtop to the same list. The Fury added a convertible and as in years past, Sport Furys were available in hardtop or convertible form.

Sales rose to 263,342 full-size cars (with an additional 225,156 Valiants), enough to pull Plymouth up to fifth place from its dismal 1962 showing.

Model 1964
Belvedere, Fury and Sport Fury
hardtop coupe ★★★★
Fury hardtop sedan ★★★★
Fury & Sport Fury convertible ★★★★★
Sedans & wagons, all series ★
426 "Wedge" V-8 regardless
of body type ★★★★★
426 Racc Hemi-INTESTIMABLE

Plymouth for 1964

Nineteen hundred and sixty-four would see the final incarnation of the "mandatory" three-year body cycle with another remake of the ill-fated '62.

Chrysler stylists under Elwood Engle had done a terrific job of hiding the '62, given the limitations they had to work with on the '63. With a little more lead time, the '64 would be even further down the evolutionary track.

Sheet metal remained identical to the '63 from the doors on back, except for a widening at the rear to accommodate a 2.1-inch-wider rear axle.

While the '63 had been stuck with Exner's speedboat cowl, this, too, had gone by the wayside. Missing, too, were the canted parking lamps on the end of the front fenders, replaced now by a peak that stuck out just enough to be targets for those who parked by Braille. A convex grille with a distinct peak about one-third of the way from the top neatly matched the centerline of the fender peaks. Nestled in the grille were quad headlamps; running down the side was a crease that began at the front fenders and ran the entire length of the body, with the forward edge of the crease giving just a hint to another of Exner's favorite styling tricks: the hair pin. Wider taillights, accented by a "rear grille" stainless panel on the Fury, gave the car an entirely different look than the '63.

Hardtop and pillared sedans still carried the heavy, Thunderbird-inspired C-pillar roof; two-door hardtops however, were another story. A distinctive, triangular C-pillar, with "convertible top" crease in the roof panel, along with a curved backlight gave the car a more streamlined appearance—and made it slipperier on NASCAR speedways.

It was here that Plymouth's newest engine was right at home. In fact, it was the *only* place it was at home, for Plymouth had resurrected a Chrysler engine it had never used: the hemispherical combustion chamber, 426 -ci "Hemi." Available only to well-connected race drivers, the Hemi pumped out 415 horsepower with an 11.1:1 compression ratio—425 horses at 12.5:1, both engines running twin four-barrel carburetors. Official Plymouth engineering sheets show the Hemi available in either Belvedere, Fury, or Sport Fury bodies but it is doubtful if anything other than a Belvedere ever carried the engine. At the running of the 1964 Daytona 500, the new Hemi led a three-car sweep of first, second, and third place, with "King" Richard Petty at the wheel of the winning car.

Three other 426-ci engines did see "street" use: all wedge engines of 365 horsepower (fed by a single four-barrel carb), the "Stage III Max Wedge" 415 (11.1:1 compression), or 425-horsepower (12.5:1 compression) with dual fours on a short-ram manifold and mind-blowing set of "snake pit" exhaust headers.

The majority of Plymouth buyers choose the 145-horsepower slant six or 230-horse 318 V-8. For those whose needs fit somewhere in between,

In its final year as Plymouth's "big" car, the 1964 Sport Fury featured a prominent crease in the grille and front fenders, along with full-length side moldings to visually make the car look bigger. *Lanny Knutson*

the 265-horse 361 and 330-horse 383 were also cataloged. As the model year came to a close, Chrysler Corporation bade farewell to its "typewriter" transmission controls. Harking back to 1956, the push buttons had been a "love it or hate it" affair. The most plausible explanation for discontinuing the push buttons came from those following the Washington safety czars, who were demanding controls be standardized between makes. Although no official edict came down regarding the push buttons, they would be missing from the '65 models.

Body style and model names were unchanged from the previous two years. Both Savoy station wagons, six and nine-passenger, were available with either six- or eight-cylinder engines, but the Belvedere and Fury wagons, along with the Fury four-door hardtop and convertible—as well as the two Sport Furys—mandated the V-8.

Full-size car sales came to 297,293 units, enough to move Plymouth up one notch to fourth for the model run.

Model 1965
Belvedere, Super Stock hardtop coupe-INTESTIMABLE
Satellite & Belvedere II hardtop coupe ★★★★
Satellite convertible ★★★★★
361, 383 or 426 V-8 ★★★★★
Fury III & Sport Fury hardtop coupe ★★★★
Fury III hardtop sedan ★★★★
Fury III & Sport Fury convertible ★★★★★
Sedans & wagons, all series ★
for full size with 426 "Wedge" V-8 ★★★★★

Plymouth for 1965

If the '62 Plymouth had been considered radical, Elwood Engle's first clean sheet of paper design for 1965 could only be labeled "conservative." Engle, who had penned the neoclassic 1961 Lincoln Continental, preferred straight lines, and that is just what he ordered for the new Plymouths. Gone were all visages of the 1962 disaster, as Plymouth returned to the "big time" in vehicle size.

The front featured a fine mesh grille flanked by vertical headlights—a styling gimmick introduced some years earlier by Pontiac. The rear featured a triple-light per side that also came from GM design. Chrysler styling had been a leader in 1957, its second attempt at styling leadership in 1962 had been a disaster, and for 1965 it would be content to be a follower. Regardless of where the styling cues came from, the new Plymouth was a most attractive automobile.

The wheelbase was stretched 3 inches to 119 inches, bringing the car up to full-size standards against the competition. Slab sides were broken by two full-length body creases evenly spaced between the beltline and rocker panel, adding even more visual length to the car. Front fenders canted forward into the wind while the rear of the car featured a reverse angle crease from side to side.

Each model was now dubbed "Fury," as the name became even more diluted. At the bottom of the rung was the rather spartan Fury I, which took the place of the Savoy, except in Canada, where the Savoy name would live on. Replacing the Belvedere, at least in name only, was the Fury II. What had previously been the Fury line now became the Fury III. Sport Fury would still mean the top-of-the-line, performance-oriented hardtop or convertible, available only with V-8 power, fitted with bucket seats, console, and special trim.

Designated the "C" body, it would share its underpinnings with both Dodge and Chrysler, although they would each have separate, longer wheelbases. As had been done in years past, all station wagons, whether Plymouth, Dodge, or Chrysler, shared the same body on a 121-inch wheelbase.

The old "B" body, dating back to 1962, had not, however, fallen by the wayside. In answer to Chevrolet and Ford offerings of compact, intermediate, and full-size (Corvair/Falcon, Chevelle/Fairlane, Impala/Galaxie) cars, Plymouth's "B" body received a new front end and became the intermediate-series Belvedere. Like the big car, all models were called Belvedere, as in Belvedere I and Belvedere II. Instead of a Belvedere III at the top of the line, a new name, Satellite, entered the picture. Styling of the Belvedere series was a scaled-down version of the big car, with a fine-mesh grille and canted fenders. But here the similarity ended, as the Belvedere would use single headlamps, rather than duals like the big car.

Engine availability was little-changed from years past, with the exception of the 273 V-8 in the Belvedere line. Introduced the year before in the Valiant, the 273 was not available in the big Fury, and both cars differed in their next option choice: Belvedere used the "B" block 361, big Furys used the "B" block 383. Fury III wagons and the Sport Furys mandated V-8 power, but the Belvedere II's convertible was available with a six-cylinder, the first six-banger convertible since 1954. The 426 wedge was available in either the Belvedere or Fury line.

Chosen this year to provide the pace car for the Indianapolis 500 was a Sport Fury convertible. A first for Plymouth, advertising made a lot of noise that "You can buy one just like it," or at least a car with the same powertrain and in official Pace Car colors–white with a blue top and blue interior. (There are claims that "THE" pace car had an orange interior but official Speedway photos of the car used on race day show a blue interior.)

Powered by a 383 V-8, ads hinted the Pace Car was 426 powered, reading "It has power to spare in its optional four-barrel Commando 426-cu. in. V-8 engine." Exactly how many of the 6,272 Sport Fury convertibles built in 1965 left the factory as pace car replicas is unknown.

Sales of 489,485 intermediate and full-size cars showed Plymouth's conservative styling was what buyers wanted. Yet even with Valiant's total production, Plymouth couldn't knock Pontiac out of third place.

Model 1966

Belvedere, Super Stock hardtop
coupe–INTESTIMABLE
Satellite & Belvedere II hardtop coupe ★★★★
Satellite convertible ★★★★★
361, 383 or 426 V-8 ★★★★★
Fury III & Sport Fury hardtop coupe ★★★★
Fury III hardtop sedan ★★★★
Fury III & Sport Fury convertible ★★★★★
Sedans & wagons, all series ★
for full size with 426 "Wedge" V-8 ★★★★★
VIP hardtop coupe or sedan ★★★★
Belvedere II convertible ★★★★★
426 Street Hemi V-8 ★★★★★

Plymouth for 1966

With the success of the big new Fury in 1965, Plymouth turned its attention to the aging "B" body Belvedere. Due for some major revamping, the "B" had its origins with the much maligned '62. The B body would be called on to serve until the Gran Fury was demoted to the Volare chassis in 1982!

What had been Plymouth's full-size car became the intermediate-size "Belvedere" series for 1965. Styling changes included a return to single headlamps and a flatter grille. *Lanny Knutson*

Again, Elwood Engle had free reign to design cars the way he liked them—straight as an arrow. Straight, knife-edge fender lines began at a forward peak and swooped straight back to the extreme rear of the car. Sculpted side panels and single headlamps carried on the relationship with the previous year's car. The wheelbase remained at 116 inches, losing 3 inches in overall length it had gained in 1964; this done, no doubt, to bring it more in line with Ford's Fairlane and Chevy's Chevelle, against which it was competing. Still, it was the biggest car of the three.

Belvedere engine choices couldn't have covered a wider range. At the bottom end was the 225-ci Slant Six, and at the top was the awesome 426-ci hemispherical-combustion chamber "Street Hemi." Conservatively rated at 425 horsepower, detuned "just enough" to make it a street-drivable engine—provided of course, you could live with a rough idle, rumbling exhaust, and more horsepower then most knew what to do with! Magazine editors stumbled over themselves to drive the Street Hemi, and racers stood in line to buy them—then head for the nearest drag strip to become "King Of The Hill."

Most buyers opted for the 273, 318, 361, or 383 power plants. Belvederes ordered with the Hemi option naturally got heavy duty everything, including a lot of underbody restructuring. Ironically, disc brakes were introduced as options on the '66 Valiant and full-size Fury—but not the Belvedere, which was the only model in which the Hemi was available! Prices of Hemi-powered cars have gone through the roof in recent years, resulting in cars being fitted with Hemi engines that originally carried something else, giving rise to a "buyer beware" attitude and a thriving "matching numbers" business to authentic correct cars. Some 1,510 Belvederes were Hemi-powered, one of which was driven to victory at the Daytona 500 by Richard Petty.

With an all-new car the year before, the full-size Fury settled in for a minor restyle of

Returning to a full-size car for the first time since 1961, all full-size 1965 Plymouths bore the Fury name in one form or another. At the top-of-the-line was the Sport Fury hardtop coupe. *Robert Kersh*

grille and trim. Horizontal bars in a center framework gave the illusion of a split grille—again, ala Pontiac. At the rear, the taillamps were moved upward on the deck lid, which carried a new stamping, giving the illusion of a split grille like the front. Furys and Sport Furys featured brushed aluminum panels in these coves. The rear bumper was modified with the addition of letters spelling out the word "Plymouth" at the top.

In answer to Ford's LTD, which had been introduced the year before, a new model, the VIP, came on line. Originally offered only as a four-door hardtop, the VIP featured a vinyl roof (the roof covering was supposedly optional but few, if any, VIPs ever came without it), fluted aluminum taillight panel, wood-grained-insert side trim, rubber bumper strips, and special colors and medallions. Luxurious interiors included deep pile carpet and special tufted-block pleated upholstery on seats that featured fold-down armrest, front and rear. A padded dash was standard, as

were individual reading lamps on the inside C-pillars, seat-edge courtesy lights, plastic walnut interior trim, and special medallions. The standard VIP engine was the 318 V-8, with other V-8s optional. After January 1st, VIP trim was also available on a two-door hardtop. The VIP would remain in production through the 1969 model year.

At the other end of the scale, a price-leading low-level sedan, resurrecting the "Silver Special" name from 1958, was trotted out. A Fury II four-door sedan, it was painted solid silver metallic with exclusive blue upholstery. Full wheelcovers, whitewall tires, and bright window moldings completed the package. The Silver Special, like the VIPs, were not counted separately in year-end production totals.

The 14-millionth Plymouth came off the line in December of 1965, one of 507,713 intermediate and full-size Plymouths built during the model run. Again, Pontiac still managed to keep Plymouth at bay for a fourth-place finish.

For the first time in its history, Plymouth was chosen as the official Pace Car for the 1965 Indianapolis 500. Pac-ing the race was a 383-powered Sport Fury convertible. *Indianapolis Motor Speedway*

Model 1967
Belvedere, Super Stock hardtop coupe-INTES-TIMABLE
Satellite & Belvedere II hardtop coupe ★★★★
Satellite convertible ★★★★★
361, 383 or 426 V-8 ★★★★★
Fury III & Sport Fury hardtop coupe ★★★★
Fury III hardtop sedan ★★★★
Fury III & Sport Fury convertible ★★★★★
Sedans & wagons, all series ★
for full size with 426 "Wedge" V-8 ★★★★★
GTX hardtop coupe ★★★★★
VIP hardtop coupe or sedan ★★★★
Belvedere II convertible ★★★★★
426 Street Hemi V-8 ★★★★★

Plymouth for 1967
Content to play follow-the-leader in styling, the '65-'66 Plymouths did a good job of imitating GM's early '60s straight-line designs, but now the General had gone to the "Coke bottle" look of curvaceous lines. It was time for Elwood Engle to follow suit—but not to the extremes of General Motors.

In the third year of the Plymouth full-size body shell, Engle continued his trademark knife-edge along the fender top running front to back—only now there would be a slight hike in the rear fender line, just forward of the C-pillar. A slight canting inward of the fenders helped surround the still-vertical quad headlamps, effectively hiding them from side view.

Around back, the deck lid received a pronounced boattail hump, under which ran a taillight panel from side to side. Following GM leads, there were three lights per side, at least on the VIP, Sport Fury, and Fury, with aluminum trim in between. Reflecting their lower status, the Fury I and II had just two lamps and painted panels. Bodies were slab-sided with larger wheel openings, surrounded by bright trim on upper level models. The only carryover sheet metal was found on the roof of sedans and station wagons.

A new roofline on Fury III and Sport Fury two-door hardtops had nearly constant-width C-pillars, giving the car a light and airy look. The Sport Fury's optional "Fast Top" completely changed the look to formal with a heavy triangular C-pillar. This heavier roofline, covered in vinyl, was standard for the VIP two-door hardtop. Four-door hardtop C-pillars were also reworked to give a more formal appearance.

Under the hood, an all-new 318 V-8, coded the LA block, was derived from the 273 introduced in 1964 for the Valiant. The two looked alike and did share the same cylinder head and other external components. Internally, the 318-LA carried the same crankshaft, rods, and pistons as the old A block 277 and 303 from 1956. Externally, it used the same water pump. It became the standard V-8 for all VIPs, Sport Furys, and the Fury II and Fury III hardtops and convertibles. Standard powerplant for all Fury I, II, and III sedans was the Slant Six.

Intermediate-size Belvederes received only minor trim changes, as dual headlamps replaced the singles of years past, and the only sheet metal change was a concave indentation on the deck lid. New for the year was a bottom-of-the-line station wagon called simply "Belvedere," without any numbers. Joining the Belvedere I wagon, it was a replacement for the discontinued Valiant wagon.

At the other end of the scale, and much more memorable, was the addition of a luxury performance car in either coupe or convertible form. For those wanting near-maximum performance but unwilling to put up with the temperament of the Hemi, the GTX 440 was the ticket. Unlike the Hemi, which found its way into some of the plainest (lightest) machines for racing, the GTX 440 was a stand out in any crowd. The fiberglass, simulated hood scoops, optional racing stripes, blacked-out grille, and pop-out racing-style gas cap all spelled high-speed luxury. Interiors were gussied up as well to go along with the optional electric tachometer and 150-mile-per-hour speedometer.

The standard engine was the car's namesake, a 440-ci, 375-horsepower V-8. There was an optional engine—14 ci smaller but producing 50 more horsepower—the Hemi. Only 125 buyers opted for the Hemi. It would be a one-year-only offering in the GTX.

Other Belvedere models included the Belvedere I two-door, four-door, and station wagon; Belvedere II hardtop, convertible, four-door, and wagon in six- or nine-passenger form; and Satellite and GTX hardtops and convertibles.

Full-size cars included the Fury I two-door, four-door, or wagon; Fury II two-door, four-door, or wagon in six- or nine-passenger sizes; Fury III

As in years past, most Plymouth buyers in 1966 opted for the four-door sedan, seen here in Fury III trim. *Willard Stein*

hardtop, convertible, four-door sedan, and hardtop and wagons for six or nine; the VIP two- and four-door hardtop; and Sport Fury in convertible or coupe, in regular or fastback top.

Sales of 465,390 intermediate and full-size cars again kept Plymouth in fourth at the end of the model run.

Model 1968
Satellite, Sport Satellite convertible ★★★★★
Satellite, Sport Satellite hardtop coupe ★★★★
Road Runner-all body types ★★★★★
GTX-all body types ★★★★★
VIP, Sport Fury & Fury III hardtop
coupe or sedan ★★★★
Fury III, and Sport Fury convertible ★★★★★
Sedans & wagons, all series ★
440 V-8 ★★★★
426 Street Hemi ★★★★★

Plymouth for 1968
Styling for 1968 was still slab-sided but a closer examination revealed all-new rear quarter-panels that did much to straighten out the "hump" of the '67's fender line. A new rear door stamping and new deck lid eliminated the boattail look and gave the car its own identity. Front fenders and sheet metal remained the same with an obligatory grille change for model identification. The lower half of the grille became a fine mesh painted body color. Headlamps remained vertical dual quads; side marker lights, a government-mandated safety feature, sat at the extreme ends of both front and rear fenders; small and round, they looked very much like last-minute additions. Other standard safety (i.e., mandated) equipment included a dual brake system with warning lamp, emergency flashers, back-up lights, and a left-hand outside rear-view mirror. Optional on

Clean, crisp styling continued to characterize the 1966 Belvedere line. Performance enthusiasts had a potent machine in the form of the Satellite coupe, which was powered by a 383-ci V-8 with four-speed transmission. *Dwayne Daddario*

wagons was a rear window washing system that cleaned the glass as it rolled down.

Models names and numbers remained the same except the Fury II station wagon was discontinued—or was it? Station wagons again got their own Suburban nomenclature of Custom and Sport Suburban from years past. What would have been the Fury I wagon was offered only in six-passenger form, and Custom and Sport wagons were offered in either six or nine-passenger capacity.

The Fury III came in convertible, two- or four-door sedan, or hardtop forms with a choice of regular or Fast Top roof styles. The Sport Fury came in convertible or choice of top for the hard-

top, while the VIP hardtop came only with the fastback-style roof.

The biggest news for the year was not in the full-size car line, but in the intermediate Belvedere camp. For sometime Chrysler officials had been noting that performance buyers, specifically those buying Hemi engines, were putting them into the cheapest, most stripped-down models possible. If Plymouth were to drop a big engine into the lightest, no-frills body available, would there be a market for it? The answer was an astounding "YES."

Belvedere two-door sedans had gone by the wayside for 1968, but there was a pillared coupe that shared the hardtop's sheet metal, even its frameless doors. Powered by a 383-ci, 335-horsepower V-8 priced at $2,896, the Road Runner was an instant success. Nearly making it out the door with the name Chaparral, it took instead the name of the chaparral cock as its namesake—a bird most people know as the roadrunner. Somewhere the association was made between the name of the car and Warner Bros. Saturday morning cartoon character, and when the dust settled, Plymouth had rights to use the cartoon figure's likeness on the car. Clever engineering replaced the car horn's aluminum windings with copper—presto, even the horn sounded like the cartoon character.

Optimistically cautious, 2,500 Road Runners were projected—yet over 10 times that number rolled out the door, joined shortly thereafter by a true hardtop coupe, of which an additional 15,000 would be built. Not bad for a dirt-cheap, dog-dish hubcap, taxi interior, bottom-of-the-line pillared coupe.

While the Road Runner stole thunder from everything else, few people noticed that the Belvederes were now called just that—Belvedere, available in sedan, wagon, or swing-window pillared coupe like the Road Runner. Replacing the Belvedere II line was the Satellite four-door, wagon, hardtop, and convertible. What had been the Satellite was now the Sport Satellite in hardtop or convertible, and two wagons in six- or nine-passenger form.

At the top of the list was the GTX, a car that was everything the Road Runner was—and more. The bucket-seat, luxury high-performance hardtop or convertible was powered by a standard 375-horsepower 440 or the optional 425-horse 426 Hemi.

Spurred by sales of the Road Runner, Plymouth built 262,098 intermediate and 349,540 full-size cars, ending the year, once again, in fourth place.

Model 1969

Satellite, Sport Satellite convertible ★★★★★
Satellite, Sport Satellite hardtop coupe ★★★★
Road Runner-all body types ★★★★★

New for 1967 was a high-performance, luxury sport coupe in the genre of the old Fury called the GTX. It was powered by a potent 440 V-8 and capable of showing its tail feathers to just about everything else on the road. *Lanny Knutson*

GTX-all body types ★★★★★
VIP, Sport Fury & Fury III hardtop
coupe or sedan ★★★★
Fury III, and Sport Fury convertible ★★★★★
Sedans & wagons, all series ★
440 V-8 ★★★★
426 Street Hemi ★★★★★

Plymouth for 1969

"Fuselage" was the word for all full-size Chrysler products for 1969. Following aircraft principles, Chrysler designed bodies of a single arc from one rocker panel over the roof to the other rocker panel. Although forward-looking, since it is used by nearly every car builder in the 1990s, the fuselage style did not catch on with the buying public of the time. Critics claimed the cars looked too bulbous and that the fuselage design was better suited for smaller cars.

Although all-new, the full-sized 1969 Plymouths had an appearance of continuity with previous years' models. A rather plain single-tier stamped grille was flanked by horizontally paired headlights, a change from the stacked quads that had been a trademark of the big Fury since its 1965 inception. Sport Fury and VIP models were given a more interesting diecast-appearing grille.

Horizontal taillights rested above massive rear bumpers. Upscale models had a die-cast panel between the red lenses.

The three models—Furys I, II, and III; Sport Fury; and VIP—were identified by an inset panel behind the front wheels. The VIP came standard

Full-size Plymouths' top offering for 1967 was the VIP coupe with fast top roof style. Engine options included everything from the mundane 318 to the potent 440. Only the 426 Hemi was excluded from the option list. *Don Hermany*

with pillow-pleated upholstery, vinyl roof, fender skirts, and many other luxury appointments. It and the Sport Fury had wheel openings outlined with bright trim. The Sport Fury and VIP two-door hardtops had ventless front door glass. All other cars continued with conventional vent windows, and all had concealed windshield wipers.

A midyear addition was the Formal Hardtop, which was created by installing the wider C-pillar four-door hardtop roof to the two-door body.

The base Fury I two-door was actually a pillared hardtop coupe that shared the true hardtop's doors. The Suburban station wagon had an integral roof spoiler to cleanse the rear window.

The Fury engine list included the 225 six and the 318; 383 two-barrel; 383 four-barrel; and 440 engines of 145, 230, 290, 330, and 375 horsepower, respectively. The optional 383 for the Suburban was limited to 350 horsepower.

Setting the pace on the super speedways was the Hemi-powered Plymouth of Richard Petty.

Styling changes for 1968 were minimal for the full-size Fury III. *Merrill Berkheimer*

The hugely popular Road Runner was rewarded with an expanded role in the intermediate series. It kept the hardtop it gained at midyear 1968, to which a convertible was added for 1969.

A new cross-hatch grille was installed on the Belvedere, Satellite, and Road Runner models. On the latter, it was given an argent finish rather than a bright finish. A dual-bar diecast-appearing grille was reserved for the Sport Satellite and GTX lines. The line name appeared in the center of this grille.

Sheet metal changes were reserved for the rear fender caps to accommodate redesigned taillights and the deck lid, which was given an oval indentation. This indentation was filled with a diecast molding on the upper-scale models.

Although the intermediate Plymouth series offered a full complement of sedans and wagons, it is best remembered for its "post" and hardtop coupes that were the basis for the Road Runner and GTX musclecars.

The vertical hood vents could be made functional with special underhood ducting. When so equipped, the vent openings were covered with red plastic mesh.

The 440 was a GTX exclusive until spring, when the two-barrel version was installed in a Road Runner. A flat-black, big-scooped fiberglass hood that was held in place by four chrome pins gave the car a special identity. It also came *sans* hubcaps with only chrome lug nuts setting off the plain wheels.

Model 1970
Satellite convertible ★★★★★
Sport Satellite hardtop coupe ★★★★
GTX-all body types ★★★★★
Road Runner-all body types ★★★★★
Superbird-INTESTIMABLE
Fury, Sport Fury hardtop coupe ★★★★
Sport Fury S/23 ★★★★★
Sport Fury GT ★★★★★
Sedans & wagons, all series ★
440 V-8 ★★★★
426 Street Hemi ★★★★★

Plymouth for 1970
Plymouth's musclecar era reached its zenith with its 1970 Rapid Transit System of five high-performance cars. The Duster 340 is covered

Marked by a smoother roofline, the 1968 GTX still carried the basic design themes of earlier years. *Lanny Knutson*

elsewhere. The others were the Barracuda, Road Runner, GTX, and Sport Fury GT.

The Barracuda was Plymouth's all-new car for the year. No longer a Valiant-based car, it has its own E-body chassis. For the first time the Barracuda was a long-hood/short-deck sporty car of the Mustang/Camaro genre. Yet, unlike its competitors, it was not built on a compact-car platform. Instead, Chrysler engineers shortened the B-body chassis so it would more easily accommodate the big engines and heavy-duty axles, brakes, and suspension components the market was demanding.

The grille was a simple design in argent finish with a single vertical divider. Genuine driving lights flanked the license plate of the 'Cuda. A flat, inset valence panel, housing the plate and ribbon taillights/back-up lights, was finished in body color on the Barracuda, in flat black on the 'Cuda, and argent on the Gran Coupe. Protruding through the under-bumper pan were large rectangular exhaust tips on the 'Cuda.

As a regular Barracuda, the car could be docile enough, powered by a 225 Slant Six or 318 V-8. Optional was a 383 two-barrel engine.

Only minimal changes were made to the intermediate cars for 1969. Extremely popular was the Satellite hardtop coupe. *Luc Grondin*

"Fuselage" styling was the name applied to the full-size Plymouth design for 1969. This was the first redesign of the full-size Plymouth since 1965. *Lanny Knutson*

The 'Cuda engine line-up began with a choice of standard 340 or 383 four-barrel V-8s, and the optional 440 and 426 Hemi engines. The engines were identified by numbers on the simulated dual "shaker" hood scoops, which were actually functional as an option, and by optional "hockey stick" stripes on the rear quarters. The fabled Hemi-Cuda, especially the extremely low-production convertibles, has long been the darling of collectors, and can be extremely high-priced today.

Another Barracuda offering was the Gran Coupe, a luxury version with high-level interior appointments and exterior trim. It could be ordered in conjunction with standard or high-performance engines.

A spring offering was the AAR 'Cuda. Named for the All American Racers company of Dan Gurney, hired to race 'Cudas on the Trans Am circuit, the car was powered by a three two-barrel carb 340 engine and marked by side-dump exhaust pipes, large rear and small front E70 tires, flat black paint on the hood and the fender tops, and special strobe stripes.

The mid-sized Plymouths, in the third and final season of a styling cycle, bore a few more sheet metal changes than did the previous year's model.

An upside-down "telephone receiver" loop grille forecast what was to appear in more dramatic fashion the following year. Behind the doors on the coupes were simulated air scoops. A new taillight panel was installed with inward-pointing arrow-shaped taillamps. The

Performance buyers many times choose a Sport Satellite like this 1970 model as the basis for their muscle machine. Even with a 318 V-8 under the hood, the car looked like it was ready to race. *Jeffrey Robinson*

deck lid now opened from above this panel rather than the bumper.

The GTX offered optional stripes that began at the headlights and exited into the rear fender scoop. As a bit of whimsy, the Road Runner bird "ran" out of the scoop, leaving a dusty circular trail all the way to the front of the car.

The muscle models featured a "power bulge" hood. Optional was the Air Grabber, a functional scoop that opened by vacuum power when needed.

Four-speed manual transmissions were coupled with Hurst shifters topped with an unique pistol grip.

Simply "fantastic" was the Road Runner Superbird. Dominated by a huge rear wing and pointed nose, it could not be missed. A limited production of 1,920 were built (one car for every two dealers) to qualify it for NASCAR competition. Actually, it was

The ultimate in performance machines—and the most outrageous Plymouth ever built and sold to the public—is the 1970 Road Runner Superbird. Just 1,902 were built, most with the 440 V-8. With its long sloped nose and towering tail fin, the Superbird became the car to catch on the NASCAR super speedways. With its success rate, it was soon outlawed. *Plymouth Owners Club*

a Dodge Charger body modified to accept Plymouth pieces such as the side scoops and taillight panel. Still, its wing and nose cone were different from those found on the similar Dodge Charger Daytona. Standard power was the 440; optional was the 426 Hemi. The car enjoyed success on NASCAR tracks, including a Daytona 500 win, before such special-bodied cars were virtually banned.

The standard-size (as the line was first called in 1969) Plymouth featured a few changes for the second year of its fuselage body. Grille/bumper and taillight/bumper combos were in style, and

Right
The Road Runner took its name from the Warner Bros. Saturday morning cartoon character. Under special licensing agreements, the cartoon character appeared on every car built—here with helmet in hand on the tail fin of a Superbird namesake. *Jim Benjaminson*

Fuselage styling and a heavy roofline mark this full-size 1971 Gran Coupe. *Robert Hoffman*

Plymouth joined the fashion parade. The loop bumper gave the '70 Furys a stronger frontal appearance. Headlight doors hid the lamps on the upper trim models. The rear bumper was moved up, and the taillights were moved down, to become a single unit. The modified hood featured twin bulges. On high-performance models, the engine's cubic-inch size was displayed on the bulge edge.

New models included a Sport Fury four-door sedan and the Fury Gran Coupe. The latter, a once-lowly two-door "post" sedan, was fitted with premium appointments. Of the last full-size Plymouth convertible, just 1,952 units were made.

The new version of the Sport Fury was the GT. With standard 440 four-barrel and optional 440 six-barrel power, it was marketed as a gentleman's hot rod in the tradition of the Chrysler 300. For those who wanted the GT look but not necessarily the power was the S/23. It could be ordered with engines ranging from the 318 to the two-barrel or four-barrel 383s.

Model 1971
Satellite Sebring & Sebring Plus
hardtop coupe ★★★★
GTX-all ★★★★★
Road Runner-all ★★★★★
Fury II, Fury III, Sport Fury
hardtop coupe ★★★★
Sport Fury GT coupe ★★★★ 1/2
440 V-8 ★★★★
426 Street Hemi ★★★★★

Plymouth fleet sales catered to the taxi and police car trade. Superior handling and outstanding performance made this 1972 Fury I pursuit sedan a favorite with law enforcement officers everywhere. *Jim Benjaminson*

Plymouth built police cars for every purpose, from six-cylinder-powered "prowlers" for city work, to V-8-equipped "pursuit" vehicles for freeway use. This 1973 police pursuit was powered by a 360 V-8. *Jim Benjaminson*

Plymouth for 1971

Fuselage styling came to mid-size Plymouths in 1971. Called the Satellite series, it actually was comprised of two mid-size Plymouth lines. The two-door hardtop coupe with a 115-inch wheelbase and the four-door sedan with a 117-inch span were two different cars sharing not one piece of sheet metal.

The dramatically styled coupe was dominated by a huge "telephone receiver" loop bumper. The C-pillars were integral with the rear quarter-panels. Large bulges reached out to cover the tires. Inset into the rear bumper were rectangular taillight/back-up-light units.

Satellite, Sebring, and Sebring-Plus represented the lower- to upper-trim levels of the standard power coupes; the Road Runner and GTX did likewise for the high-performance cars. The latter two boasted hoods with non-functional dual inset vents on which the engine displacement size appeared. Optional was a "power bulge" hood with a functioning vacuum-opening Air Grabber scoop.

The GTX featured wide, dramatic stripes flowing out of the standard hood vents and down to the wheels on both sides. Additional stripes outlined the lower-body character line, up and over the wheels, from front to back. The Road Runner was available with strobe stripes running over the roof from rear wheel to rear wheel.

Without a mid-size convertible for the first time, Plymouth offered the coupes with optional sliding-panel sunroofs.

The 383 four-barrel, 440 four-barrel, 440 six-barrel, and 426 Hemi comprised the Road Runner engine list. The GTX offered all but the 383. The other coupes were available with 225, 318, and 383 two-barrel and four-barrel engines.

The sedan, a fraternal twin to the coupe, was similarly styled but actually different. Most notably the grille, which hinted at the coupe grille shape, sat above, not within, the bumper. Trim levels ascended from Satellite to Custom to Brougham.

The top wagon received Regent nomenclature. All wagons were styled after the C-body wagons.

The Barracuda received numerous add-on trim changes, causing some detractors to dub it the "J.C. Whitney 'Cuda."

Some critics had complained that the '70 Barracuda grille appeared too docile for a

Sleek, new styling marked 1973's Satellite Sebring.
Lanny Knutson

performance car. Perhaps overreacting, Plymouth designers created a grille comprised of three D-shaped openings per side to suggest barracuda fish teeth. Flanking the openings were the Barracuda's first and only quad headlights. The grille pan itself was painted argent on most models, body color on others.

Flanking the cowl were chrome-simulated inset louvers that suggested fish gills. The taillight/back-up lights were changed slightly into two separate units per side.

Optional on 'Cudas were large flat-black decals that covered almost the entire rear quarter-panel, ending on the doors where the engine displacement number was incorporated into the design.

All body styles and engine choices offered in 1970 were repeated for '71. This was the last year for both the convertible and the Hemi engine. Only 1,014 Barracudas and just 374 'Cuda convertibles—the very last Plymouth droptop—were sold.

The Barracuda lines took a precipitous fall from a combined production total of 54,799 in 1970, to just 18,690 for 1971.

The standard-size Fury carried on with minimal sheet metal changes. The pillared coupe—almost a hardtop already—was given the standard hardtop roof. A wider C-pillared "formal" hardtop was offered on upper lines. All Furys had ventless side glass.

The twin "power bulges" were gone from the hood. The open-headlight grilles slanted in from top and bottom to leave a narrow opening that stretched from side to side. The "headlight door" grille was comprised of four sets of twin ovals with vertical insets.

Only 375 Sport Fury GTs, identified by large "GT" letters on the hood, were made. Most popular was the Fury III hardtop sedan.

Plymouth's first captive import was brought in to engage the Vega and Pinto in the sub-compact wars. A rebadged British-built Hillman Avenger, the Plymouth Cricket, appealed to very few buyers over the three years it was offered.

Model 1972
Satellite Sebring & Sebring Plus
hardtop coupe ★★★★

Road Runner-all ★★★★★
Fury II, Fury III, Sport Fury
hardtop coupe ★★★★
Gran Fury GT coupe ★★★★ 1/2
440 V-8 ★★★★
426 Street Hemi ★★★★★

Plymouth for 1972

The Barracuda, reflecting its drop in sales, was drastically cut in both model choices and engines. Just the Barracuda and 'Cuda remained in coupe form only. Engine choices were limited to the 225 and 318 for the plain Barracuda, and the 318 and detuned 340 for the 'Cuda.

The grille returned to a design similar to that of 1970. Simulated driving lamps again served as parking lights. Taillight/back-up lights became twin round units—Camaro-style—set within the rear valence panel.

The Satellite series changed little from '71. Grille textures were different, especially on the Road Runner, which seemed to have a '70 'Cuda grille installed inside its loop bumper. A new rear bumper exhibited dominant, sideways-D-shaped taillights.

The slow-selling GTX was dropped, leaving the Road Runner as the sole performance car. It was available with the small-block 340 for the first time, although the new 400 (which replaced the 383) was considered the standard Road Runner engine. Optional were 440 four-barrel and six-barrel engines.

The remaining coupe, sedan, and wagon lineup was basically unchanged.

The Fury fuselage body received a major revamping as the hood, fenders, and quarter-panels were all redesigned. The latter featured forward-slanting rear-wheel bulge sculpting that extended to the rear bumper. This bulge was sculpted from both the front and the back on the "informal" two-door hardtops only.

Dramatic twin-loop front bumper/grilles dominated the front. Both open-headlight and hidden-headlight grilles were available.

The Gran Fury replaced the Sport Fury. The remainder of the model line-up was similar to the previous year but with reduced model offerings.

The standard engine was the 318, with a 400 two-barrel and a 440 four-barrel as the only options until midyear, when the new 360 small block V-8 was introduced. Chrysler's new electronic ignition, which saw limited installation on certain '71 models, was optional on early '72 cars and was later standard on all V-8 engines.

Model 1973
Sebring & Sebring Plus hardtop coupe ★★★★
Road Runner ★★★★★

Fury III, Gran Fury hardtop
coupe or sedan ★★★★
Sedans & wagons, all series ★
440 V-8 ★★★★

Plymouth for 1973

Plymouth toned down the frontal appearance of its mid- and full-size offerings by lopping off the loop bumpers in favor of the more-conventional grille-over-bumper arrangement. The change was due more to government requirements for energy-absorbing bumpers than style considerations.

The Satellite coupes received new front sheet metal with headlights that were slanted back slightly surrounded by a bright rectangular bezel. Between was a grille consisting of a double row of rectangles with parking lights set in the lower outside corners.

The window edge of the C-pillar was moved into a nearly vertical position. The lower body character ridge was eliminated. The taillights still resided in the rear bumpers but as inset ovals.

The Road Runner had a large "Power bulge" with simulated vents on the forward corners. Stripes on the sides identified the engine size. When a 440 engine was installed, the stripe read "440 GTX." Although the separate GTX model was dead, its name lingered as the 440 package for the Road Runner.

The Road Runner engine selection ran from the 318 through the 340, 400, and four-barrel and six-barrel 440s. The horsepower ratings of all were down due to emissions and fuel economy considerations.

The Satellite sedans were given a new grille inset. A surface-level, argent-colored panel had a center oval cutout for an egg crate-patterned grille that was deeply recessed at the ends. The effect was of a more formal appearance.

The taillight/back-up lenses were altered into a rectangular pair per side. Flanking the license plate were heavy rubber bumper guards.

Although extensively restyled the previous year, the standard-size Fury received a new hood, grille, bumper, and fender caps. For the first time in five years, hidden headlights were not an option. Each quad light had its own bright bezel and was set in a body color panel. A wide radiator-shape grille resided between them. Its fine horizontal bar texture extended into bumper cutouts. To add some character to the much plainer front end, a prominent, wide, arrow-shaped raised center section was stamped into the hood.

The taillights were changed significantly to vertical elongated teardrop-shaped units rising out of the bumper corners. Somehow, they brought to mind 1957. A single-unit rectangular back-up light resided in the upper center of a massive chromed bumper.

Specialty models built on the Satellite chassis for 1974 included the Sebring Sundance, which sported unique striping across the roof and interesting upholstery patterns. The Sundance name would later be applied to a line of small Plymouths. *Wayne Farough*

As in 1972, the Fury was a V-8-only series. The 318 was standard on all models except the Suburban, in which the 360 was standard. Other engines available were the 400 two-barrel and 440 four-barrel.

The Fury I was limited to a single four-door sedan. Fury II had only the sedan and the Suburban wagon. The largest line was the Fury III with the sedan, hardtop coupe and sedan, and two- and three-seat Custom Suburban wagons. The Gran Fury came as a hardtop coupe and sedan as well as two Sport Suburbans.

The Barracuda was still around as base and 'Cuda hardtop coupes and the same selections as 1972. The grille and taillights were unchanged. The side marker light positions were slightly changed. About the only other visible difference was a 'Cuda body-side stripe that had a flat bottom edge.

Model 1974
Sebring & Sebring Plus hardtop coupe ★★★★
Road Runner ★★★★★
Fury III, Gran Fury hardtop
coupe or sedan ★★★★

Sedans & wagons, all series ★
440 V-8 ★★★★

Plymouth for 1974

An all-new Fury greeted the Plymouth buyer for 1974. Unfortunately, following the 1973 gasoline shortage crisis, it was not a good year to promote a large car. With the usual three-year lead time in car development, it was more from lack of luck than foresight that Plymouth had a brand-new full-sized car and a seven-year-old compact on the market at the time.

The conservatively styled car was elegantly attractive with square lines and straight sides. Its frontal appearance—actually forecast by the '73 Fury—included a grille made up of narrow horizontal bars set between quad lights in bright rectangular bezels. Rectangular "ribbon" taillights dipped into slight recesses in the rear bumper.

Body styles consisted of a four-door sedan, a hardtop coupe and sedan, and two- and three-seat wagons. The mid-seventies opera window fad hit Plymouth that spring as the Gran Fury hardtop coupe was modified with vinyl-covered panels in which the small side windows were set.

The 225 six was again available on base Furys. The 360 was the base V-8 but cars could be ordered equipped with the 318. The 400 two-barrel became the Gran Fury and Suburban standard engine.

The Satellite coupes were only slightly changed with a similar-patterned grille that was more recessed than in 1973. The rear bumper lights consisted of a triple-square lens unit, with the inside lenses serving as back-up lights.

The Sundance was a spring special coupe. The Aztec Gold or Spinnaker White body was set off by ornate filigreed gold stripes that incorporated a sunburst design on the C-pillars. Of course, this special package lent its name to a Plymouth model 13 years later.

The Satellite sedans received a new cross-hatch-designed grille insert. All Satellites except the Road Runner came standard with the 225 six. V-8 selections included the 318, 360 four-barrel, and 400 four-barrel. The big 440 four-barrel remained a Road Runner-only option.

In its tenth and final season, Barracuda came with a continuation of its 1973 cars with a couple of changes. The rear side windows on the base Barracuda were fixed, making it a coupe like the Duster. The 'Cuda—now with a 360 replacing the 340—came with a color-keyed grille. With a production of 11,734, the Barracuda became history.

The market was going in a different direction, causing Plymouth to reenter the "truck" market after a 33-year absence. The Voyager and Trail Duster were rebadged renditions of the Dodge Sportsman "window" vans and Ramcharger sport utility vehicles. Both carried the Plymouth name boldly across blacked-out grille centers.

Chapter 2

1960-1976 Valiant and Barracuda

Chrysler was late getting into the compact market. Perhaps the market's rejection of its "Smaller On the Outside, Bigger On the Inside" marketing strategy a decade earlier in favor of "bigger is better," left Chrysler wary of jumping back in the small car wars. But the ever-increasing popularity of the European imports and the domestic Rambler drove General Motors and Ford to plan models of their own. Still, Chrysler dawdled. Ford and GM were well on their way in designing their compacts when Chrysler finally entered the fray.

To make up for lost time, Chrysler's compact became one of the first automobiles to be designed with the aid of computer simulation, however primitive it was compared to 1990s technology.

Originally to be called Falcon, after a Chrysler dream car, the proposed compact had to be renamed when Ford registered the same name for its compact. Eventually, "Valiant" was chosen.

Ford had chosen thoroughly American styling and engineering for its Falcon. Chevrolet enveloped the European-style rear-engine chassis of its Corvair with fairly conventional domestic styling, while Chrysler stylist Virgil Exner incorporated European styling for the Valiant's relatively conventional chassis.

Most of the styling cues favored by Exner appeared on the Valiant: radiator-sized grille opening, headlight shapes flowing back onto the fender sides, full wheel openings, and a spare-tire stamping on a semi-fastback deck lid.

The Valiant also featured quad headlights, a rounded six-window greenhouse, and cat-eye taillights that capped canted mini-fins. It was Chrysler's first car in six years not to be blatantly finned.

In dimensions, it was slightly larger and heavier than its competition and its new six-cylinder engine was a bit more powerful.

Chrysler's first all-new six-cylinder engine since 1931 was canted 30 degrees to the right to aid hood clearance and, as a bonus, create room for a mini-ram-effect intake manifold. With 170 ci, it was given a 101 brake horsepower rating. The Slant Six,

Chrysler Corporation's entry into the compact car field in 1960 was the Valiant. During the first year of its existence, the Valiant was not aligned with any of the other corporate divisions. Advertised as "Nobody's Kid Brother," the Valiant was aligned as part of the Plymouth-DeSoto-Valiant Division. European styling showed a few of Virgil Exner's favorite touches, including the fake spare tire on the deck lid, open wheel wells, and full radiator-size grille opening. *Barry Levittan*

as it quickly became known, proved to be an extremely reliable powerplant that would remain in production more than a quarter-century.

Traditional Chrysler torsion bars and rear leaf springs suspended the 106.5-inch wheelbase, unibody chassis. Push buttons, another Chrysler tradition, controlled a version of the TorqueFlite automatic transmission called the 904. Especially designed for the Slant Six, it was the first with an aluminum case. A three-speed manual transmission, with floor shift, was standard.

Two model series were offered: the base V100 and the slightly upscale V200. The latter was identified by thin bright trim that followed the edge of the rear fenders and the doors' lower character lines. Wheel covers were unavailable but trim rings could be ordered to supplement the small hubcaps on 13-inch wheels.

The V200 interiors featured color-keyed cloth and vinyl upholstery with matching carpet. Gray upholstery and black rubber mats were installed in V100 cars.

At midyear, a station wagon was introduced. Featuring six-window styling to utilize the sedan doors, it had a tailgate with a roll-down window and spare tire well beneath a flat floor. For its inaugural season only, Valiant's wagon was available in a three-seat as well as a two-seat configuration.

Another midyear addition was the Hyper-Pak for the new Slant Six engine. Designed specifically for racing applications, it consisted of a long, tuned ram intake manifold with a four-barrel carburetor and cast-iron dual exhaust manifolds. The package increased the 170 engine's horsepower to 148 brake horsepower but racing mechanics were able to raise it as high as 185 with domed pistons and a high-lift cam. Led by Lee Petty, the seven Valiants entered in the inaugural NASCAR Compact Division race placed first through seventh. When Valiant similarly dominated the 1961 race, the series was canceled.

Unlike its competitors, Valiant was an independent marque in the Chrysler corporate line-up. Although built in a Dodge plant, Valiant was sold exclusively by Plymouth dealers in the United States. In Canada it was sold at both Dodge and Plymouth dealerships.

Total U.S. production was 253,432.

Valiant 1961
Sedan ★
Station wagon ★
Hardtop ★★★★
Signet ★★★★★
Any model with Hyper-Park ★★★★★

Minimal changes were made to the Valiant for 1961, which had officially become a Plymouth (at least as far as U.S. sales were concerned). A rare and unusual accessory are the rear wheel fender shields. *Lanny Knutson*

1961

Valiant became a Plymouth model in 1961, identified as such only by a diminutive "By Plymouth" plate under the Valiant script on the trunk lid. In Canada, it continued as an independent make with the plate reading "By Chrysler" instead.

Primary news for the model year was the introduction of two-door models. The V100 two-door was a sedan with framed glass. The V200

At the low end of the Valiant totem pole for 1961 was the two-door V100 sedan. A bare-bones model, this car sports two accessories: whitewall tires and fender skirts. *Lanny Knutson*

Still basically unchanged, with the notable exception of round taillamps, the 1962 Valiant was available with two-tone paint. *Bill Burge*

version was a hardtop. Both continued the four-door's six-window styling with fixed quarter-windows.

The grille was restyled into an egg-crate design with the use of flat black paint. The side trim was redesigned into a single spear on the door character line of V200 models. Bright trim also swept back, following the upper front fender flare onto the front door, where a Valiant medallion was mounted. Full wheel covers were available for the first time.

Supplementing the 170 engine was the optional 225 Slant Six introduced as a midyear option. Called the Super 225, the 145-brake horse-power powerplant was borrowed from the full-size Plymouth line. An aluminum-block version of this engine was also available. However, quality-control problems led to most being replaced by cast-iron engines. An aluminum-engined Valiant is a rare find today.

Production, in the United States, dropped to 143,078.

Valiant 1962
Sedan ★
Station wagon ★
Hardtop ★★★★
Signet ★★★★★
Any model with Hyper-Park ★★★★★

1962

For its third season, Valiant's sheet metal remained unchanged except for the deletion of the spare-tire stamping on the deck lid. The grille opening was outlined with a heavier chrome frame with Valiant stamped onto the upper edge. A new, finely-textured grille of horizontal strips filled the cavity. The hood latch, which previously had been the emblem in the center of the

grille, became a chrome lever centered beneath the upper grille frame.

The taillights were changed to round units mounted below the now capped-off fins. The lower body side trim on the V200 models was a wide molding featuring three rectangular "ventriport" markings just ahead of the rear wheels. A two-tone option in the Spring featured a contrasting color beneath this molding and back onto the rear fender. Also on V200 models only was a large, circular Valiant nameplate that somewhat compensated for the lack of a spare tire impression.

The instrument panel was redesigned. Manual transmission cars lost their floor shifters in favor of Chrysler's new concentric steering column shifter.

A new sub-series was the sporty Signet 200. The two-door hardtop featured bucket seats and unique outside markings. A large, circular Valiant medallion was mounted in the center of the blacked-out grille. The headlight frames received a similar treatment. The upper fender flare was highlighted by a color-filled trim spear. The lower body and rear-fender character lines were left unadorned to lend a sporty flavor to the car.

To preserve the uniqueness of the Signet, the standard V200 two-door was changed from a hardtop to a pillared sedan. Neither of Valiant's primary competitors, Falcon and Corvair, had hardtop models.

Production rose slightly to 157,294.

Valiant 1963
Sedan ★
Station wagon ★
Hardtop ★★★★
Signet hardtop ★★★★★
Convertible ★★★★★
Barracuda ★★★★★
Any with Formula S package ★★★★★

1963

Valiant's first major restyle brought it a more conventional appearance. Although designer Virgil Exner had departed the company by the time of the car's introduction, it did bear some of his styling cues. The grille remained a radiator-shaped entity but it was widened to stretch to the new single-unit headlights. The headlight shape continued to flow onto the fenders just below another of Exner's favored cues: the hairpin. A bent ridge was stamped into the upper edge of the fender to provide some character to an otherwise rather plain design.

The rear of the car bore a rounded, sloping appearance not unlike the 1996 Mercury Sable. Elwood Engel, Exner's successor, muted the design by squaring off the rear quarter panels with vestigial fins. Horizontal strip taillights were mounted below these "fins." Similarly squared-off were the previously fully-radiused rear wheel openings. An unbroken molding—an Engel trademark—ran along the upper beltline from front to back on V200 models.

Although its wheelbase was reduced by a half an inch to 106 inches, the '63 Valiant's overall length was increased by 2 inches. Mechanically, the car was virtually unchanged from 1962.

A convertible was added to the Valiant line-up for the first time. In the V200 series it featured a bench front seat. A bucket seat version joined the Signet 200 hardtop. All convertible tops were manually operated, although there are reports of power lift mechanisms being installed by the end of the model year.

Again the hardtop was a Signet exclusive. The Signet grille was blacked out, as were its wheel cover centers. A midyear Signet hardtop offering was an optional vinyl-covered roof, the first on any Plymouth.

Chrysler Canada modified its Valiant by using the new Dodge Dart 111-inch wheelbase body, to which Valiant front fenders, hood, and grille were added. Other Valiant trim was used, as were the Valiant dash and other interior appointments. Since it was sold by both Plymouth and Dodge dealers, the Valiant remained an independent Chrysler make in Canada.

Reflecting the popularity of its new styling, Valiant's production jumped to 225,156 in the United States.

Valiant 1964
Sedan ★
Station wagon ★
Hardtop ★★★★
Signet hardtop ★★★★★
Convertible ★★★★★
Barracuda ★★★★★
Any with Formula S package ★★★★★

1964
For a restyle that was only in its second year, the 1964 Valiant offered numerous changes. Exner's radiator-shaped grille disappeared in favor of a fully horizontal unit. A protruding center section created a distinctive grille that, in one way or another, would be a Valiant trademark for the rest of its existence. Centering the grille was a round, inset Valiant emblem. The leading edge of the hood was redesigned to match the raised middle grille section.

The side edges of the sedan and hardtop roofs received a beveled crease. Each mini fin received a vertical taillight with small square back-up lenses at the base.

Inside, the heater controls were moved from a panel below the dash to its upper center. The plastic instrument surround was also slightly modified.

A new Chrysler-built, Hurst-shifted four-speed transmission could be ordered installed in any Valiant. By December, Valiant's first V-8 engine was offered.

Although the new engine owed its heritage to the 318 V-8, it was essentially a new design with thin-wall casting which made it 55 pounds lighter than the 318. This first of Chrysler's LA engine series—which is still in production in the late-1990s—had a 273 ci displacement and produced 180 brake horsepower. Cars in which it was installed were identified by a V-8 emblem located at the open end of the fender hairpin stamping.

On April 1, a sporty Valiant with a fastback roofline was introduced to the public. Called "Barracuda," it was a Valiant with a roof dominated by a huge 14.4-square-foot, hand-formed rear window. The deck lid was unique to the car. A carpeted trunk space could be opened to a large cargo area beneath the rear glass. This area could be expanded even further by lowering the rear-seat back, station wagon-style, making a sporty car very practical.

The Barracuda was further identified by a special three-piece grille. The center section was painted body color while the side sections were blacked out with single bars extending inward to parking lights styled like driving lamps. The fenders bore hairpin stampings that were narrower than those on the regular Valiants. The V-8 emblems, on cars so-equipped, were mounted just behind the headlights.

Standard wheel covers were regular Valiant items with simulated knock-off hubs added. Optional were wheel covers styled with a mag-wheel appearance through which real chrome lug nuts protruded.

Mechanically, the Barracuda was no different from any other Valiant.

Although it was introduced just before Ford's Mustang, the Barracuda wasn't intended to be a Mustang competitor, but simply a sporty Valiant.

A 1964-1/2 Barracuda can be differentiated from the '65s by its push-button controls, if it has an automatic transmission, and by the Valiant script under the right corner of the deck lid.

Combined Valiant/Barracuda production of 251,028 in the United States nearly matched Valiant's first-year record.

Chrysler Canada continued the practice of mounting a Valiant front clip on a Dart body and selling it as Valiant at both Dodge and Plymouth dealers. The 273 V-8 wasn't available in Canadian Valiants until 1965. The Barracuda, however, was introduced at approximately the same time as it was south of the border. Since it, like the Valiant, was sold as an independent make, the Plymouth name did not appear on the car. The block letters on the trunk read Valiant instead of Plymouth.

Valiant 1965
Sedan ★
Station wagon ★
Hardtop ★★★★
Signet hardtop ★★★★★
Convertible ★★★★★
Barracuda ★★★★★
Any with Formula S package ★★★★★

1965

In the third year of its styling cycle, the '65 Valiant sported a new stamped grille and fenders that appeared on the 1964-1/2 Barracuda. The Barracuda's round back-up lenses also were installed on all Valiants.

The Barracuda was unchanged except for the deletion of the Valiant script that had appeared under the lower deck lid corner. Although it still bore a Valiant medallion, the Barracuda was being divorced from Valiant identity and soon would be known simply as the Plymouth Barracuda. Optional racing stripes were also made available.

Between the bucket seats, a mini-console with an automatic shift lever could be installed. Other automatic transmission cars bore a column shifter since all Chrysler products had abandoned push-button controls.

New to the engine line-up was the Commando 273. With 10.5:1 compression and a four-barrel carburetor, it produced 235 horsepower. Since the Valiant chassis wasn't designed for dual exhausts, a single exhaust system was installed. It ended with a large square-tipped resonator, which produced more noise than most dual systems.

Although available on all Barracudas and V200 Valiants, the Commando 273 was found primarily in Barracudas with the Formula S package. In addition to the engine, the package included heavy-duty suspension parts and extra-wide rims on which were mounted Goodyear Blue Streak tires. (Fourteen-inch wheels became a midyear option on V-8 cars.) Formula S medallions replaced the usual V-8 emblems just behind the headlights.

U.S. Valiant/Barracuda production dropped back to 231,749.

Chrysler Canada offered two distinct Valiant lines in 1965. The V200, including Signet, was the complete Dodge Dart body but with Valiant

Completely redesigned for 1963, Valiant added a convertible. *Robert Gibson*

nameplates, wheel covers, and interior. The V100 line was the complete U.S. Valiant body. The Custom 100 was the same as the U.S. V200. Both lines, along with the Valiant-badged Barracuda, were sold by Dodge and Plymouth dealers.

Valiant 1966
Sedan ★
Station wagon ★
Hardtop ★★★★
Signet hardtop ★★★★★
Convertible ★★★★★
Barracuda ★★★★★
Any with Formula S package ★★★★★

1966

In the final year of its styling cycle, the Valiant received significant one-year-only styling changes. Displaying Engel's influence, the fenders, quarter-panels, deck lid, and roof pillars were all squared-off. Massive bumpers eliminated the need for under-bumper pans. All Valiants received a Barracuda-style painted grille center section. The side sections contained fine mesh on the Valiants; cast-aluminum-appearing egg-crate stampings appeared on the Barracudas. The Barracudas lost their driving lamp-style parking lights.

The Barracuda was further distanced from Valiant as it received new medallions bearing a fish likeness to replace the familiar Valiant emblem in the grille and under the rear window. However, the Barracuda had to share Valiant's vertical taillights, which bore large rectangular reflectors with small, square back-up lenses mounted underneath.

Unlike the other Valiants, the lower-production station wagon remained unchanged behind the cowl.

Argent paint treatment was available for the lower body panels on Signet models. Lacquered beltline pinstripes were standard on Barracudas; redesigned racing stripes could be applied. Fender-mounted turn signal indicators were standard on Barracudas, optional on other Valiants.

A redesigned instrument panel contained two large nacelles. The left one contained the speedometer. On manual-transmission Barracudas, an optional tachometer was mounted in the right nacelle; or a vacuum gauge in automatic-transmission cars. Between new thin-shell bucket seats, a full-length counsel could be installed from which protruded a Hurst four-speed shifter or an automatic selector, depending on how the car was equipped.

The engine line-up remained the same this year, but the Commando 273 could be installed in any Valiant except the station wagon. Identifying V-8-equipped cars was a small rectangular plate mounted low behind the front wheels.

Production in the United States dropped further to 176,166.

Chrysler Canada returned to a single Valiant body for 1966. A complete Dodge Dart body was given Valiant identification and sold as such. This was Valiant's final year as an independent make in Canada. The Barracuda was just that—Barracuda. No Valiant or Plymouth scripts appeared anywhere on the car.

Valiant 1967
100 Sedan ★
Station wagon ★
Signet ★★★
Any with Formula S or 4 speed ★★★★

Barracuda 1967
Hardtop ★★★
Fastback ★★★★★
Convertible ★★★★★
'67 Formula S with 273 V-8 ★★★★★
1968-69 with 340 V-8 ★★★★★
1967-1969 with 383 V-8 ★★★★★
1969 with 440 ★★★★★
1968 Hemi Cuda-INESTIMABLE

1967
Valiant's third and final complete restyle came this year. Fully the product of Engel's design philosophy, it bore a tasteful blend of squared-off lines and beveled edges. The styling, surprisingly formal for a low-priced compact car, led some to dub the new Valiant a "mini Mercedes."

The wheelbase of the revised car was increased to 108 inches. Although unchanged in

Introduced in midyear 1964 was the Barracuda sports fastback. Sporting a huge rear window, divided grille, and redesigned front fenders, many people saw the Barracuda as a last-minute challenge to the Ford Mustang. In actuality, the Barracuda preceded the Mustang but it never became the run away success the Mustang did. *Tom Zorn*

length, the new Valiant was 1 inch taller than its predecessors. This Valiant was the first compact to have curved side glass. It had a split grille divided by a body color panel bearing a filigreed Plymouth emblem. Its taillights were vertical items that curved onto the fender tops.

The model line-up was significantly changed. The slow-selling station wagon was dropped; the

The 1965 Barracuda (left) continued with minimal changes, and it would receive a new frontal design like that of the '66 Valiant Signet convertible pictured here. *Jim Benjaminson*

At this angle, this 1966 Barracuda looks like the 1964-65. Only the cut of the front fender indicates the difference in the front-end design. *Jim Benjaminson*

hardtop and convertible were shifted to the expanded line of the redesigned Barracuda.

The V200 was dropped as a model line but retained as a decor option for the V100. The V100 and Signet lines each had a two- and four-door sedan. The former was a bare-bones economy car; the latter was dressed up with bright window surrounds; rain gutters; moldings on the lower trunk, rocker, and wheel lip; as well as interior dress-up items. The Signet sedans could be ordered with either a bench or bucket front seats.

The 200 decor option offered colors and upholstery midway between the two lines and was identified by full-length bright side moldings and a nameplate with "Valiant two hundred" fully spelled out.

The 170 engine was given the 225's camshaft to increase its horsepower to 115. The 225 engine was standard for the Signet line, but the 170 could be ordered as a delete option. Both 273 V-8s were available in all Valiants. The four-speed manual transmission was now available only with V-8 engines.

Introduced on November 25, 1966, was an all-new Barracuda. It was specifically designed from the ground-up as a sporty car rather than as a revamped Valiant. Featuring curved and flowing lines, it was quite a contrast to Engel's general preference for more angular styling.

Barracuda's usual driving lamp-style parking lights returned to the split grille. Taillights were set in the ends of a concave rear panel. The gas cap was a racing-style flip-open unit.

It shared the 108-inch wheelbase of Valiant but was 4.4 inches longer.

No longer an exclusively fastback line, the '67 Barracuda picked up the hardtop and convertible dropped by the Valiant.

The fastback, called the Sport Barracuda, remained the flagship of the Barracuda line-up. Its rear window, much smaller than that which made previous Barracudas famous, fit the body lines in a very natural manner. As before, its rear seat and trunk divider panel could be folded down to provide a large, uninterrupted storage area.

The two-door hardtop had a unique concave rear glass and a sedan-type deck lid, a first for Barracuda. The convertible was basically a reinforced hardtop body with a choice of manual or power tops.

Dominating attention in the engine lineup was a B-block 383. Due to space limitations, it could not be ordered with either air conditioning or power steering. Also, redesigned exhaust manifolds cut its horsepower to 280, 45 less than the four-barrel 383s in larger Plymouths. The standard engine for Barracuda was the 225 six. The base V-8 was the 180-horsepower 273. The Commando 273 was still offered. Although the new Barracuda chassis was designed for dual exhausts—as used on the 383 engine—the Commando 273 carried on with its single-exhaust, square-resonator system.

The Formula S option continued as a sports suspension and instrumentation package. It was identified by the usual circular medallions mounted low, behind the front wheels.

A slight drop in production led to a total of 171,503.

Valiant 1968
100 Sedan ★
Station wagon ★
Signet ★★★
Any with Formula S or 4 speed ★★★★

A car with a history is this 1966 Valiant sedan. Its original owner was Neta Snook who taught Amelia Earhart how to fly. Its current owner, Ann Pellegreno, is herself a flyer, and in 1967—30 years after Earhart's disappearance—flew the same route in the same type of airplane Earhart flew, successfully completing the trip. *Jim Benjaminson*

Completely redesigned for 1967, the Barracuda featured split grilles and a complete line of body styles.
Andrew G. Weimann II

Barracuda 1968
Hardtop ★★★
Fastback ★★★★★
Convertible ★★★★★
'67 Formula S with 273 V-8 ★★★★★
1968-69 with 340 V-8 ★★★★★
1967-1969 with 383 V-8 ★★★★★
1969 with 440 ★★★★★
1968 Hemi Cuda-INESTIMABLE

1968

All-new in 1967, the Valiant and Barracuda lines had minimal changes for 1968.

The new Valiant could be identified by a narrower separation piece between the split grilles, which featured a slightly changed mesh texture. The taillights were changed to three-section units with the lower segment housing back-up lights. Some of the exterior bright trim, such as the Signet trunk molding and the 200 decor option side trim (which featured an indented red stripe), were changed. The hood bulges had insert panels that identified the high-performance engines, if the car was so-equipped.

The Commando 273 was discontinued (replaced by the 340 in the Barracuda line). In compensation, the 273 base V-8 was upped to 190 horsepower and the 230-horsepower 318 from the larger Plymouth lines became Valiant's most-powerful engine.

Like all other makes, all Valiant and Barracuda cars featured mandated side-marker lights, four-way flashers, and dual brake systems.

Barracuda exterior changes were limited to grille, taillight, and body stripe and trim changes. The former consisted of inserts of finely spaced convex vertical bars. The taillight and back-up lights were reversed. However, when taillights, brake lights, or turn-signal lights were activated, the white back-up lenses glowed red to compensate for the small red lenses.

The hardtop's concave rear glass was abandoned after one year in favor of a more conventional window that was straight from top to bottom.

The standard V-8 for Barracuda became the 318. Replacing the Commando 273 was the new 340, a high-revving small-block engine of underestimated 274 horsepower that would gain legendary status during its five-year life span. For 1968 only, the four-speed manual transmission 340 had a hotter cam than the engine installed in TorqueFlite-equipped cars.

New heads and a redesigned intake manifold combined to increase the 383's horsepower to 300. Ordering either the 340 or 383 engine automatically got you the Formula S package.

For racing applications only, a 426 Hemi-equipped Barracuda could be ordered from your local dealer. In addition to a special drag-racing chassis, the cars featured fiberglass front fenders and hood with a large scoop. These cars quickly became dominant at sanctioned drag strips.

Another decrease in production: 156,207.

Valiant 1969
100 Sedan ★
Station wagon ★
Signet ★★★
Any with Formula S or 4 speed ★★★★

Barracuda 1969
Hardtop ★★★
Fastback ★★★★★
Convertible ★★★★★
'67 Formula S with 273 V-8 ★★★★★
1968-69 with 340 V-8 ★★★★★
1967-1969 with 383 V-8 ★★★★★
1969 with 440 ★★★★★
1968 Hemi Cuda-INESTIMABLE

1969

Minor sheet metal changes in the form of a new hood, greeted the '69 Valiant buyer. A new one-piece horizontal grille with parking lights at the ends was set in a dished satin-finished panel that included the headlights. A Plymouth "rocket ship" emblem was mounted in the center of the Signet grille but not those of the 100 or 200 decor-option cars. The taillights returned to a single-lens unit similar to those of 1967 but with flat lenses that did not curve onto the fender tops.

Mechanically, the Valiant was unchanged from the previous year.

The Barracuda, too, had a new hood, which necessitated a change in the grille surround cap. The split grille shapes were slightly changed and filled with a mesh pattern similar to that of 1967. The taillights also returned to a configuration similar to that of '67 but with larger red lenses. The rear-cove insert panel was wider and came with either flat black or brushed aluminum finish.

New to the line-up were the 'Cuda 340 and 'Cuda 383. Officially named what many had commonly called the cars for years, the 'Cudas were intended to be no-frills musclecars in the vein of the previous year's hugely popular Road Runner. Either of the two performance engines was coupled with a standard four-speed manual transmission and Formula S suspension package installed in a fastback body with a bench front seat and non-folding rear seat. Non-functional twin hood scoops and tape stripes were also a part of the 'Cuda package.

More upscale were the 383-S and 340-S packages, which included bucket seats and other more plush appointments such as map pockets and bright pedal trim.

These cars were externally identified by a wide stripe that flowed through the left-side racing-style gas cap, extending from taillight to headlight. Just ahead of the doors, the numbers 383 or 340 appeared in the stripe, denoting the engine under the hood.

Initially, aluminum sport wheels were offered on Barracudas, as well as other Plymouths. Defects led to their early recall and they were never replaced. The few that escaped recall are highly prized among collectors today.

A sign of the times was the Mod Top, a vinyl hardtop roof with a floral "flower power" pattern that could be combined with a similar floral-patterned vinyl upholstery. The fastback also got optional vinyl—a panel with painted sheet metal around the edges.

The engine line-up remained unchanged until midyear. Then, a 375 horsepower 440 engine was made available as an optional for Barracudas. A "limited number" were installed; actual production figures are unavailable.

Only 139,205 Valiants and Barracudas were produced, the lowest number ever. It was merely the calm before a Valiant sales storm.

Valiant 1970
Sedans ★
Duster ★★★★
Duster 340 ★★★★★
Duster 360 ★★★★★
'74 Valiant Brougham sedan or hardtop ★★★★
Scamp hardtop ★★★

Performance enthusiasts were not overlooked by Barracuda. Rarely seen today is the Hemi-Cuda. More common was the 1969 'Cuda 340, such as the one seen here. *Ernest Fodor*

Barracuda 1970
Coupe ★★★★ (add ★ for Gran Coupe)
Convertible ★★★★★
Cuda coupe ★★★★★
'Cuda convertible ★★★★★
1970-71 with 340 or 383 V-8 ★★★★★
1972-74 with 340 or 360 V-8 ★★★★★
1970-71 with 440 V-8-INESTIMABLE
1970-71 Hemi-Cuda coupe or convertible-INESTIMABLE

1970

Description of Valiant's 1970 model year can be reduced to one word: Duster. The new model was single-handedly responsible for Plymouth regaining its traditional number three spot in sales for the first time since 1959.

Plymouth created the new car to replace the Barracuda, which had moved up to its own E-body series. A sporty looking fuselage-styled semi-fastback coupe was put on the A-body platform behind carryover Valiant front sheet metal.

The only other Valiant was a four-door sedan, offered at a single trim level. However a host of options could make a plain car rather fancy. The only change on the sedan was found in the taillights—which returned to a style similar to those introduced in 1967—and the grille, which it shared with the Duster. The grille consisted of black horizontal bars with a raised center section. On this section was a Plymouth emblem. Next to the headlights were prominent rectangular parking lights.

Although the Duster's body appeared to be a hardtop, its rear windows did not roll down but could be flipped out from the rear. The door glass was frameless, as on a hardtop, and came without vent windows. Its taillights were two pairs of frameless ovals sunk into the rear panel. Decals and a cartoon character carried the Duster's identity. Optional stripes could be applied between the taillights.

The Duster 340 was a true mini-musclecar. Powered by the potent 340 engine, the high-performance model came with a new heavy duty three-speed floor shift or optional four-speed manual or automatic transmissions, as well as disc brakes and wide tires on Chrysler's new rally wheels. It was a full $600 cheaper that the 340 'Cuda and, given its lighter weight, more potent. Many buyers snapped up the bargain.

The Duster 340 used the 1967-1969 Barracuda dash with integral tachometer. The other Dusters and the sedan continued with the Valiant dash.

The standard six was increased to 198 ci, which brought its horsepower rating up to 125. The 225 six and 318 V-8 continued in the Valiant line-up. The 340 engine could be ordered only with the entire Duster 340 package.

The standard three-speed manual transmission continued with a column-shift lever. The new all-syncro three-speed, which was standard with the 340 and optional with all other engines, had a floorshift.

A Spring special model was the Gold Duster, which included as standard equipment a number of otherwise optional items, such as wheel covers and whitewall tires. True to its name, it was identified by gold-colored stripes on the front and rear and special "Gold Duster" decals. It also featured an argent grille surround that would become standard the following year.

Nearly three out of every four Valiants sold was a Duster. With production at 323,501, Valiant accounted for nearly half of the total sales of all Plymouths.

Valiant 1971
Sedans ★
Duster ★★★★
Duster 340 ★★★★★
Duster 360 ★★★★★
'74 Valiant Brougham sedan or hardtop ★★★★
Scamp hardtop ★★★

Barracuda 1971
Coupe ★★★★ (add ★ for Gran Coupe)
Convertible ★★★★★
"Cuda coupe ★★★★★
'Cuda convertible ★★★★★
1970-71 with 340 or 383 V-8 ★★★★★
1972-74 with 340 or 360 V-8 ★★★★★

In 1970 Plymouth signed race driver Dan Gurney to promote and race its 'Cuda. Gurney's All American Racers name was applied to the AAR Cuda as shown here. *Bill Edwards*

1970-71 with 440 V-8-INESTIMABLE
1970-71 Hemi-Cuda coupe or convertible-INESTIMABLE

1971

The only visible change to the Valiant sedan and standard Duster coupe was the deletion of the Plymouth emblem from the grille center. However, sharing the showroom was an "all-new" Valiant, the largest yet. Actually, the car was a carryover 111-inch wheelbase Dodge Dart hardtop body with Valiant front sheet metal and interior appointments. Dubbed the Scamp, it was the result of an inter-division exchange with Dodge which had been given the Duster body to create its new Demon coupe.

The Scamp's taillights were mounted in the bumper, as were the Dart's, but were single rectangular units rather than the dual lights found on the Dodge.

The Duster 340 received a bolder look with its own grille, a vast series of narrow vertical ovals that stretched from headlight to headlight and appeared to be made of cast-aluminum, although it was really plastic. For those who wanted to advertise, there was an optional flat-black hood with huge 340 numerals angled on one side.

For those who just wanted the look of muscle, the Twister package was introduced. It featured numerous Duster 340 appearance items plus some tape stripes and fake hood scoops of its own, yet it was powered by either a slant six or 318 V-8 engine.

Valiant's total production dropped slightly to 296,081, two-thirds of which were Dusters. The sedan and Scamp split the remaining 90,000.

Valiant 1972
Sedans ★
Duster ★★★★
Duster 340 ★★★★★
Duster 360 ★★★★★
'74 Valiant Brougham sedan or hardtop ★★★★
Scamp hardtop ★★★

Barracuda 1972
Coupe ★★★★ (add ★ for Gran Coupe)
Convertible ★★★★★
Cuda coupe ★★★★★
'Cuda convertible ★★★★★
1970-71 with 340 or 383 V-8 ★★★★★
1972-74 with 340 or 360 V-8 ★★★★★
1970-71 with 440 V-8-INESTIMABLE
1970-71 Hemi-Cuda coupe or
convertible-INESTIMABLE

1972

Narrower but wider taillights were installed on the '72 Duster coupes. Above was a slightly modified deck lid featuring a raised center ridge. The new deck lid was actually a running change instituted late during the 1971 model year. The only other Duster changes occurred when the rear side-marker lights were moved higher on the quarter-panel and cast-Duster nameplates replaced the decals behind the front wheels.

The Twister package continued and the Gold Duster returned after a one year hiatus.

While the 225 and 318 engines remained unchanged, emissions requirements caused the 198's net horsepower to fall to 100 and the 340's to drop to 240, the latter because of a reduction in compression from 10.3:1 to 8.5:1. For this year only, the 340 could be installed in any Duster, Scamp, or even Valiant sedan.

A 1972 Scamp can be identified by the "Scamp" decal above the Plymouth nameplate on the lower-right trunk edge. The sedan remained unchanged.

Total Valiant production increased to 348,843 for 1972. A reported 2,001 Duster hardtops were built for either the Canadian or overseas markets.

Valiant 1973
Sedans ★
Duster ★★★★
Duster 340 ★★★★★
Duster 360 ★★★★★
'74 Valiant Brougham sedan or hardtop ★★★★
Scamp hardtop ★★★

Barracuda 1973
Coupe ★★★★ (add ★ for Gran Coupe)
Convertible ★★★★★
Cuda coupe ★★★★★

'Cuda convertible ★★★★★
1970-71 with 340 or 383 V-8 ★★★★★
1972-74 with 340 or 360 V-8 ★★★★★
1970-71 with 440 V-8-INESTIMABLE
1970-71 Hemi-Cuda coupe or
convertible-INESTIMABLE

1973

A significant frontal change brought a new appearance to 1973 Valiants. A new hood was matched by the wide, raised center section of a new three-section grille flanked by squared headlight bezels. Below was a massive bumper with large rubber guards designed to meet more-stringent protection requirements.

Large single-unit taillamps were shaped to flow with the Duster's rear sheet metal. The other Valiants remained unchanged from the rear.

In addition to the returning Twister and Gold Duster were the new Space Duster and the Special Coupe packages. The former resumed the old Barracuda concept of a folding rear seat and fully carpeted trunk and cargo space that could extend to 6.5 feet. A sliding sunroof was optionally available for the car. The Special Coupe was intended to be a luxury Duster. Pleated vinyl seats, a full vinyl roof, and vinyl-insert side trim enhanced the upscale package, which also included the Spacemaker Pak created for the Space Duster.

The 340 returned as the engine exclusive to the Duster 340. The standard six for all other models was the 198, reduced again to 95 horsepower. The 225 six and 318 V-8 continued as the other available engines.

Helped in large part by the 1973 gasoline shortage crisis, Valiant production rose to 402,805, approximately 265,000 of which were Dusters. Another 2,614 hardtops were reportedly built for Canada.

Valiant 1974
Sedans ★
Duster ★★★★
Duster 340 ★★★★★
Duster 360 ★★★★★
'74 Valiant Brougham sedan or hardtop ★★★★
Scamp hardtop ★★★

Barracuda 1974
Coupe ★★★★ (add ★ for Gran Coupe)
Convertible ★★★★★
Cuda coupe ★★★★★
'Cuda convertible ★★★★★
1970-71 with 340 or 383 V-8 ★★★★★
1972-74 with 340 or 360 V-8 ★★★★★
1970-71 with 440 V-8-INESTIMABLE
1970-71 Hemi-Cuda coupe or
convertible-INESTIMABLE

1974

Since Plymouth had enjoyed success since 1971 using the Dodge Dart body for its Scamp hardtop, the division decided to appropriate the Dart sedan body as well. Its 111-inch wheelbase provided greater interior and trunk room. Buyers approved of the move, purchasing more than twice the number of Valiant four-door sedans as in 1973.

The flagship among the sedans was the Valiant Brougham, a midyear addition to both the sedan and hardtop lines. It featured crushed velour upholstery and many other luxury interior appointments. Color-keyed or simulated wire wheel covers were offered. Vinyl roofs, chrome grilles, and stand-up hood ornaments were standard equipment.

Government bumper protection requirements forced the abandonment of the Scamp's (and Dart's) taillight-bumper combo. New strip taillights were installed above the bumpers of the Scamp and the "new" sedan.

Government requirements also dictated rubber bumper guards on the rear of Duster coupes. Otherwise, save for tape stripe treatments, the Duster remained unchanged.

The Gold Duster, Space Duster, and Twister packages continued.

The 340 engine—devoid, because of emission requirements, of its former powerful glory—was dropped in favor of a 360-ci version of the same block. Its horsepower was set at a net 245, just five more than the 340 it replaced. Though potent enough in a light-bodied car, the 360 just was not a high-performance engine like the 340.

Valiant production shot up to 470,817, thanks to continuing gasoline crisis concern and Plymouth's efforts to provide variety to the expanding compact car market. One of every four compact cars sold in the United States during 1974 was a Valiant.

1975-76

Valiant entered its final two years with a new fine-mesh grille for all its models. The Brougham sedan offered even more luxury. A new Valiant Custom sedan offered a trim level between the Brougham and the base sedan.

Radial tires, a Fuel Pacer system, tighter torque converter, and lower gear ratios helped increase the

The complete 1968 Barracuda line included a fastback, convertible, and coupe. *Jack Sexton*

fuel economy of the unchanged engine line-up.

Dusters got more luxury appointments with full-length rocker and taillight panel moldings on the Gold Duster and new Duster Custom Coupe.

Valiant spent its final year sharing the showroom with its replacement, the Volare. Plymouth was following an industry trend to give a totally redesigned car a new name. Thus, the popular Valiant came to the end of its road.

Although reduced in selection variety, the Duster line-up featured a couple new packages: the Silver Duster and the Feather Duster. The former, which replaced the Gold Duster, featured unique red-and-black tape stripes that followed the lower-body character line to set off its silver paint. It was available in optional Boca Raton cloth and vinyl upholstery.

The lightweight, economy Feather Duster featured aluminum parts such as the engine intake manifold and inner-fender and hood-brace parts. About 22 percent of 1976 Dusters were so-equipped and identified by "Feather Duster" lettering on the front fender.

Although the Volare was a much fresher design than the decade-old Valiant, it was unable to earn the reputation for reliability the Valiant enjoys to this day. Twenty years after its demise, Valiants are just beginning to disappear from common view on the roads.

Chapter 3

1975-1996 Plymouth Vehicles

1975-1976 Duster ★★★★
Silver Duster ★★★★★
Feather Duster ★★★★
Duster 360 ★★★★★

1977-1978 Volare
California Custom ★★★★★
1978 Richard Petty Kit Car ★★★★★

Any V-8 power Police Pursuit ★★★★
package sedan

1983 Scamp pickup ★★★★
1983 Scamp GT pickup ★★★★★
1997 Prowler ★★★★★

Of historic interest:
1977 Gran Fury (loaded)-last
full size hardtop ★★★
1981 Reliant coupe-(loaded) ★★★
1982 Gran Fury with 118" wb-
last full size Plymouth ★★★
1984 Voyager minivan-(loaded) ★★★

The Late-1970s

Nineteen seventy-four saw introduction of the Plymouth Trail Duster 4x4 sport utility vehicle. Like earlier Plymouth Commercial Cars, the Trail Duster was a badge-engineered Dodge Ramcharger. Available with a completely convertible top or an optional, removable hardtop, the Trail Duster would be part of the line-up through 1980. Offered at first as a four-wheel-drive-only, a two-wheel-drive version was made available in 1975.

On the passenger-car side, the full-size Plymouth became known as the Gran Fury, with the Fury name relegated to the mid-size cars that had previously been called Satellite. Nineteen seventy-five would be the first year Plymouths were built using a catalytic converter system for emission control. Built on the Fury chassis, Road Runner buyers were given the choice of five V-8 engines, up to a maximum 235-horsepower, 400-ci V-8.

Duster models, with such clever names as Feather Duster (an economy tuned Slant Six model), Silver Duster, and Gold Duster, continued to find favor with buyers. For the performance enthusiast, there was the Duster 360, its name taken for the 360-ci V-8 under its hood.

Plymouth debuted the Volare in 1976, a car which earned *Motor Trend*'s "Car Of The Year" Award. Volares sold like hot cakes, but safety recalls (Volare and its Dodge clone, the Aspen, set

Designed and built for the California Plymouth dealer network was the Volare-based California Custom. First offered in 1977, it used an Aspen hood, tube grille, "California" style padded top, and non-functional lakes pipes. *Rick Moehring*

a record for the number of safety recalls) and early rust problems soon found these same customers clamoring at Chrysler's doors. The rust problem was so bad that Chrysler was forced under government mandate to recall the cars to replace front sheet metal.

Nineteen seventy-six would see the Duster and full-size Fury phased out at the end of the year. The Road Runner, with a standard 318 V-8 and optional 360, was transferred to the Volare platform, which featured a cross-mounted torsion bar suspension. All Chrysler products received lean-burn electronic engine controls. The Feather Duster was fitted only with the 225 Slant Six that made use of more aluminum than normal.

California Plymouth dealers, apparently with the blessing of the home office, began offering a special Volare model called the California Custom in 1977. Utilizing the hood and front bumper from the Aspen, the California Custom featured a 318 V-8 as standard equipment. Custom touches included a tube bar grill, non-functioning lakes pipes running the length of the rocker panels, baby moon hubcaps, and a special, blind-quarter-window, padded "Carson type" top. Adding $1,892 to the Volare's base price, it is unknown how many California Customs were built. The California Custom was continued into 1978.

Chrysler announced in 1976 it had inked a deal with Volkswagen to purchase four-cylinder engine and transaxle assemblies for use in a new model. This car debuted in 1978 as the Plymouth Horizon. The Horizon was again cloned with a Dodge model called the Omni, both of which helped Chryslers CAFE (corporate average fuel economy) figures and launched the corporation on its drive to strictly front-wheel-drive vehicles. Boxy little five-door sedans (counting the rear opening hatch) powered by a 105-ci 70- or 75-horsepower four-cylinder engine, the Horizon would be a mainstay for the next few years. *Motor Trend* magazine would again award Chrysler "Car Of The Year" honors for the Horizon-Omni combination.

Nineteen seventy-eight can be considered the year Plymouth died—at least as a full-size automobile, as it discontinued production of the Gran Fury and intermediate Fury lines. With the demise of the full-size cars, so too came the end of the road for the 440 V-8. Taking up the slack was the Volare, which now advertised a series of "Fun Runner" models including the Volare Super Coupe, Front Runner, and Sun Runner, the latter being a T-top roof option. Road Runners were available with either a 165- or 175-horsepower 360 as its biggest powerplant. Chrysler Canada, however, saw to it that its customers had more models to choose from, bringing out the Car-

By 1978 the Road Runner was based on the Volare. Options included the Sun Runner T-top roof panels. *Greg Berkheimer*

avelle line. It would be several years before the Caravelle would make its appearance south of the border.

Rarely seen was the "Richard Petty Kit Car." For those wishing to plunk down an extra thousand dollars or so, Plymouth offered a Volare coupe decked out like a short-track race car. Available in both Dodge and Plymouth versions, the Plymouth came in standard two-tone blue, dark blue sides with a light blue hood and fender flares (the Dodge version was two-tone red). Standard equipment included a 318 V-8 with choice of two- or four-barrel carburetion or a

The limited-production 1978 Volare Richard Petty Kit Car was designed to look like a short-track race car. Buyers with enough jingle in their pockets could order a real factory-built race car complete with a Petty Engineering chassis. *Jeff Berkheimer*

The 1979 Horizon TC3 was a highly styled version of the econo-box Horizon sedan, the first of the Chrysler-built front-wheel-drive cars. *Lanny Knutson*

four-barrel 360 V-8 and automatic transmission. (Canadian kit cars were available with manual transmissions.) Kit cars came with a huge door number decal (it was shipped in the trunk for dealer installation) bearing the number 43, which, of course, was the number on Richard Petty's race cars, which were also painted blue. The 360-equipped kit cars were shipped with hood decals denoting the larger powerplant.

The Petty Kit Car was more than just looks. It was fitted with a heavy-duty suspension, factory-installed rear anti-sway bar, special 15x8-inch wheels with negative offset, and GR15 Aramid-fiber radial tires. The wheels were held in place with chrome lug nuts. Dress-up items included windshield "locks" and hood pins like real NASCAR race cars, front air dam, quarter-window louvers, deck lid spoiler, and wheel flares which helped keep the larger-size tires inside the body work. Sales of the kit cars were to be kept to 1,000 units, but how many were actually built is unknown. While the Petty Kit Car was fully streetable, those with the urge to race and with an extra $10,000 in their pockets could order a *real* factory race car built on a tubular chassis actually built by Petty Enterprises. This car was available in several versions, from a bare chassis to rolling chassis, with or without sheet metal, or as a complete race car.

Enter Iacocca—And Government Help

If 1978 was not a banner year for Plymouth, there were events taking place in Dearborn, Michigan, that would have a profound effect on the industry. On July 13, Henry Ford II, grandson of the founder and namesake to the Ford Motor Company, fired the president of Ford, a brash, cigar-smoking, tough-talking executive named Anthony Lido Iacocca. It was a move that startled not only Iacocca, but the entire industry as Iacocca had taken credit for Ford's wildly successful Mustang and highly profitable Lincoln Mark-series luxury cars.

Iacocca, it seemed, had overshadowed Henry Ford II, and that was something "the Duce" couldn't handle. For Chrysler, it would be a godsend as Iacocca walked in the door as president on November 2, 1978. Within months, he would become Chrysler's CEO as chairman John Riccardo stepped aside.

As 1979 dawned, things looked bleak for Chrysler. Iacocca took the reigns as the second OPEC oil embargo began, Chrysler's market share had slipped to less than 10 percent, ledger books showed a $1.1 *billion* loss, and employees—27,000 of them—had been laid off.

One of his first acts would be to fire 33 of Chrysler's 35 vice-presidents. From all appearances it seemed the corporation was doomed. Iacocca had no choice but to seek aid from the U.S. Government, and appearing before Congress, he pleaded his case. It was a move unprecedented in the automobile industry and there were those who said Chrysler should be allowed to die—with or without dignity. Had this been allowed to happen, America would have lost the 10th-largest Fortune 500 industrial corporation. Despite its financial woes, Chrysler was still bigger than U.S. Steel, bigger than International Telephone and Telegraph (ITT), and bigger than RCA, Firestone, and 3M combined.

Going to the government for help was a bitter pill for Iacocca to swallow but it had to be done. To secure the loan, Chrysler laid its cards on the table. In an industry where new models and product development are top secret priorities, Chrysler unveiled its plans for a series of front-wheel-drive automobiles. There for Congress—and the competition—to see, was an automobile carrying the engineering code-letter K. It was a "shoot the works, carry all your eggs in one basket" proposition. This automobile would be one of two things: It would either be the Kar that Killed Krysler, or the Kar that saved Krysler.

The aid package that was finally approved amounted to some $3.5 billion, $1.5 billion of which was guaranteed by the U.S. Government if Chrysler should fail to pay it back. The package also called for $475 million in wage concessions from the United Auto Workers and $125 million in concessions from Chrysler management.

Among the requirements was another precedent-setting move in the industry, that of placing a high-ranking member of the United Auto Workers on the Chrysler Board.

Although controversial, the Chrysler Loan Guarantee Act of 1979 was signed into law by President Jimmy Carter. Despite his troubled presidency, which saw interest rates over 20 percent and runaway inflation, President Carter followed the precedent set by President Dwight D. Eisenhower in 1956 to rescue Studebaker-Packard. (A deal to merge Chrysler and Ford fell through in 1981.)

Plymouth for 1979 and
The Coming of the K Car

Plymouth offered just two cars lines for 1979: The sub-compact Horizon and the Volare with its tarnished reputation. Engine choices were pared to the Horizon four-banger, the 225 Slant Six, and two V-8s in familiar 318 and 360 displacements.

By now, Plymouth had fallen to ninth place in industry sales, worse even than its eighth-place finish after the disastrous 1962 model year. Until the K car could get into production, Plymouth soldiered on with the Volare, which would be laid to rest at the end of the 1980 production run. A sporty version of the Horizon called the TC3 made its debut and Plymouth once again built a full-size car, the 118.5-inch wheelbase Gran Fury, a near-identical clone of the Dodge St. Regis (which owed its existence to the Chrysler Newport). The Gran Fury would prove to be most popular with police departments across the country.

Nineteen eighty saw another staggering loss of $1.7 billion. Plymouth sales, which had remained around a half-million units per year, began a precipitous slide in 1979, to slightly more than 372,000 units. For 1980, sales declined to less than 291,000 units, only slightly better than the recession year of 1938! Plymouth sales would continue to free fall until beginning a gradual upturn in 1984, but it would take over a decade for sales to surpass the half-million plateau again.

Nineteen eighty-one saw the debut of the much-written-about K series of cars. But could they pull the rabbit out of the hat for Chrysler? Proudly, Iacocca climbed behind the wheel of the first car to drive it onto the stage, but the car wouldn't start. Its battery stone-cold dead! Was it an ominous warning from some strange power? If nothing else, it was a black eye on Chrysler's already sullied reputation.

The K car would debut as a two-door coupe, four-door sedan, and "five" door wagon. Plymouth Reliant K cars was available in three trim levels, base, Custom, or SE. The standard engine was a

By 1980 Plymouth (and Dodge) was supplying 80 percent of the nation's police departments with pursuit sedans. This Gran Fury pursuit was used by the North Dakota State Patrol.

belt-driven, overhead-cam 2.2-liter Chrysler-built four, or optional 2.6-liter Mitsubishi-built four.

Most cars were shipped with SE trim and loaded to the hilt with accessories, which gave the cars amazingly high sticker prices, a fact that kept buyers away in droves. Sales didn't really take off until less-expensive stripped models began hitting showroom floors. As a move to further induce buyers, Chrysler resurrected its five-year, 50,000-mile warranty program.

Buyers of full-size Plymouths found their engine choices pared down to nothing more than the old, reliable 318 V-8.

Leading Chrysler Corporation into front-wheel-drive technology was the Horizon. This is a 1981 Horizon Custom. *Robert Gibson*

Cute as a bug's ear and twice as rare is the 1983 Plymouth Scamp pickup based on the Horizon TC3. Built only one year, slightly more than 2,000 were manufactured. *Jim Benjaminson*

The last of the full-size Plymouths were the 1988 Gran Fury sedans—the last police package cars the company would build. This sedan saw use with the East Hartford, (Connecticut) Police Department.

Sales of full-size cars had fallen to less than 16,000 units. Horizons sold nearly 95,000 copies and Reliant K's nearly 152,000 units.

Full-size Plymouths were down-sized for 1982, with the wheelbase being reduced from 118.5 inches to 112.7 inches. Sales of these cars increased by 3,000 units over 1981. Sales of Horizons and Reliants dropped slightly, although the Horizon added a sporty model called the TC3. Engine choices for the year included 2.2- and 2.6-liter four-cylinders, the Slant Six, and 318 V-8.

Total Plymouth sales of 232,386 units was the lowest production figure the company had seen since 1932!

If ever there was a year for rejoicing at Chrysler, 1983 was it. For one thing, Chrysler paid back its loan seven years early. Iacocca announced the pay back on July 13—five years to the day since he had been fired at Ford. The check was made out for the staggering sum of $813,487,500.

Chrysler also managed to post a profit at the same time. As the end of the model run came to a close, so too came the end for Chrysler's workhorse Slant Six. First introduced in 1960, the Slant Six had powered everything from full-size Plymouths to light-duty Dodge trucks and even motor homes.

Reliant sales remained nearly level while the Horizon saw a substantial gain, as did the Turismo, which was little more than a renamed TC3. Added to the sales line-up was a cute little car-based pickup featuring TC3 styling called the Scamp. A one-year-only model, the Scamp found only 2,129 buyers.

Full-size cars sales fell to 1981 levels, a good number of which were fleet vehicles sold to police departments. Plymouth had offered its first police package back in 1957 and now found itself (along with Dodge) supplying about 80 percent of the nation's police cars. Total production for 1983 came to just 8,500 units more than 1982, beginning what would be a long, hard climb back to former levels.

The Mini-Van and the Late-1980s

If the K car had saved Chrysler, it was the mini-van that resurrected the company. An idea that had died on the drawing boards at Ford, the mini-van was an automobile in search of a market, and how much of a market was in search of a mini-van surprised even Chrysler.

Once again, Plymouth would share a cloned version with Dodge. Plymouth's was called Voyager, and Dodge's was the Caravan. Powered by the 2.2-liter Chrysler-built four or optional 2.6-liter Mitsubishi four, the vans could seat seven comfortably, offered tons of cargo carrying space, and could easily fit into any garage stall in America.

Plymouth's version sold more than 64,000 units (Dodge built about 3,000 more for the year). Bolstered by level sales of the Reliant K, an upsurge in Horizon and Turismo production (full-size Plymouths remained static at the 15,000 car level), Plymouth was shy (by 176 units) of breaking the 400,000 mark for the model run, still below sales levels set back in 1936.

Sales increased slightly for 1985, helped by the addition of the Caravelle in the United States (it had been sold in Canada since 1978). Sales declined slightly for 1986, slowly climbing to the magic half-million mark in 1989.

Nineteen eighty-seven saw Chrysler purchase American Motors, which netted the company Jeep and Eagle, as well as a new assembly plant in Bramalea, Ontario, Canada. The Horizon "America" arrived on the scene (subtly hinting consumers should buy American) in 1987, as did the Sundance (In Canada, the Horizon "America" became the "Expo" to honor the Vancouver World's Fair). The last Caravelle and Reliant station wagons came off the line in 1988. The Reliant wagon was survived by Reliant sedans for one more year before being replaced by the Plymouth Acclaim. Nineteen eighty-nine also marked the demise of the last Gran Fury's and with it Chrysler's dominance of the police car market.

The 1990s

If there is to be a bona fide early-90's Plymouth collectible, it will be the Plymouth Laser.

Coming through the Chandelier Tree in Redwood National Forest is a 1988 Sundance RS. *Lanny Knutson*

Built in a joint venture with Mitsubishi called Diamond Star Motors, the Laser was a clone to the Mitsubishi Eclipse and Eagle Talon. Puzzling is the fact Lasers received mediocre reviews while the Eclipse and Talon received rave reviews, yet all three were identical with the exception of the final nameplates as the car came off the line!

Nineteen ninty marked the final year for the Horizon. Nineteen ninety-one saw the arrival of the four-wheel-drive mini-van and, at the steps of the Henry Ford Museum in Dearborn, arrival of a 1984 mini-van for permanent display, recognizing the importance of the mini-van concept to the automobile industry.

Lee Iacocca stepped down in 1992, but not altogether voluntarily. By 1995 he and investor Kirk Kerkorian were attempting a ill-fated takeover of Chrysler.

Plymouth had seen its ups and downs but now talk was rampant that Plymouth would go the way of DeSoto. Like DeSoto, the marque lacked its own identity. Truly it seems Plymouth lost its mentor when Walter P. Chrysler died in 1940. Back in 1932 Walter Chrysler had asked the buying public to "Look At All Three"—Ford, Chevrolet, and Plymouth. Having floundered since the late 50's, it would have been easy to simply let the name die.

Steve Torok, Chrysler-Plymouth general manager, announced formation of the Plymouth Renaissance team in 1994 to prevent that from happening. "In the past, we would have kicked this problem to the ad agency and said 'Give us a new campaign,' but we are looking at Plymouth's foundation," Torok stated. "The team is modeled after those that planned the LH cars. The image they will seek to create for Plymouth is that of an inexpensive, no-frills but well-equipped car targeted for the 'young families and singles entering their 30's' market. The new Neon and Voyager vans are part of the plans."

"Dragging Plymouth out of moth balls means a major monetary commitment from Chrysler— and some of the most savvy marketing in Detroit," stated Fara Warner of *Brandweek* magazine. Steve Goodall of J. D. Power called it "the classic marketing problem (salvaging a dying brand)— Oldsmobile and a few others come to mind."

It's estimated the "re-launch" will cost $50 to $100 million dollars. The problem, according to Torok, is "to some people, especially those under 35, Plymouth means absolutely nothing."

It is a program now in full swing as this is written in April of 1996. Test markets of "Plymouth Place," a computer kiosk located in shopping malls initially in Portland, Oregon, and Milwaukee, Wisconsin, (and eventually expanding cross country) enable prospective buyers to print out information about new Plymouth products without high-pressure salesmen looking over their shoulders. A multi-media ad campaign prominently featured the new Mayflower sailing ship emblem along with the slogan, "Plymouth, One Clever Idea After Another."

When Chrysler's LH line of "cab-forward" cars was introduced in 1993, as the Chrysler Concorde, Dodge Intrepid, and Eagle Vision, Plymouth was conspicuously absent. Still there was a glimmer of hope in the most unlikely of places, a neo-30's hot-rod concept car called the Plymouth Prowler. Designed by Chrysler Vice President of Styling Tom Gale, the Prowler utilized modern technology throughout, including the body. Powered by a V-6 intended for front-wheel drive, the Prowler reversed everything to drive through the rear wheels. Shown across the country (there were originally two prototypes, a drivable machine and a static model for photography), customers began to line up asking "when can I take delivery?"

Concept cars had been shown by Chrysler before—for over 45 years, the corporation had teased the public with these vehicles—but each time the cars failed to see production. That would change with the Dodge Viper RT/10 sportster. First shown in prototype form in 1989, the Viper, with its snarling 10-cylinder 488-ci motor, began production in 1992. But it was a Dodge.

The Neon, Breeze, and the Prowler

Plymouth fans would wait through 1994, seeing the last Sundance roll off the assembly line to be replaced by the Neon, a car it would again share with Dodge. This time there would be absolutely no differences between the two cars with the exception of the badge on the hood. Powered by a 2-liter 132-horsepower four-cylinder, the '94 Neon, originally built only as a four-door sedan, was joined by the Neon coupe for '95.

Nineteen ninety-five would see the demise of the Plymouth Laser and Acclaim and a redesigned, sleeker-looking mini-van.

What's new for '96? It's called the Breeze, part of the Plymouth Renaissance built on the JA platform (shared with the Chrysler Cirrus and Dodge Stratus) but it will have its own identity, even resurrecting the Plymouth Mayflower sailing ship used from 1928 through 1959.

But it is 1997 most Plymouth fans are waiting for, when the first production Prowler hits

A future Plymouth collectible is the 1990 Laser. *Norman Townsend*

the street. Sharing assembly lines with the Dodge Viper RT/10, the Prowler features a "purpose-modified" 3.5-liter 24-valve single-overhead cam V-6 with dual-throttle-body fuel induction mated to a rear-wheel-drive, four-speed, fully adaptive, electronically controlled "Autostick" transaxle.

Weighing around 2,800 pounds, the 113-inch wheelbase car comes standard with: dual air bags; air conditioning; ventilated disc brakes; manual cloth top (black only); remote deck lid release; rear-window electric defroster; time-delay electric door locks; side-impact protection; 12-gallon fuel tank; dual, power, outside rear view mirrors; AM/FM cassette radio with seven speakers; remote keyless entry system with theft alarm; leather seats; cruise control; power windows with locks; intermittent windshield wipers; and tilt steering column.

Interior space is the same as a Corvette roadster (and 10 cubic-feet more than a Viper). The Prowler will ride on extended mobility (run flat) P225/45R17 tires on the front, P295/40R20 on the rear, with a low-pressure sensor system and gauge-cluster warning lamp! Optional will be a two-wheel trailer, designed in the same shape as the Prowler body, for extra carrying capacity.

How can a $35,000, two-seat, 1930's-styled automobile save a brand name? It's the classic idea revived from the past, when dealers parked a shiny new convertible in the showroom window—it draws in potential customers. Chances are the family man who stopped to looked at that

First shown in prototype form in 1993, the Plymouth Prowler street rod is scheduled to go into production as a 1997 model, built on the same assembly line as the Viper RT/10. *Jim Benjaminson*

new Belvedere convertible back in 1956 drove out the door with a plain-Jane four-door sedan—but it was the convertible that brought him into the showroom in the first place. It would appear the Prowler will do the same thing. Already customers are lining up for a crack at buying a Prowler; how many will actually get to own one remains to be seen.

Can you sell cars out of a computer kiosk located in a shopping mall? Or over the telephone—or the Internet? Plymouth's Renaissance Team has tapped into the youth market.

For those with an on-line computer at home, if you don't believe me, punch up http://www.plymouthcars.com on your PC. Or, if you're not on-line, grab the phone and call 1-800-PLYMOUTH. Despite its earlier history of intra-corporate rivalry and lackluster model offerings of the last few decades, Plymouth is making a robust attempt at reversing its fortunes. Perhaps in the not-too-distant future, car buffs will again talk of the big three: Chevrolet, Ford—and *Plymouth*.

This Neon sedan just doesn't say "Hi"—it shouts a big "HELLO!" Displayed at the Neon assembly plant in Belvidere, Illinois, this special show Neon gives viewers an inside look at how the car is put together. *Jim Benjaminson*

Chapter 4

DeSoto

Hernando DeSoto would have been proud, had he lived long enough to see his name, family coat of arms, and even his bust displayed on this contraption called an automobile. The 16th century explorer gets credit for discovering the Mississippi River during his travels—just how his name became associated with the line of automobiles introduced by Chrysler Corporation in the summer of 1928 is something of a mystery. Perhaps it was the connection with travel and adventure that brought his name to the forefront.

DeSoto joined the growing ranks of the Chrysler Corporation during the halcyon days of 1928 along with the Plymouth and Fargo commercial cars. Much speculation had taken place when the Plymouth name first surfaced in Detroit but there was no doubt who was behind the DeSoto project, the first announcement appearing in the trade publication *Automobile Trade Journal* on April 23, 1928. The headline read, "DeSoto Six, New Motor Car, To Be Built By Walter P. Chrysler." Under the headline *ATJ* continued, "DeSoto Motor Corporation is a division of the Chrysler Corporation, owned 100 percent by the parent company and will build a car which is non-competitive with any of the four Chrysler lines. DeSoto Corporation, officered by executives of Chrysler, with J. E. Fields, president; C. W. Matheson, vice-president in charge of sales; B. E. Hutchinson, vice president and treasurer; and W. P. Chrysler, chairman of the board. Above officers and W. Ledyard Mitchell, vice president and general manger of operations of Chrysler; F. M. Zeder, vice president in charge of engineering, Chrysler Corporation; K. T. Keller, Chrysler vice president in charge of manufacturing; constitute the DeSoto board. New car will be sold by entirely new dealer organization now being formed."

DeSoto's first model, the K, shared the same bodies, chassis, and wheelbase as the Plymouth Q. *R. Bird*

That announcement was all it took for 500 would-be dealers to ask for a DeSoto franchise—without even seeing a prototype of the new car.

DeSoto was incorporated on May 6, 1928, exactly four days after Chrysler had successfully purchased Dodge Brothers. Production began that July, and DeSoto shared facilities with the new Plymouth and Chrysler cars at the corporation's Highland Park headquarters near Detroit. It would come to share more than just production facilities. Major body panels were shared with the new Plymouth to the point where one had to ask, "Is DeSoto simply a six-cylinder Plymouth, or is Plymouth just a four-cylinder DeSoto?" Like Plymouth, the new DeSoto was considered a 1929 model.

Introduced to the public on August 4, 1928 (there had been a private dealer showing in Detroit on July 7th), by year's end over 34,000 cars had been shipped to more than 1,500 dealers, most of whom handled DeSoto exclusively. DeSoto would set a sales record for a new make of automobile that would not be broken for over 30 years. Unfortunately, DeSoto's initial sales success would not be an indication of the trials and tribulations to follow.

DeSoto K
Roadster, phaeton, rumble seat coupe ★★★★★
Business coupe, Deluxe sedan ★★★★
Two-door and four-door ★★

DeSoto for 1929
"Multum pro Parvo" in Latin means "Much For Little," the motto for the new DeSoto. It was a motto many first-time DeSoto buyers found fitting of the new automobile. Conventionally styled, there was little mistaking the family resemblance between Chrysler or Plymouth. Like its corporate stablemates, DeSoto featured the thin line radiator shell, with the hood overlapping the radiator core, giving the car a longer appearance. Hood louvers were grouped into three separate clusters, and headlamps, cowl lamps, cowl band, taillamps, and door handles were chrome-plated, and on the Deluxe, the headlight tie bar was chromed.

Plymouth dealers had been asked to dress like Pilgrims when the first cars were delivered. Whether DeSoto dealers were asked to dress like Spanish explorers is a question. When it came to naming body styles of the new DeSoto, the Spanish connection was clear. What was normally called the business coupe was the "cupe business." The Deluxe coupe (with non-folding cloth top and landau irons) became the "cupe de lujo." The Deluxe sedan carried the moniker "sedan de lujo" (there was also a regular sedan), with the roadster (with rumble seat) becoming the "roadster Espanol." The touring car took on the name "faeton," and the two-door was the "sedan coche." Needless to say, it wasn't long before the fancy titles faded into oblivion. A three-door, blank quarter-window "commercial sedan" was built in prototype form but it would appear none were sold at retail.

Known as the Model K, the DeSoto rode the same 109-inch wheelbase chassis as the new Plymouth. In nearly every aspect, the cars were identical with the exception of the powerplant: the K series DeSoto was powered by a 175-ci, 55-horsepower six. Both DeSoto and Plymouth shared a 4 1/8-inch stroke, but the DeSoto's bore, at 3 inches, was fully 5/8-inch less than the four-cylinder Plymouth. With just 5 more cubic inches, the DeSoto developed 10 more horsepower than the Plymouth four. Unlike the Plymouth, the

The survival rate of early DeSotos has been dismal, despite setting sales records when it was first introduced. *WPC Club*

DeSoto six had a water pump, although fuel was supplied by a vacuum tank, and ignition was by Delco-Remy. Four-wheel Lockheed hydraulic brakes, 5.00x19-inch balloon tires, and automatic windshield wipers were standard equipment. Standard upholstery was mohair, although Deluxe models received a better grade, along with dual fender-mounted spare tires. Prices for the new DeSoto ranged from $845 to $995.

DeSoto finished calendar year 1928 in 18th place, rising to 14th by end of 1929.

DeSoto CF and CFH 8
Roadster, phaeton, convertible, rumble seat coupe ★★★★★
Business coupe, Deluxe sedan ★★★★
Four-door ★★

DeSoto K
Roadster, phaeton, rumble seat coupe ★★★★★
Business coupe, Deluxe sedan ★★★★
Two-door and four-door ★★

DeSoto CK
Roadster, phaeton, convertible, rumble seat coupe ★★★★★
Business coupe ★★★★
Four-door ★★

DeSoto for 1930
Effective with cars built after July 1st (some sources say August 15, 1929), the Model K DeSoto became a 1930 model for sales purposes, with no other changes made to the car. Within 14 months, DeSoto surpassed the 100,000 mark in sales.

Like Plymouth, Model K DeSotos' main production centered on closed cars. DeSoto and Plymouth were purposely designed to look like their Chrysler progenitors. *National DeSoto Club*

Nineteen thirty would mark debut of the CF series, the first straight eight-cylinder engine in the Chrysler line-up. (It should be noted that at this early date, DeSotos were being coded with the letter "C," which in later years would designate Chrysler cars. DeSoto would begin using the letter "S" to designate DeSoto models with the 1931 model SA.)

At a time when the number of cylinders was an indication of a car's status, it is surprising Chrysler Corporation chose to let DeSoto build the first straight-eight from the company rather than reserve the honor for the Chrysler nameplate. The reasoning may have been that Marmon's Roosevelt had already gone on the market, advertising the first straight-eight at a price of less than $1,000. At $965 for the business coupe, DeSoto could advertise itself as the lowest-priced straight-eight on the market. (Dodge, too, would also get its own straight-eight.) With a bore of 2 7/8 inches and stroke of 4 inches, the eight displaced 208 ci, and developed 70 horsepower.

Production of the CF Eight began in December of 1929 and continued through November of 1930.

Differing from the six-cylinder DeSoto, the CF Eight featured an undivided vertical louver arrangement on the hood side panels. The thin line radiator of the six-cylinders was abandoned in favor of the more conventional deep radiator with a chrome-plated radiator shell. Like previous cars, bumpers were two-piece, and like all Chrysler products, DeSotos employed four-wheel hydraulic brakes. Eight-cylinder cars sat on a seven cross-member 114-inch frame (5 inches longer than the six).

Later in the year, the six-cylinder series CK "Finer DeSoto Six" came on line. Like the CF Eight and the 30U Plymouth, the CK abandoned the thin line radiator in favor of the more conventional full radiator shell. Also setting the CK apart were the cowl lamps mounted on the crown of each front fender.

Boring the engine 1/8-inch increased displacement to 190 ci, 15 more than the K series, raising horsepower to 60. A new mechanical fuel

The DeSoto CK is most easily identified by the fender-mounted park lamps, as seen on this example. *National DeSoto Club*

pump replaced the trouble-prone vacuum tank.

Body styles in the CK series were the same as the K, with the addition—like Plymouth—of a real convertible coupe with fixed windshield posts and roll-down windows. CF Eight body styles included the same line-up as the K and CK of roadster with rumble seat, phaeton, business coupe, Deluxe coupe (with rumble seat), four-door sedan, Deluxe sedan, and convertible coupe. The Spanish model designations were, thankfully, laid to rest.

Calendar-year production for 1930 came to 34,889 units, good enough to bring DeSoto up one spot to 13th in industry sales.

DeSoto CF and CFH 8
Roadster, phaeton, convertible, rumble seat coupe ★★★★★
Business coupe, Deluxe sedan ★★★★
Four-door ★★

DeSoto SA
Roadster, phaeton, convertible, rumble seat coupe ★★★★★
Business coupe, Deluxe sedan ★★★★
Two-door, four-door ★★

DeSoto for 1931
The SA series DeSoto made its debut in January at the New York Automobile Show although production had begun a month earlier. The SA had a restyled body, but again used the thin line radiator design with vertical radiator shutters and vertical hood louvers patterned after the Imperial.

New for the year were dual cowl ventilators. The engine was again bored, this time an additional 1/8 inch, resulting in a 3 1/4-inch bore. Displacement was up to 205 ci, bringing horsepower up to 72. Both the SA and CF boasted an "Easy Shift" transmission, in addition to offering free-wheeling as a $20 option. (Free-wheeling would become standard later in the model run.) Like Plymouth, DeSoto used a wide array of transmissions throughout the year, beginning production with a spur-gear transmission used since the start of DeSoto production in the summer of 1928. This was replaced by two different transmissions, one using left-cut helical gears, the other using right-cut helical gears. Production of the 1931 DeSotos was transferred from Highland Park to Plymouth's Lynch Road facility on April 31, 1931. Goodyear became the official tire supplier to Chrysler, replacing the Fisk brand used since both Plymouth and DeSoto came on line.

SA DeSotos came in the usual assortment of body types, including a roadster with rumble seat, phaeton, standard coupe, Deluxe coupe with rumble seat, convertible coupe, two-door sedan (in midyear), four-door sedan, and Deluxe sedan.

Bumpers were now of the one-piece variety, with the cowl lamps moving back to the base of the windshield. Wheelbase was increased 3/4-inch as well.

The DeSoto Eight, now known as the CF* remained the same with the exception of being stroked 1/4-inch to 221 ci, raising horsepower to 77. The * in the model code indicated the larger-displacement engine in a car that had otherwise unchanged. The eight-cylinder DeSoto would be phased out at the end of the model year. As in previous years, the six-cylinder DeSotos continued to share major body stampings with the four-cylinder Plymouths. Model

Touring cars were fast losing their popularity with buyers, making them among the rarest and most desirable of the early DeSotos. *National DeSoto Club*

The DeSoto CF series featured a straight-eight engine. Selling for under $1,000, it was the lowest-priced eight on the market. *WPC Club*

year designations continued to be confusing with cars being sold as both 1931 and 1932 models. Both the SA and CF* series were considered next year's models after July 1st, 1931. The CF* phaeton was added to the model line-up after January 1, 1932, but it, like the roadsters, would be discontinued before the true 1933 models came on the scene.

Calendar-year sales of 29,835 slipped DeSoto back to 14th in industry sales.

DeSoto SC
Roadster, rumble seat coupe, convertible, convertible sedan, phaeton ★★★★★
Business coupe, seven-passenger ★★★★
Brougham, four-door ★★

DeSoto for 1932
If DeSoto styling had been conventional since its inception, the "true" 1932 DeSoto series SC was about to set the industry on its ear. Featuring a rounded grille patterned after the popular Miller racing cars running on the nation's race tracks, DeSotos would not be mistaken for anything else on the road. Stories were told of a blind man who was asked to run his hands over the front fascia of the car. After so doing, the man proclaimed DeSoto to be the most beautiful car he had ever seen!

Available in two trim levels, Standard and Custom, the Custom series featured external trumpet horns, dual taillamps, dual windshield wipers, cigar lighter, safety glass, adjustable seats, and fenders painted to match body color. Chrome headlamps were standard on all models. Unique to DeSoto was what appeared to be a split windshield. Although stylish, the windshield was actually one piece!

Body styles in the Standard SC series included a two-passenger roadster, phaeton, busi-

ness coupe, rumble seat coupe, two-door "brougham," and four-door sedans in both five- and seven-passenger formats. Custom body styles included a rumble seat roadster, rumble seat coupe, convertible coupe with rumble seat, four-door sedan, four-door Town Sedan, and two-door convertible Victoria. The convertible Victoria was a top-of-the-line offering also offered by sister Plymouth; DeSoto production of this model came to just 275 units. All DeSotos featured forward-opening "suicide" doors on all body styles. Two open-front Town Cars were also built (probably to special order) but were not regularly cataloged models.

The engine was again stroked 1/8-inch for 211 ci with an increase in horsepower to 75, just 2 horses short of the previous year's eight-cylinder car. Chassis features included a double-drop frame on a 112-3/8-inch wheelbase and adoption of "Floating Power" introduced the year before by Plymouth. "Floating Power" mounted the engine at three points, suspending the powerplant along the axis of its own center of gravity. Developed to reduce vibration from Plymouth's four-cylinder engine, Floating Power made the six- and eight-cylinder DeSoto engines silky smooth. DeSoto's lone seven-passenger car shared a 121-inch wheelbase with the seven-passenger PB Plymouth and seven-passenger Dodge.

Famed Indianapolis race car driver Peter DePaolo had driven a CF* DeSoto Eight on a promotional tour

The 1931 SA DeSoto returned to the "thin line" radiator design of earlier years. Motorists who enjoyed open-air motoring but disliked drafty, side-curtained roadsters could opt for the convertible coupe with folding top and real windows. *James Shillito*

the previous year and was this year called on to make a 10-day promotional trip culminated by a 300-mile race track trial at speeds up to 80 miles per hour.

Calendar-year sales of 27,441 helped moved DeSoto into ninth place in industry sales.

DeSoto SD
Rumble seat coupe, convertible, convertible sedan ★★★★★
Business coupe, seven-passenger ★★★★
Special Brougham ★★★
Brougham, four-door ★★

DeSoto for 1933
DeSoto claimed 52 changes to the 1933 SD Standard series (with an additional 28 improvements to the Custom) while telling its dealers, "the DeSoto car, as now produced, will not be essentially changed during the 1933 selling season."

Even die hard auto buffs had to look hard to see the differences. The rounded radiator grille was retained, featuring a horizontal rather than vertical motif but other changes, such as "silent upholstery springs" went unnoticed. Again offered in two trim levels, top-of-the-line cars could be easily identified by the vertical trim divider over the headlamp lens. Other Custom equipment included twin sun visors, dual trumpet horns, and taillamps, but this equipment was made standard on both trim levels later in the model run. Wire wheels were discontinued in favor of wood wheels and smaller tire sizes. Prices were unchanged at introduction time and reduced by $30 to $100 on March 27, 1933, probably as a sales incentive. In addition, a $20 accessory package (called combination #2) offered dual taillamps, dual windshield wipers, cigar lighter, and special paint, and was released for all Standard models.

Unlike Plymouth, which discontinued the convertible Victoria at the end of the 1932 model run, this model was continued into 1933 in Custom trim level only. President Roosevelt was one of just 132 people who would take delivery of this unusual body style. Standard body styles included the two-passenger business coupe, rumble seat coupe, two-door Brougham, two-door Special Brougham, and four-door sedan. Custom models included only the rumble seat coupe, convertible coupe, four-door sedan, and convertible Victoria. The Special Brougham was discontinued midyear

The SD DeSoto got a 2-inch increase in wheelbase and the engine was again stroked to bring displacement up to 218 ci with rated horsepower of 86 for both trim levels. Making their debut as standard equipment on all models was an automatic choke and coincidental starter, the latter activated by stepping on the accelerator pedal, a feature that became a Buick trademark in later years.

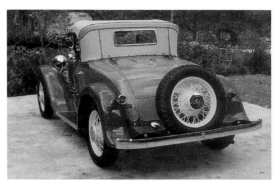

The car that all other SA roadsters are judged by, Charlie Black's 1931 roadster.

DeSoto assembly would move from the Plymouth plant at year's end, to the Chrysler Jefferson Avenue plant, as DeSoto moved up a notch in the corporation hierarchy. In years past, Chrysler's price ladder had found Plymouth at the bottom, DeSoto directly above Plymouth, then Dodge, Chrysler, and Imperial at the top. With the switch to the Airflow body in 1934, DeSoto leapfrogged Dodge. In the long run, it was a move that would eventually spell doom for DeSoto.

As a prelude to introduction of the Airflow, a specially prepared '33 DeSoto sedan was built by Aero Dynamics of New York City. Driven across country by veteran race driver Harry Hartz, the car had the body mounted backward on the chassis to prove the point that the automobile as it was then known was more efficient in reverse than it was in forward motion. Fitted with a special wrap-around rear window, Hartz' zany stunt drew a lot of attention, not all of it favorable, especially from police who ticketed him for driving the wrong way!

A special close-coupled "pillarless" sedan was exhibited at Chrysler's pavilion at the Chicago World's Fair. With both front and rear doors open, the sedan lacked a center door post, but it never got beyond the prototype stage. (A pillarless sedan wouldn't see production until the 1957 Cadillac Eldorado Brougham.)

Year-end totals fell to 20,186 units for calendar-year 1933, dropping DeSoto back to 12th in industry sales.

DeSoto Airflow SE
Coupe, Town Sedan ★★★★★
Brougham ★★★★
Four-door ★★★

DeSoto for 1934
To say there had never been another car like it would be an understatement when DeSoto unveiled

Probably the rarest 1932 DeSoto is the SC Convertible Victoria. It shared its body with the PB Plymouth convertible Victoria. *D. Kramer*

its "Airflow" for 1934. Credit—or blame—for the car lies with Carl Breer, of Chrysler's famed Zeder, Skelton, and Breer engineering trio. Breer himself told the story of how he came up with the idea of designing an aerodynamically shaped car, based on the principle of birds in flight. The result of five years of research, Breer took the accepted "norms" of automobile engineering and literally threw them out the window. Tested in the woods of northern Michigan, the airflow principles were established in a

DeSoto for 1932 featured a rounded grille inspired by Harry Miller's race cars. Absolutely gorgeous is this three window coupe. *National DeSoto Club*

prototype known as the "Trifon Special." When it appeared in the showrooms, the Airflow established new standards in the construction of the automobile.

Called "completely and unmistakably new," the Airflow DeSoto was literally "born in a wind tunnel," the contour of the car designed according to aerodynamic principles. With a gracefully rounded front to "bore" through air currents, the radiator was completely hidden behind a chrome grille. Headlamps were fared into the body, something other Chrysler lines would not adopt until 1939. Fenders, usually designed to add length to a car, were streamlined to form a cover over the wheels, with the rear wheels further protected by the addition of "wheel shields." At the rear, the body curved downward in true "stream line form."

The result was a car that was unconventional and unusual—and to many, just plain ugly. The Airflow DeSoto was the type of car that evoked one of two responses—either you liked it or you hated it and there was little ground in between. Even today, 60 years later, the Airflows still evoke these emotions.

The Airflow claimed 40 percent less wind resistance to a car of similar size. Body and frame construction was discarded in favor of an all-steel welded body trussed by bridge-like steel girders, over 40 times stronger than a conventional automobile. One can only wonder why the Airflow retained a tube front axle, while both Dodge and Plymouth adopted independent front wheel suspension for 1934. Because of the teardrop shape, engineers moved the engine 18 inches over the front axle. The passenger compartment was also moved 18 inches forward of the rear axle (again the result of the teardrop shape), resulting in a much improved ride; DeSoto called it "Floating Ride." Capitalizing on the shape, the front seat was increased 8 inches in width, allowing three front seat passengers to sit comfortably. Wind noise was reduced by employing special body and window vents. Front windows, like those of the PE Plymouth for 1934, featured a disappearing vent wind wing. (While Plymouth would discontinue it at model end, the Airflows, both DeSoto and Chrysler, would continue using the complicated system.)

Interiors were as unusual as the exterior. Front seats were surrounded by chrome tubing, with several inches of air space beneath the cushion. Four-door sedans capitalized on reducing costs by having front and rear doors interchangeable—that is, the left front door interchanged with the right rear door.

Powering the Airflow was a 100-horsepower 241.5-ci six-cylinder engine. Proving its mettle, the Airflow established 25 AAA speed records, including an 86.2 mile per hour "flying" mile, and a record 80 miles per hour for 100 miles,

DeSotos for 1932 and 1933, including the roadster, utilized forward-opening "suicide" style doors. *WPC Club*

prompting DeSoto advertising to crow you could read a book or write a letter at 80 miles an hour (hopefully while someone else was doing the driving!). Harry Hartz piloted an Airflow cross-country, recording an average of 21.4 miles per gallon for the trip. No doubt this car was equipped with the Borg Warner overdrive, a $30 option (developed by Chrysler engineering).

Only four body styles were offered, all built on a 115-1/2-inch wheelbase, including a five-passenger coupe, whose access to the luggage compartment was only through the rear seat of the car and trunk-mounted spare tire. There was also a two-door "brougham," four-door sedan, and four-door Town Sedan with blind quarter-windows. The price of $995 bought any body style, a significant jump over the prices of the 1933 DeSoto.

Introduced at the New York Auto Show, the cars (along with the Chrysler Airflow) stole the show. Sales, however, were another story. Actual cars for retail sales were slow in coming, giving the competition more than ample time to circulate stories the cars weren't any good. Being priced $200 more than the highest-priced '33 DeSoto, in the

Unique split headlamp trim was found on 1933 Custom DeSotos. *Jim Benjaminson*

midst of one of the worst years of the depression, helped take a toll on Airflow sales. Buyers flocked to the more conventional Plymouth and Dodge, which sported some of the most beautiful cars built. Despite public exposure at the Chrysler Pavilion at the Chicago World's Fair, setting stock

Built in just four body styles, the most commonly seen Airflow was the regular four-door sedan. Abbreviated fenders and flush grille and headlamps were uncommon sights in 1934. *Jim Benjaminson*

car records, and receiving the Grand Prix Award at the Monte Carlo Concours D'Elegance, Airflow production came to a measly 13,940 units, with most buyers choosing the regular four-door sedan.

Calendar-year sales of 15,825 cars kept DeSoto in 12th place in industry sales but it was soon clear the buying public was not yet willing to accept the radical Airflow styling. Surprisingly, the Airflow design was soon copied around the world, most notably by Sweden's Volvo, Japan's Toyota, and France's Peugeot.

DeSoto SF (Airstream)
DeSoto SF Rumble seat coupe, convertible ★★★★★
Business coupe, ★★★★
Two-door and four-door Touring Sedan ★★★
Two-door, four-door ★★

A redesigned grille (retrofitted to many 1934 Airflows) gave the 1935 Airflow a more conventional look. All Airflows had the rear wheels skirted. *Plymouth Owners Club*

DeSoto SG (Airflow)
Coupe, Town Sedan ★★★★★
Brougham ★★★★
Four-door ★★★

DeSoto for 1935
Realizing the need for a more conventional car, but not giving up on the Airflow design, DeSoto entered the model year with two completely different series of cars. The Airflow continued, now coded SG, with a more prominent vee'd front end which made the car look longer. (Dealers would install an "update" grille on '34 Airflows to give them the appearance of the '35 Airflow.) The wheelbase remained at 115 1/2 inches. Hood louvers decreased to just three horizontal louvers compared to the previous year's 11. The same four Airflow body styles were continued with prices increasing to $1,015, regardless of body type.

Despite the Airflows controversial looks, it received, for the second time, the Grand Prix Award at the Monte Carlo Concours D'Elegance. Added to the line was the SF series of conventionally styled automobiles. Body types included both business and rumble seat coupe, convertible coupe (featuring a separate "X" brace frame mounted on top of the regular frame, designed to prevent sagging and twisting commonly found in regular open cars), and two- and four-door sedans, in either flatback or humpback "Touring Sedan" format. Like the '35 Plymouth, the SF DeSoto applied many of the Airflow principles to the design of a regular automobile. Styling took on a more rounded look. Called "Airstream," the SF was built on a 116-inch wheelbase shared with Dodge, 3 inches longer than the PJ Plymouth. Styling included a sloping V-type radiator, with two rows of horizontal hood louvers and bullet-shaped headlamps. The front bumper had a V-shaped dip in the center, with three chevron hash marks on the lower front fenders.

A Deluxe equipment package included two-tone paint, small front fender lamps, dual taillamps and trumpet horns, two windshield wipers, wheel trim rings, chrome fender and running board molding, cigar lighter, and front compartment carpet.

Both the Airstream and Airflow were powered by the 241.5-ci six, with the Airstream developing 93 horsepower to the Airflow's 100 horsepower (achieved by a higher 6.5:1 compression ratio). Differing from the Airflow, the Airstream had independent front suspension. Airflows continued to offer overdrive, but dropped Free-Wheeling.

Priced $200 less than the Airflow, the Airstream outsold its companion by a better than three-to-one ratio. Just 6,797 Airflows were built compared to 20,784 Airstreams. Calendar-year

DeSoto's 1934 Airflow changed the way all cars looked and were built. Built with a bridge truss-like structure, bodies were complete from front to back when they went into the paint room.

sales of 34,276 cars saw DeSoto slip one more notch, to end the year in 13th place.

DeSoto S1 (Airstream)
DeSoto S1 Rumble seat coupe, convertible, convertible sedan ★★★★★
Business coupe, Traveler Sedan, seven-passenger ★★★★
Two- and four-door Touring Sedan ★★★
Two-door and four-door ★★

DeSoto S2 (Airflow)
Coupe, Town Sedan ★★★★★
Brougham ★★★★
Four-door ★★★

DeSoto for 1936
Nineteen thirty-six would mark the last year for the Airflow DeSoto. (Its companion Chrysler Airflow would soldier on for one more year.) A new diecast grille with vertical moldings, curved diagonal trim pieces, and twin "pennon" style hood louvers, along with new bumpers and revised body side moldings, set the Airflow apart from previous years.

Body styles were pared to just two, the five-passenger coupe and four-door sedan. Prices had continued to escalate, with either body style now commanding $1,095. The DeSoto Airflow passed into history after only 5,000 1936 S2 models, 250 coupes and 4,750 sedans, had been built. Mechanical specifications of the last Airflows remained the same as previous years, with a 115 1/2-inch wheelbase and power from a 100-horsepower 241.5-ci six.

The S-1—or Airstream—series was built on a 2-inch-longer wheelbase than in 1935, and was powered by the 93-horsepower version of the 241. For the first time, overdrive was optional on all Airstreams. Custom models were fitted with a hypoid rear axle

The 1935 Airflow sedan was again the most popular body style in the Airflow series. Note the twin-opening windshields for ventilation. *National DeSoto Club*

as standard equipment, with Deluxes retaining the old-style spiral bevel differential. When ordered with overdrive, Deluxes also came with hypoid gearing. Available in two trim levels, Deluxe or Custom, the Airstream carried conventional bodywork with a new horizontal bar grille and "pennon" style hood louvers. Deluxe Airstreams had a flat one-piece windshield while the Custom (with the exception of the convertible) had a vee'd two-piece windshield. Other Custom touches included two instrument-panel glove compartments, dual cowl-mounted windshield wipers (Deluxes had a single wiper on the header board), chrome moldings on the top of the headlamps, chrome chevrons on the front fenders, fender skirt and running board moldings, rear wheel shields, and two-piece rear windows.

Body types for the Deluxe series included a business coupe, two-door Touring Brougham, and four-door Touring Sedan. Custom models included those already mentioned along with a rumble seat coupe, convertible coupe, and four-door convertible sedan. Both series featured full steel roof panels replacing the customary fabric center (the steel panel was still an insert, however), and all closed cars featured built-in trunks.

Added to the line for this year was a series of Custom models on an extended 130-inch wheelbase, including a four-door five-passenger Traveler Sedan, four-door seven-passenger sedan, four-door seven-passenger limousine with fixed divider window, and 2,500 seven-passenger taxis for New York City's "Sunshine" Cab Company, all built with sliding sunroofs.

Nineteen thirty-six was a good year for the corporation as it built, for the first time, 1 million cars in a calendar year, surpassed Ford Motor Company as the nation's number-two auto maker, and embarked on building a new plant on Dearborn's Warren Avenue to become the exclusive home of DeSoto. Calendar-year sales of 52,789 cars were not enough, however, to move DeSoto out of 13th place in industry sales.

DeSoto S3
Rumble seat coupe, convertible,
convertible sedan, limousine ★★★★★
Business coupe, seven-passenger ★★★★

In its final year, 1936 Airflows were pared to just two body types. A redesigned grille and pennon-shaped side panels set it apart from earlier Airflows. *National DeSoto Club*

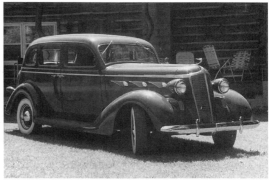

Seen here is an example of the conventionally styled Airstream S-1 series, which easily outsold the Airflows. The Airstream series shared much of its body with Dodge. *National DeSoto Club*

Brougham Touring, four-door
Touring Sedan ★★★
Two- and four-door Sedan ★★

DeSoto for 1937

Having discontinued the Airflow, DeSoto offered just one model series, coded the S3 for 1937. Conventionally styled, the S3 featured a horizontal grille bar divided by a center panel painted body color. The top six grille bars continued along the length of the hood. An unusual change was adoption of a front opening "Alligator" style hood. Bullet-shaped headlamps and unusual ribbed bumpers characterized the new DeSoto. The ribbed bumpers, both front and rear, proved to be a popular item with customizers who soon adapted them to many other makes of cars.

As with the rest of the corporate line, safety became a big issue. Dash knobs were located beneath the raised instrument panel, the back of the front seat in sedans was heavily padded and door handles, both inside and out, were redesigned to prevent snagging of clothing and accidental opening.

Built on a 2-inch-shorter wheelbase (116 inches), the S3 came in business coupe, rumble seat coupe, convertible coupe, two-door fastback Brougham, two-door Touring Brougham (with built-in trunk), four-door fastback or Touring Sedan, as well as a four-door convertible sedan that shared its body with Chrysler. Bodies for the four-door convertible were built by Murray rather than Chrysler's normal body supplier Briggs. Most DeSoto bodies were supplied by Kercheval, a Chrysler-owned subsidiary.

Extended wheelbase models rode on a 3-inch-longer 133-inch wheelbase, and included a four-door seven-passenger touring sedan, seven-passenger limousine, and a California seven-passenger taxi. Power came from a 93-horsepower, 228-ci six, a destroked version of the previous year's engine. Hypoid axles were now used across the board and the once-popular option of fender-mounted spare tires was discontinued. Also on the option list was the $35 "Gas-Saver" overdrive transmission, which was claimed to gave "one mile free in every five."

A special DeSoto convertible sedan served as official car for the secretary of the AAA race board during the running of the Indianapolis 500 (not as the pace car, as has been erroneously reported elsewhere). And to the chagrin of criminals everywhere, DeSoto police cars of the Eastchester, New York, Police Department were the first in the world to install three-way radio communication allowing car-to-car or car-to-base communications.

Calendar-year sales of 86,541 units carried DeSoto to an all-time-high 11th-place finish in industry sales.

DeSoto S5
Rumble seat coupe, convertible,
convertible sedan, limousine ★★★★★
Business coupe, seven-passenger ★★★★
Brougham Touring, four-door
Touring Sedan ★★★
Two- and four-door Sedan ★★

DeSoto for 1938

Like the rest of the corporate line, the '38 DeSoto received a mild facelift from the previous year. Gone was the alligator-style hood, replaced by a shorter and more conventional butterfly type. A heavy, shorter

The 1936 Airstream convertible was a body style Airflow buyers had been deprived of. This would be the last year for side-mounted spare tires on a DeSoto. *National DeSoto Club*

diecast grille flanked an aluminum chevron-style center grille. Headlamps were now integrated into the tops of the fenders, windshield wipers were moved to the cowl, and for the first time, the windshield was fixed in place, with fresh air coming to the passenger compartment via a cowl-mounted ventilator.

The wheelbase increased 3 inches to 119 inches, the longest of any DeSoto up to that time. Under the hood sat the same powerplant as the previous year, a 93-horsepower six displacing 228 ci.

Again offered in just one series, coded S5, buyers had the choice of business coupe, rumble seat coupe (the last rumble seat coupes DeSoto would build), two-door Touring Brougham (with trunk), flatback two-door, four-door Touring Sedan, four-door fastback sedan, convertible coupe, or four-door convertible sedan (also the last four-door convertible DeSoto would build).

Long-wheelbase models also gained 3 inches in wheelbase to 136 inches in four-door seven-passenger, seven-passenger limousine, and seven-passenger California-taxi body styles. A handful of chassis were shipped to the Cantrell company for installation of station

wagon bodies and at least one special Town Car was built by Derham.

An unusual option was the DeSoto Ambulance conversion. Unlike the Plymouth ambulance conversions, which allowed a stretcher to be inserted through the trunk, the DeSoto Ambulance featured a removable center door post and removable passenger front seat. Held in place by dowels and thumb screws, the center post could be easily removed to allow insertion of a gurney into the passenger compartment. In later years, a more modern version with swing-out-of-the-way center post would be offered.

Wounded by the Recession of 1938, calendar-year sales of 32,688 were off 62 percent compared to the record year of 1937. Despite the drastic decline, DeSoto slipped only one notch, to 12th, for the year.

DeSoto S6
Hayes body Custom Club Coupe,
limousine ★★★★★
Seven-passenger, business coupe,
auxiliary seat coupe ★★★★
Two-door and four-door sedan ★★

DeSoto for 1939

Gambling the recession of 1938 would be brief, Chrysler Corporation spent $15 million revamping its car lines for 1939. Dodge, DeSoto, Chrysler, and Imperial would all receive new bodies, while Plymouth would be forced to soldier on with its old body, although a major redesign cleverly hid that fact.

Coded the S6 series, DeSoto again offered two trim levels in Deluxe or Custom form. Oddly enough, even long-wheelbase models would be available in either trim level.

Streamlined styling featured a prow-like front end, the nose of the car covered with horizontal chrome grille bars on either side of the main grille, whose bars stretched back toward the hood. A vee'd, two-piece windshield added length to the cowl and interior compartment. Headlamps and taillamps were an integral part of the fenders, giving the cars a streamlined appearance. Four square vents decorated the lower hood panels, which were now fastened into place but removable for service of the engine.

Custom series equipment included dual sun visors, dual horns, dual taillamps, and darker colored interior fabrics. All cars received electric windshield wipers and column-mounted gearshifting.

Missing from the DeSoto line-up was the convertible sedan and convertible coupe—only Plymouth would offer any open cars in the corporation this year—and the rumble seat coupe. With the new bodies, the old-style "humpback" Touring Sedan body was discontinued, and all cars were now designed with a built-in rear luggage compartment. Deluxe buyers had the choice of three-passenger business coupe, three- or five-passenger auxiliary seat coupe, or two or four-door sedans. Long-wheelbase Deluxe models included a seven-passenger taxi, sedan, or limousine.

Custom models offered the same line-up with two exceptions: there was no Custom seven-passenger taxi, and only Custom buyers could opt for the Custom Club Coupe.

Built by Hayes, the Custom Club Coupe featured a special roofline with thin window-pillar posts. A one-year-only model shared with Chrysler, Imperial, and Dodge, only 1,000 Hayes bodies were supplied to the corporation. Of these, just 264 DeSoto Custom Club Coupes were built.

The wheelbase remained the same 119 inches as in 1938 (136 inches on long-wheel base cars), with power from a 93-horsepower, 228-ci six. New for the year was a column-mounted shift lever, a "Safety Signal" speedometer that changed colors as the car's speed increased, and electric windshield wipers. With the discontinu-

With the demise of the Airflow, DeSoto offered a single series called the S3 for 1937. Featuring an alligator hood opening and ribbed bumpers, DeSoto began sharing its heritage with Chrysler rather than Dodge. The ribbed bumpers became a popular item with customizers. *National DeSoto Club*

ance of open cars, DeSoto circulated photographs of sunroof-equipped coupes and sedans. Dealer letters indicate there was an intent to produce these sunroof cars for sale. Dealer price sheets, while listing the sunroof, did not indicate any price for the option, which was later quietly dropped, apparently due to lack of interest. Cars photographed with the option were probably prototypes that never reached the public. If any such cars did find their way to a customer, they would be extremely rare vehicles today.

With the improving economic picture, DeSoto sales rebounded to 53,269 for the calendar year, yet DeSoto found itself slipping to 14th place, a position it had last seen in 1931.

Cars with the humpback-style trunk were known as Touring Sedans. *National DeSoto Club*

Changes to the rear of the S5 DeSoto were minimal. Plain bumpers and redesigned deck lid trim were the only changes. *National DeSoto Club*

Completely redesigned for 1939, DeSoto eliminated the humpback-style trunk on all sedans, and fared the headlamps and taillamps into the fenders. *National DeSoto Club*

Changes to the S5 DeSoto included heavy cast grilles on either side separated by vertical grille teeth, a return to a butterfly opening hood, loss of the ribbed bumpers, and headlamps mounted on the fenders rather than the radiator. This would be the last year for a rumble seat coupe. *National DeSoto Club*

DeSoto S7
Convertible, limousine ★★★★★
Business coupe, auxiliary seat coupe, seven-passenger ★★★★
Two- and four-door sedan ★★

DeSoto for 1940
Redesigned for 1940, the S7 DeSoto again featured a split grille motif of horizontal chrome grille bars centered between fender-mounted sealed-beam headlamps. Buyers could again

Among the rarest of all DeSotos is the Custom Club Coupe with body by Hayes. Featuring thin window pillars and a peaked roof that ran into the deck lid, just 265 were built. *Collectible Automobile Magazine*

choose between two trim levels, again called Deluxe and Custom, with either model easily identified by the script found on the lower rear hood panels, spelling out the trim level. In addition, Custom models had chrome trim around the windshield, windows, and above and below the taillamps, trim not found on the Deluxe.

The wheelbase increased 3 1/2 inches to 122 1/2 inches and to a whopping 139 1/2 inches on extended-wheelbase cars, which again were available in either trim level. Power was provided by a 100-horsepower six displacing 228 ci, marking the first time since the Airflow that a DeSoto reached a triple-digit horsepower rating. Deluxe buyers could choose between the three-passenger business coupe, three- or five-passenger auxiliary seat coupe, and two- or four-door sedans (still carrying the title of Touring Sedan, although the luggage compartment was now an integral part of the body). Only two long-wheelbase cars, a

Eliminating convertibles for 1939, DeSoto circulated photographs of its "Sunshine Roof" option. Despite the publicity, it appears the option was never implemented.

Although DeSoto did build a series of taxi cabs for a New York company that did have sunroofs, no cars are known to exist with this feature. *Collectible Automobile Magazine*

seven-passenger sedan and the seven-passenger California taxi, came in Deluxe trim.

Custom body types were the same as the Deluxe, with the addition of a convertible coupe (with power-operated top), which returned to the line-up for this year. Long-wheelbase Customs included a seven-passenger sedan and limousine. At midyear DeSoto brought out the "Sportsman," a gussied-up four-door sedan featuring two-tone paint in three combinations of green, gray, or blue over gunmetal. Colors were split along the beltline and extended over the hood. Other Sportsman features included two-tone interior fabrics, chrome trim on door panels, a color steering wheel, two-tone woodgrain on the instrument panel, and additional exterior chrome trim, including the windshield divider bar, chrome strips on the hood nose, and chrome speedline strips on the fenders. The Sportsman name would become more familiar in the 1950s when applied to the hardtop convertible bodies. Optional for all models were "Safety Rim

Wheels," which held the tire on the rim in case of flat or blowout. Safety rim wheels would become standard equipment on all Chrysler lines for 1941.

Added to the option list was a semi-automatic transmission called "Fluid Drive." Although it would be years before Chrysler Corporation would offer a truly fully automatic transmission, "Fluid Drive" would be a staple of all car lines except Plymouth for years to come. Fluid Drive discarded the conventional flywheel in favor of a fluid coupling. There was no metal-to-metal contact as found in a regular clutch/pressure plate combination. Fluid Drive provided two gear-lever positions: "low," controlling first and second gear (used mainly for extra pulling power), and "high," which engaged third and fourth gears. Fluid Drive still required a clutch, which was needed when shifting to reverse or initially into high range. Once under way, it was necessary to release the accelerator pedal to allow the transmission to shift in final high, usually accomplished with an audible "thump."

Some 83,805 DeSotos found homes by end of calendar-year 1940, good enough to move it into 10th place in industry sales.

DeSoto S8
Convertible, Limousine ★★★★★
Business coupe, auxiliary seat coupe, Town Sedan, seven-passenger ★★★★
Two- and four-door sedan ★★

DeSoto for 1941

Longer, wider, and with a lower beltline, DeSoto launched its "Rocket" line of bodies for 1941. Returning to the alligator-style hood opening first used in 1937, the hood latch was released from inside the passenger compartment. Latching the hood from the inside foiled battery thieves after DeSoto moved it from under the driver's seat, where it had resided since 1929.

Carrying the same styling motif of years past, the grille was made up of 14 curved, vertical bars on either side of the center body panel, only now the bars ran vertically rather than horizontally, setting a DeSoto styling trend that would last for the next 15 years. Three short, horizontal trim strips decorated the nose of the car. Running boards were now fully concealed on all models.

Coded the S8, Deluxe or Custom trim levels were offered for both regular and long-wheelbase vehicles. Deluxe models were fitted with the familiar 100-horsepower, 228 six, achieved at a 6.5:1 compression ratio. Custom models now boasted 105 horses, reached by raising compression to 6.8:1. The wheelbase was decreased by 1 inch, to 121.5 inches, and long-wheelbase models continued to be built on the 139.5-inch wheelbase.

The 1940 DeSoto was the first to use sealed-beam headlamps. *Jim Benjaminson*

Deluxe body styles were the same as 1940, while the Custom differed by the addition of the four-door Town Sedan. Unlike the regular four-doors, where the rear door opened backwards (suicide style), the Town Sedan opened in conventional fashion. Rear quarter-windows normally found in the roof-body side structure, were carried in the door frame on Town Sedans. The Town Sedan was an across-the-board addition to all Chrysler lines with the exception of Plymouth, which wouldn't get that body style until next year. Custom models were easily identified by the vertical chrome strips decorating the taillamps and by chrome reveal body moldings. The word DeSoto was prominently stamped into each rear bumper bar. Two-tone paint were available on any closed model at a slight extra cost, and running boards could be deleted as a no-cost option.

This model year's Sportsman was a club coupe fitted with convertible type upholstery of leather and whipcord. DeSoto ambulance conversions continued to be available, now featuring a hinged (rather than removable) B-pillar.

Fluid Drive, now coupled with "Simplimatic" transmission, was continued. To prove how easy a DeSoto with Fluid Drive was to operate, two young ladies, Virginia Campbell and Joselyn Reynolds, were given a car to drive cross-country. Recording 13,611 miles in five months, the two women claimed they never once had to shift the car during the entire trip.

Calendar-year figures showed a slight increase in sales, to 85,980 units, not much higher than 1940, but enough to keep DeSoto in 10th place overall for the year.

DeSoto S10
Convertible, limousine ★★★★★
Business coupe, auxiliary seat coupe, seven-passenger, Town Sedan ★★★★
Two- and four-door sedan ★★

DeSoto for 1942

DeSoto's 1942 models are among the most sought-after of the prewar cars for two reasons: their relative scarcity caused by early production shut-down for the duration of the war, and their one-year-only hidden headlamps.

Mildly restyled, DeSoto took on dramatic new dimensions through the use of the hidden-headlamp concept. Pioneered by the 1936 Cord 810, DeSoto's "Airfoil" lamps hid beneath retractable panels at the leading edge of the fenders. Advertised as "out of sight except at night," the clean fenders drew attention to the heavier, 37-tooth vertical grille. Chrome fender trim that wrapped from side to side provided the break line between the expanses of painted sheet metal and the tooth grille, culminating as the grille peaked below the forward edge of the hood. Rectangular parking lamps and a hood medallion that fell to join the upper grille cavity and concealed running boards were among the remaining changes to the car.

Coded S10, the 1942 DeSoto was again offered in two trim levels: Deluxe and Custom, both available in two wheelbase lengths, 121.5 inches and 139.5 inches. Power came from an engine bored slightly to 3 7/16 inches, displacing 237 ci, and developing 115 horsepower. Power was transmitted by the standard three-speed manual transmission, with Fluid Drive and Simplimatic transmission optional.

Deluxe buyers had their choice of business coupe, club coupe, two- or four-door sedan, four-door Town Sedan with blind quarter-windows, and a convertible coupe. Only 79 ragtops were built before DeSoto production was shut down on January 30, 1942. (Dodge production came to a halt a day earlier, and Plymouth and Chrysler production ended the next day.)

Long-wheelbase Deluxes included a seven-passenger sedan and seven-passenger California taxi. Custom models included a business coupe, club coupe, convertible coupe (489 built), two-door Brougham, four-door sedan, and four-door Town Sedan. Long-wheelbase Customs included a seven-passenger sedan and seven-passenger limousine. Never built in large quantities, these big cars saw production of just 79 and 20 units, respectively.

Ever rarer were cars equipped with the "Fifth Avenue Ensemble," a dealer-ordered accessory package available on virtually any body type. A one-year-only offering (the "Fifth Avenue" name would appear in later years on Chryslers), the

Among the more unusual features of the short-lived 1942 DeSoto were the hidden headlamps set above a toothy vertical grille. *National DeSoto Club*

"ensemble" included Fluid Drive with Simplimatic transmission 8-tube pushbutton radio, electric radio antennae (on all but the convertible), electric clock, turn signals, parking brake lamp, four bumper guards including license plate holder, exhaust pipe extentions, cigar lighter, lighted hood ornament, rear wheel shields with special stainless steel mouldings, pushbutton starter mounted on the instrument panel, and five whitewall wheel trim rings. Perhaps the most unusual feature was a special steering wheel with built-in cigarette dispenser! Not mentioned but included in the ensemble were Fifth Avenue nameplates front and rear.

Nineteen forty-two production amounted to slightly better than 25,000 units, but calendar-year sales came to just 4,186, dropping DeSoto to 14th for the year.

DeSoto S11
Convertible, Suburban, Limousine ★★★★★
Business coupe, club coupe,
seven-passenger ★★★★
Two- and four-door sedan ★★

DeSoto for 1946–49

Like the rest of the Corporation, DeSoto was late getting back into the business of building automobiles after the war. Building just 367 Deluxes and a single Custom car in December of 1945, the new 1946 DeSotos were based on the short-lived 1942 body.

Restyling included a new hood, new front fenders that blended back into the door, and restyled rear fenders. Gone were the hidden headlamps, but the grille design left little doubt as to DeSoto's heritage, made up of vertical grille teeth like the '42. Larger parking lamps sat below the front fender molding, which curved over the grille

A lowered beltline gave the 1941 DeSoto a sleeker look, but it was the vertical grille teeth that would set DeSoto's styling trends for the next 15 years. *Jim Benjaminson*

Restyled after the war, the S11 series DeSoto would be virtually unchanged for three years. Gone were the hidden headlamps, with redesigned fenders running into the doors. Open DeSotos such as this 1947 model are hard to find today. *Rusty Tillotson*

cavity. Prominently exposed headlamps and a wrap-around front bumper completed the package.

Coded the S11 series, the Deluxe line was given the additional code letter of S (Custom models became the S11-C) series. Two wheelbase lengths, unchanged from 1942, would be offered, but now only in the Custom line. Body style choices were likewise pared down, the Deluxe to just four, including three-passenger coupe, club coupe, and two or four-door sedans. Customs were available in club coupe, convertible (now offering four top fabric color choices), and two-or four-door sedan on the regular chassis, or an eight-passenger sedan or limousine, and new-to-the-line, eight-passenger Suburban.

Not appearing in the sales line-up until November of 1946, the Suburban was designed for use in posh hotel settings or for the well-healed buyer who needed hauling capacity along with room for many passengers. The Suburban featured a fold-down rear seat with no partition between the trunk and passenger compartment, a

metal-and-wood roof rack for even more carrying capacity, and beautifully finished wooden interior panels. Seats were upholstered in a heavy plastic called Delon. Priced at $2,093, it was the most expensive DeSoto built, yet 7,500 of them were sold.

Like the rest of the corporate line, there would be no discernible changes in the S11 series until it was phased out of production in favor of the "second series" DeSoto in March of 1949. The engine and drivetrain remained unchanged from postwar models, and even the huge two-ton Suburban would be hauled around by the 237-ci six, now rated at 109 horsepower (down from 1942). Tire sizes were changed late in 1947, from 6:00x16-inches on regular-chassis cars, to 7.60x15-inches. Due to shortages, whitewall tires were not available until April 1947, and most of the early cars were fitted with a plastic inner wheel liner that gave the effect of whitewalls. Transmission changes came in the form of Chrysler's M6 hydraulically controlled (rather than

S11 production continued into the early months of 1949 before being replaced by all-new postwar designs. Cars sold after December 1, 1949, such as this S11-C club coupe, were considered to be "first series" 1949 models. *Robert & Hope Ricewesser*

vacuum-controlled) four-speed known as Gyrol Drive with Tip Toe Shift.

Cars built after January 1, 1947, were considered to be 1947 models, likewise cars after January 1, 1948, were 1948s. Anything built after December 1, 1948, was considered by the factory to be a 1949 model. When the "true" '49s came on line, they were called, for lack of anything better, the "second series" 1949s.

Calendar-years sales of 62,860 for 1946 put DeSoto up one notch to 13th place over its 1942 showing. Despite increased sales, DeSoto's market share slipped in each of the following two years: 81,752 for calendar-year 1947 saw DeSoto move back to 14th, and 92,920 units for 1948 slipped DeSoto back another notch to 15th.

DeSoto S13
Convertible, Suburban, wood-body
station wagon ★★★★★
Club coupe, Carry All Sedan,
eight-passenger ★★★★
Four-door ★★

DeSoto for 1949

Among the last of the Big Three to introduce its true 1949 models, Chrysler Corporation spent $90 million bringing the new cars on line. Not one single piece of sheet metal or trim interchanged with previous models as the old turtle-back body shell was finally replaced by modern styling, at least by Keller's standards. Although it was a radical change from prior years, the new DeSotos were conservatively styled—too conservative for some in what is now derided as the Keller "three box" school of styling.

A half-inch shorter, 2-1/2 inches narrower, and considerably lower than the S11, DeSoto shared its basic body and engine block with Chrysler. Despite a 4-inch-longer wheelbase for regular-chassis cars, the new DeSotos looked shorter and boxier than they actually were. Different ornamentation and a smaller-displacement engine told the world DeSoto was one step beneath Chrysler in the corporate pecking order. A vertical grille of alternating wide and narrower bars (two narrower bars to each wide bar) did little to help the cars' rather high appearance, but it gave DeSoto instant recognition. Windshields were still two

The second series 1949 DeSotos was completely new, not sharing one piece of glass or sheet metal with previous cars.

This Custom Club Coupe sports an accessory windshield visor and door handle scratch guards. *National DeSoto Club*

pieces of flat glass, a move made more for cost reduction than style, making for a pronounced beltline where the roof met the body. Riding on the leading edge of the hood was a DeSoto coat of arms medallion beneath a lighted ornament featuring the bust of Hernando DeSoto. Taillamps sat in little pods on top of the detachable rear fenders.

Trim levels still carried the names Deluxe and Custom, coded S13-1 and S13-2, respectively. Deluxe buyers were given a choice of club coupe, four-door sedan, or the all-new Carry-All and four-door station wagon. The wagon, a first for DeSoto, offered the marque's first "factory" wagon, a four-door affair with a wood body. (The only other wagons had been built by outside body builders, although the DeSoto body was provided by Chrysler's "house" builder, U.S. Body & Forging.) Although the body (and roof) were all steel, it was trimmed with ash trimming and DiNoc panels. Only 850 wagons would be built.

Perhaps more significant was the Carry-All. Similar to the Suburban but built on the short-wheelbase chassis, the Carry-All's rear seat folded down to provide cargo-carrying capacity. Like the Suburban there was no partition between the trunk and passenger compartment with the rear deck and seat back trimmed with wood protected by steel skid strips. Unlike the Suburban, the Carry-All did not have a roof rack. Until the introduction of an all-steel station wagon, the Carry-All combined the best of both worlds. Sales of 2,690 clearly showed buyers preferred a maintenance-free body to that of the woody wagon.

Custom buyers again could choose either regular- or long-wheelbase models. Regular-chassis body types included a club coupe, convertible coupe, and four-door sedan, while long-wheelbase models included the eight-passenger sedan or nine-passenger Suburban. Gone was the long-wheelbase limousine.

Powered by the same 237-ci six as before, horsepower was raised to 112 via increased compression ratio (yet it was still 3 horsepower less than the 1942 DeSoto). Custom buyers were treated to Gyrol Fluid Drive with Tip Toe Hydraulic shift as standard equipment, an option that ran Deluxe buyers an extra $121.

Calendar-year sales of 108,440 DeSotos carried the marque back to 13th place for the year.

DeSoto S14
Same as S13 with addition of metal
station wagon ★★★
Sportsman hardtop ★★★★★

DeSoto for 1950

Like Plymouth, DeSoto's 1950 models were essentially restyled '49s. Making for easy identification of the 1950 DeSoto was the addition of a body color panel in the center of the grille, dividing the 14 grille teeth, which by this time had become a DeSoto trademark. Minor trim differences such as round rather than vertical park lamps, DeSoto script replacing the DeSoto coat of arms on the hood (the coat of arms was inset into the center painted grille panel), and an all-metal DeSoto-bust hood ornament set the two cars apart. Around back, it took an observant eye to notice the rear fenders had been extended slightly and now featured recessed taillamps, the first since 1939. There had been significant, albeit nearly imperceptible, changes in the body structure, with the 1950 model receiving a larger rear window than 1949 models.

Mechanically the same and on the same wheelbase as the '49, the Deluxe was coded S14-1, and the Custom was S14-2. Major changes for the year came with the addition of several new body types. Deluxe models were available in club coupe, four-door, or four-door Carry-All form. A long-wheelbase Deluxe, an eight-passenger sedan, was added to the line-up.

It was the Custom series that saw the greatest number of changes. Added to the customary four-door sedan, club coupe, and convertible coupe was the Sportsman hardtop convertible. Chrysler had pioneered the "two-door hardtop" concept when it built a handful of Town and Country hardtops right after the war. For whatever reason, Chrysler dropped the idea only to see it picked up by General Motors. Wildly popular on Cadillacs, Buicks, and Oldsmobiles—even Chevrolet had a hardtop—Chrysler was forced to play catch-up to an idea it had pioneered! Known as a "hardtop convertible," the body was essentially that of a convertible with a steel roof panel welded in place of the folding cloth top. Doors, interiors, and trim panels interchanged between the two body types. Rear windows of the Sportsman consisted of three pieces separated by attractive dividers. Sales of 4,600 Sportsmen trailed only the four-door sedan and club coupe in popularity. The addition late in the year of an all-steel four-door station wagon (featuring a roll-down

Most popular of the 1949 DeSotos was the Custom four-door sedan. Vertical grille teeth gave DeSoto its own identity. *National DeSoto Club*

rear window), along with the four-door wood body wagon, gave buyers a choice. Only 100 all-steel wagons would be built, compared to 600 wood body wagons, the last wood wagons DeSoto would offer.

Only two long-wheelbase Customs, the eight-passenger sedan and nine-passenger Suburban were cataloged. As before, Gyrol Fluid Drive with Tip Toe Shifting was standard on Custom and optional on Deluxe DeSotos.

DeSoto, as well as Plymouth, enjoyed the best sales years in its history, DeSoto ending with a calendar total of 127,557 units. Despite this increase, DeSoto's market share decreased, dropping one notch to 14th for the year.

DeSoto S15 & S17
Convertible, Sportsman, Suburban ★★★★★
Club coupe, Carry All Sedan,
eight-passenger ★★★★
Station wagon ★★★
Four-door ★★ (Add ★ for V-8 engine)

DeSoto for 1951

DeSoto entered the 1951 model year under the same cloud of Korean War restrictions as the rest of the industry. Material shortages of aluminum, copper, and chromium, along with a hesitancy on the part of the government to place military orders or restrict production of civilian automobiles, played havoc with the car companies.

Mildly redesigned, the S15 DeSoto featured a sloped hood with stamped wind splits, leading to a massive nine-tooth grille and heavier front bumper. Among the more noticeable changes was deletion of the chrome trim between the hood and grille opening. The DeSoto coat of arms returned to the leading edge of the hood while an all-metal bust of Hernando rode atop the hood. Bodies were devoid of chrome trim with the exception of a rear fender spear, windshield trim, and beltline moldings. Model names remained the same, and the Deluxe line (S15-1) included a four-door sedan, club coupe, and the six-passenger Carry-All on the same 125.5-inch wheelbase. A single 139.5-inch wheelbase Deluxe, the four-door eight-passenger sedan, was also continued.

Custom models (coded S15-2) included all of the previous year's models with the exception of the wood body station wagon, which had been discontinued.

DeSoto's semi-automatic transmission was standard on Custom models and optional on Deluxes. No doubt some customers had to go without an automatic as National Production Authority restrictions kept the number of automatic equipped DeSotos at 65 percent of total production. A planned Hemi-head V-8 engine for DeSoto had to be delayed until the following year because machine tools were unavailable.

Calendar-year sales slipped slightly to 121,794 units, although DeSoto's market shared climbed to twelfth, where DeSoto would remain for the next three years.

DeSoto S15 & S17
Convertible, Sportsman, Suburban ★★★★★
Club coupe, Carry All Sedan,
eight-passenger ★★★★
Station wagon ★★★
Four-door ★★ (Add ★ for V-8 engine)

DeSoto for 1952

Like the rest of the corporate line, there was little change between the 1951 and 1952 DeSotos, at least at first. It took a sharp eye to notice the differences between the two model years. Block, rather than script, lettering on the hood, a different hood ornament, and revised taillamps were the major differences.

Because of the few changes, the 1952 DeSotos also carried the code of S15-1 for Deluxe and S15-2 for Custom trim. Serial numbers were bumped slightly to differentiate between the '51 and '52 models, but production figures for the two years were lumped together.

It wasn't until Valentine's Day, 1952, that the Firedome V-8 was introduced. Based on the Chrysler hemispherical-cylinder-head V-8 introduced the previous year, the over-square design

$3 \frac{5}{8} \times 3 \frac{11}{31}$ bore and stroke displaced 276 ci, pumping out 160 horsepower.

DeSoto's first eight-cylinder since 1930, the Firedome (S17) was basically a Custom with suitable changes to note the new powerplant. A newly designed hood with functional scoop (which was added to the Deluxe and Custom lines) and Firedome 8 fender script, along with a V-8 insignia on the deck lid, gave notice of the potent new engine. All three series rode on the 125.5-inch-wheelbase chassis and all three offered at least one 139.5-inch-wheelbase body style.

Transmission choices include manual shift with or without overdrive, Fluid Drive with Tip Toe shift or Top Toe Shift with Fluid Torque Drive as options. Fluid Torque Drive substituted a torque converter in place of the fluid coupling, providing a 2.34 to 1 torque multiplication. Also known as FluidMatic (similar to Plymouth's Hy-Drive), Fluid Torque Drive used engine oil to operate the transmission. It was optional only with the Firedome V-8. Also new for the year was power steering, electric window lifts, and tinted windows. Some 1952 DeSotos may also be found with power brakes, an option not offered until 1955 but released by MoPar parts as a retrofit service package for these models.

Deluxe DeSotos were available in club coupe, four-door or Carry-All body types, or long-wheelbase eight-passenger sedan (some long-wheelbase six-passenger taxis were also built). The Custom series continued the four-door, club coupe, Sportsman hardtop, convertible, and four-door station wagon along with the extended-wheelbase eight-passenger sedan or nine-passenger Suburban.

Firedome V-8 DeSotos included a four-door sedan, club coupe, Sportsman two-door hardtop, convertible coupe, four-door station wagon, and a single long-wheelbase eight-passenger sedan.

Calendar-year production fell to 97,558 units but DeSoto remained firmly in 12th place.

DeSoto S16-S17
Convertible, Sportsman ★★★★★
Eight-passenger, Club coupe ★★★
(add ★ for V-8)
Station wagon, four-door ★★ (add ★ for V-8)

DeSoto for 1953

Nineteen fifty-three marked DeSoto's—as well as Plymouth's—Silver Anniversary, yet the corporation chose not to dwell on the subject, nor build any anniversary models to commemorate the event. As mentioned earlier, this may have been due to the fact both Buick and Ford were celebrating Golden Anniversaries.

A new body style for 1950 was the Sportsman hardtop convertible. *Terry Huxhold*

There were major changes, however. A completely new body—again of the Keller "larger on the inside, smaller on the outside" dictate—was carried off without as stubby looking a car as either Dodge or Plymouth. The wheelbase remained at 125.5 inches for all models except the extended-wheelbase eight-passenger sedan, which used the previous year's body with the addition of the '53's curved, one-piece windshield.

At long last the names Deluxe and Custom were laid to rest, replaced by Powermaster for all six-cylinder models, while the Firedome name remained for V-8-powered cars. Eleven protruding grille teeth marked the new DeSoto's front end, the teeth coming to a peak under the center of the hood, with oval park lamps under the headlamps in the grille cavity. Integral rear fenders were a marked change from years past (the extended-wheelbase eight-passenger sedan, which used the 1952 body, still had detachable rear fenders).

The club coupe appeared to be little more than a two-door sedan (and is many times incorrectly called that).

There were no changes under the hood of either series (the Powermaster was coded S18, and the Firedome was coded S16). Horsepower in the six remained at 116, and it was 160 for the V-8. Transmission choices included manual with or without overdrive, semi-automatic Fluid Drive with Tip Toe Shift, and Fluid Torque Drive. Added to the option list for this year was air conditioning in January and chrome wire wheels.

With the end of hostilities in Korea, chrome trim became more abundant and may have marked an effort by Chrysler's new head of styling to liven up the cars.

Missing from the Powermaster line was the Carry-All sedan, replaced by the four-door

station wagon. Also in the Powermaster line-up was a four-door sedan, club coupe, Sportsman two-door hardtop, and the long-wheelbase eight-passenger sedan—a car that would have seemed better suited with V-8 power!

This entire line-up was repeated in the Firedome series, with the addition of a convertible coupe.

Calendar-year sales set an all-time record high (as did those of Plymouth) of 129,963 units, again keeping DeSoto locked into 12th place.

DeSoto S19-S20
Convertible, Sportsman ★★★★★
Eight-passenger, Club coupe ★★★
(add ★ for V-8)
Station wagon, four-door ★★ (add ★ for V-8)

DeSoto for 1954

From outward glances, the 1954 DeSoto was little changed from the previous year. Most noticeable was a reduction in grille teeth, back again to just nine. Bumpers were more rounded and ornamentation was rearranged, but the word for year 1954 was "PowerFlite." Chrysler's first true fully automatic transmission, PowerFlite combined a torque converter with a two-speed gearbox. No longer was there a need for a clutch pedal because drivers could shift from neutral to forward or reverse without needing to use their left foot. Optional at $189 on all models, Power-Flite prooved to be a popular accessory for both Powermaster six and Firedome V-8s.

Styling changes for the year included a nine-tooth grille centered between circular outboard parking lamps, all riding on the same floating bar in the grille cavity. The prominent "V" on the hood surrounding the DeSoto coat of arms and hood scoop were carried over from 1953.

Powermaster (S20) body styles included a club coupe, four-door sedan, Sportsman two-door hardtop, and four-door station wagon on the 125.5-inch-wheelbase chassis, and an eight-passenger sedan on the 139.5-inch chassis. The wagon continued to use the 1949 DeSoto body with detachable rear fenders, as did the eight-passenger sedan.

Firedomes (series S19) offered the same line-up, with the addition of a convertible coupe. Updating the Sportsman hardtop was a new one-piece rear window. Joining the line for the spring selling season was the Coronado sedan. Differing in paint and trim, the Coronado borrowed its bright work from the Chrysler New Yorker, adding Coronado medallions to the rear fenders and on the C-pillar. (The Coronado name was later relegated for use by Plymouth on a series of extended-wheelbase sedans built for

Nineteen fifty DeSotos can be easily identified by the color panel in the center of the grille. The Custom Subur-ban offered the best of both worlds between a passenger sedan and a station wagon. *National DeSoto Club*

export markets in the late 1950s and early 1960s.)

Powermaster sixes, now in their last year, still churned out 116 horsepower from 250 ci. The Firedome V-8, with increased compression, now pumped out 170 horses.

Although 1953 had set all-time production records, it soon became evident buyers were flocking away from Chrysler products. Sales and production hit all-time lows as evidenced by a decline in DeSoto deliveries to just 69,844 units for the calendar year. Despite the drop, DeSoto remained 12th in sales.

DeSoto S21-S22
Convertible, Sportsman, Special
Sportsman ★★★★★
Coronado Four-door, station wagon ★★★
Four-door ★★

DeSoto for 1955
It was the called "The Forward Look"—and it came none too soon.

Under the direction of Virgil Exner, every car in the corporate line received a major restyling. All new bodies that emphasized "the forward look of motion" were the order of the day, in an attempt to undo the damage done by Keller's boxy dictates. Designed in just 18 months, Chrysler Corporation borrowed $250 million from the Prudential Insurance Company to affect the change. Exner himself penned the lines of the Chrysler, DeSoto, and Imperial, leaving his associate Maury Baldwin to tackle Dodge and Plymouth.

What evolved was a line of cars that were lower, longer, wider, and modern in every sense of the word. Carrying on the tradition set in 1941, DeSoto featured a toothy grille, this time with seven teeth nestled between protruding "buck teeth" bumper overriders. Oblong parking lamps at the extreme ends of the grille cavity completed the front end. Separate letters spelled out DeSoto beneath what appeared to be a hood scoop-type ornament, which also carried the DeSoto medallion. Headlamps were deeply set into chromed rims.

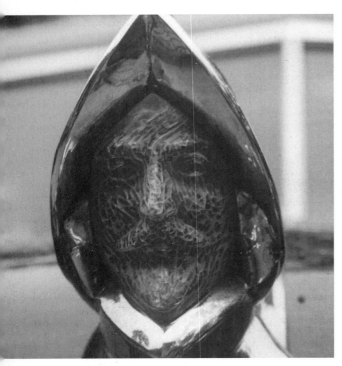

This bust of Hernando DeSoto rode proudly on the hood.

Along the side, a forward-pointing swept spear of trim provided color break lines for two-tone paint. This design, too, would become a DeSoto trademark for the next few years (on Fireflite models only; Firedomes were decorated with a single body length trim strip). Vertical taillamps capped the rear fenders. Across the deck lid DeSoto was again spelled out in individual letters set above a prominent "V."

Again, two series were offered: the S22 Firedome, which took its place at the bottom of the sales line-up, and the upscale S21 Fireflite. Under the hood, the venerable old six had been put out to pasture and for the remainder of its days, DeSoto would have V-8 power. Built on a 126-inch-wheelbase chassis (shared with Chrysler), the DeSoto Hemi now boasted 291 ci from a bore and stroke of 3.72x3.344 inches. Firedome's version put out 185 horsepower, and the Fireflite's produced an even 200, the difference coming from use of a four-barrel carburetor in the Fireflite.

Transmission choices still included a three-speed manual with or without overdrive and the fully automatic two-speed PowerFlite. Fireflites equipped with PowerFlite were fitted with a water-cooled transmission, while Firedomes had an air-cooled version. Like the rest of the corporate line, the PowerFlite's shift lever protruded from the instrument panel, but it would stay there just one year, as DeSoto adopted push buttons in 1956.

Firedomes came in four-door, convertible, Sportsman hardtop, Special hardtop coupe models, as well as the four-door station wagon. Fireflites were available in four-door sedan, convertible coupe, and Sportsman hardtop coupe styles.

Added again for the spring selling season was the Coronado sedan. Based on the Fireflite four-door, the Coronado offered DeSoto's first three-tone paint scheme of light green, black, and white applied to the top, color sweep, and body. Customers were given the choice of where the colors were applied, resulting in six possible color combinations. Coronado upholstery was leather. Extended-wheelbase sedans were dropped as sales had never really justified their existence other than the taxi trade or for use as professional cars. Chrysler and DeSoto had been among the last holdouts (with the exception of luxury builders such as Cadillac and Packard) to manufacture them.

With calendar-year sales of 129,767, DeSoto sales were about 200 cars less than 1953. It would prove to be DeSoto's last high-water mark. DeSoto once again captured the number twelve spot in industry sales.

DeSoto S23-S24
Pacesetter Convertible, regular convertible, Sportsman two- & four-door hardtop ★★★★★
Seville two and four-door ★★★★
Station wagon ★★★
Four-door ★★

DeSoto for 1956
Having received all-new bodies for 1955, DeSoto, like the rest of the corporate line, had to make due with a warmed-over restyles for 1956.

Most noticeable was DeSoto's rear quarters, which began to sprout the first vestiges of tail fins. Frontal appearance was changed by switching to a mesh grille, replacing the familiar toothy grilles of years past.

Again, two series were DeSoto's mainstays, the Firedome (S23) and Fireflite (S24). Before the end of the year, two specialty models would be added, both of which would become the most memorable DeSotos of all.

DeSoto announced in January it had been chosen to provide the pace car for the Indianapolis 500. This honor was a first for DeSoto, and the selected car was a Fireflite convertible. Built with a stock engine and beefed-up suspension, the car was appropriately dubbed the "Pacesetter." The contract with the Speedway called for two cars suitable for use as the pace car, along with 20

This extended-wheelbase 1951 Suburban is one of just 600 such cars built for 1951-52. *Mark Chandler*

support vehicles of various types for official use. It wasn't long until the Pacesetter convertible was made available to the general public.

Painted white with gold trim, the Pacesetter was identical in all aspects to the actual pace car with the exception of the pace car's lettering. All Pacesetter convertibles were equipped with power seats, electric windows, electric clock, Jiffy Jet windshield washer, special gold wheel covers, "Forward Look" emblems over a checkered flag background, gold mesh grille (with silver V medallion), and special air scoop medallion. Because the Pacesetter was based on the Fireflite convertible, it is unknown how many of the 1,485 Fireflite convertibles were built as pace car replicas.

Nineteen fifty-six was Chrysler Corporation's year for factory hot rods. It had begun with the C300 Chryslers of 1955 carrying over to both Plymouth and DeSoto for 1956, with Plymouth calling it the Fury, and DeSoto naming it the Adventurer.

Actually a sub-series of the S24 Fireflite, the Adventurer took its name from a DeSoto dream car built in 1954. The dream car had been a close-coupled four-passenger coupe built on a 111-inch wheelbase. The production Adventurer was a hardtop coupe (based on the Fireflite Sportsman) fitted with a special 341-ci, 320-horsepower "Hemi" engine. Enlarged valve ports, high-lift camshaft, larger-diameter valves, heavy-duty valve springs, modified slipper-skirt pistons, heavy-duty connecting rods, and a shot-peened crankshaft topped with two Carter four-barrel carbs meant the Adventurer was one powerful automobile.

Standard equipment included power brakes, whitewall tires, dual tailpipe extensions, dual outside rear-view mirrors, rear-mounted manual radio antennas, padded instrument panel, power front seat, electric windows, windshield washers, electric clock, and heavy-duty suspension.

Officially introduced as the Golden Adventurer on February 18, 1956, the car has often been confused with the Pacesetter convertible. Both shared the same gold vinyl with brown tweed-insert upholstery, black carpets, gold dash with black pad, and ivory-and-gold steering wheel. Both also had a stylized eagle sewn into the rear-seat backrest.

Competing with the Kaiser Traveler was the 1951 DeSoto Carry-All. From outward appearances the car was a regular sedan. *John Jung*

Pacesetter convertibles were white with gold sweep spears, while the Golden Adventurer was available in four different combinations of white and gold, gold or white, black and gold or gold and black, and white and black or black and white. Pacesetter convertibles were fitted with a gold top lined in white. Special turbine-blade gold wheel covers and gold trim were shared between the two cars. Adding to the confusion between the two cars was the fact the 1956 Adventurer was chosen to pace the Pikes Peak Hill Climb on July 4th.

A Golden Adventurer competed at Daytona Speed Weeks in Florida, recording a top speed of 137 miles per hour. Later, the same car was clocked at 144 miles per hour on the high-bank track at Chrysler's Chelsea proving grounds. Golden Adventurers were rare even when new, as only 996 were built.

DeSoto's bread-and-butter Firedome models were powered by an enlarged 330-ci Hemi, developing 230 horsepower, coupled to a standard

The interior of the Carry-All featured wood paneling and skid strips. The rear seat folded down to reveal a completely open cargo area from the back of the front seat to the deck lid. *John Jung*

three-speed manual transmission with or without overdrive. PowerFlite was standard on the Fireflite, and a $189 option on Firedomes. Fireflites also used the 330-ci Hemi, which through the use of a four-barrel carb, developed 255 horsepower. All cars switched to 12-volt electrical systems to meet the increased demands of power accessories. Push-button transmission controls came into use with the 1956 models as an across-the-board corporate change.

Restyled body side trim still incorporated the color break line for two- and three-tone paint schemes. Firedomes could easily be spotted by their chrome-plated headlamp bezels in contrast to the Fireflites' deeply hooded, painted housing. Nestled beneath the slightly upraised fin sat a triple tier of taillamps, a styling cue that would set DeSoto apart over the next few years. The color sweep spear was standard on all Fireflite Sportsman models and the convertible.

Firedomes offered two sets of hardtops, the less-expensive taking on the moniker "Seville," in either two-door or four-door hardtop form. Ironically, Cadillac would also offer a Seville model in 1956, although the name would seem more appropriate for DeSoto, as Seville was the name of the Spanish city that served as the departure point for Hernando DeSoto when he made his trip to the New World. Selling for $99 to $121 less than the Sportsman, Sevilles outsold them on a four-to-one ratio. The upscale model was the Sportsman hardtop, again in a two- or four-door format (four-door hardtops were produced by all divisions of the corporation for 1956), along with a conventional four-door, four-door wagon, and convertible coupe.

Fireflites offered just one set of hardtops, the Sportsman in either two- or four-door form, a four-door sedan, and two convertibles in regular or Pacesetter trim levels. Unusual options for the year included a gasoline-fired heater, steering wheel hub-mounted clock (it wound itself as the wheel was turned!), and an under-dash record player called Hiway Hi-Fi, playing through the car radio. Station wagon buyers could also purchase an optional "kiddie seat" that mounted behind the rear seat with room for two pint-size passengers. DeSotos were available in any of 14 solid colors and in any of 84 two-tone combinations!

Although extended-wheelbase models had been discontinued in 1955, there was still enough demand for specialty models that DeSoto's fleet sales office contracted with outside suppliers to build both extended-wheelbase, multi-door airport limousines, and raised-roof industrial ambulances. Never built in great numbers, the Memphis Coach six-door, three-seat airport limousine featured a 3-foot stretch.

DeSoto sales were off slightly for 1956, as they were for the rest of the industry. Still, calendar-year sales of 104,090 were among the best in DeSoto's history, enough to move it up one notch to end the year in 11th place. Nineteen fifty-six would also mark a high point for DeSoto as it outsold Chrysler for the first and only time.

DeSoto 1957
Sportsman two and four-door hardtop, convertible, Adventurer ★★★★★
Nine-passenger station wagon ★★★
Four-door and six-passenger wagon ★★

DeSoto for 1957
It was an unprecedented move—especially for Chrysler Corporation—but DeSoto (along with every other Chrysler division) was all-new, from the bottom up.

In an industry where the norm was utilizing a body shell for three consecutive years, Chrysler scrapped everything after just two years.

Starting with a longer, wider frame riding on unique longitudinal torsion bars with ball joints, wider wheels, and smaller rims, DeSoto was longer, lower, and wider than any preceding car. DeSoto shared "Torsion-Aire" with the rest of the corporation, and *Motor Trend* magazine named all five Chrysler lines as its "Car Of The Year." But there was more than just new engineering to crow about.

Exner's styling of the 1957 DeSoto took the dart shape of his earlier concept cars: long, smooth sides with a gently rising tailfin beginning just aft of the front door, rising to what seemed, at the time, to be towering heights. Falling down the back side of the fins were the now-famous triple-tower taillamps residing above oval-shaped exhaust ports built into the rear bumper. At the front, a flattened oval grille and bumper combination rode above protruding bumper overriders so reminiscent of prior toothy grilles. Nestled into the fender tops were headlamps in either single or dual pattern, depending on which state the car would be sold in (eight states had not certified the use of dual headlamps when the 1957 came on line). A double-compound curved windshield folded neatly into the A-pillars without creating the "dog-leg" windshield post found on GM and Ford products, as well as curving into the roof. And then there was the "razor-thin" roofline, giving the cars a light and airy appearance. It was a stunning design that brought customers running.

Plymouth's advertising campaign of "Suddenly, it's 1960;" spilled over to the rest of the corporate offerings. Truly, the cars were three years—heck, light years—ahead of the competition, especially perennial style-leader General Motors. GM's

The 1952 Custom Club Coupe is often incorrectly referred to as a "two-door." *National DeSoto Club*

1957 products were at the end of a three-year cycle and the 1958 bodies were already wrapped up. The shock waves felt from Chrysler's styling coup caused GM top brass to counter act, scrapping the 1958 after just one year in a mad scramble to redesign the product line in time for the 1959 model run. Chrysler Corporation sales soared to new heights but the euphoria would be short-lived. Poor quality, shoddy workmanship, and rust problems would soon plague these outstanding designs, causing a slump in sales that would prove to be nearly fatal. Victory would come at a terrible price.

DeSoto buyers were given three model choices for 1957, adding a line of shorter-wheel-base models called the Firesweep (S27).

In designing the 1957 models, orders had come from above that all Chrysler Corporation station wagons would share the shame body, be they DeSoto, Plymouth, Dodge, or Chrysler. This entailed designing the body so the entire "front clip" from any particular make could be bolted to it. Through clever engineering, this was accomplished by making sure all door skin panels would mate to the front fenders. The only draw back to this move was that all wagons would rely on Plymouth rear fenders. Yet the DeSoto rear fenders canted rearward, while the Plymouth wagon fender canted forward!

Chrysler had a long habit of playing name games, making one car into another, as witnessed by the Canadian and export Dodges which were thinly disguised Plymouths, as well as the export-only SP series DeSotos, which were also little more than a Plymouth in drag.

This time it was Dodge's turn to dress up, to become the Firesweep DeSoto. Built in the Dodge assembly plant, Dodge hood and front fenders were modified to look like the full-size DeSoto. Powered by a 325-ci, 245-horsepower Dodge polyspherical Red Ram "wedge" V-8 on a 122-inch wheelbase, Firesweeps were available as a Sportsman hardtop in either two- or four-door form, as a regular four-door sedan, and in either of two station wagon models: the four-door, six-passenger "Shopper" or four-door, nine-passenger "Explorer." The nine-passenger featured a rear-facing third seat, an idea pirated from the 1956 Plymouth Plainsman concept wagon that debuted the year before.

The "Shopper" carried its spare tire behind a removable panel in the right rear fender (another idea taken from the Plainsman). The "Explorer" on the other hand, eliminated the spare

Nineteen fifty-three DeSotos received all-new sheet metal, but the marque's Silver Anniversary was not noted. Powermaster name plates on this car indicate this club coupe is powered by a six. *Pete McNicholl*

altogether, relying on Goodyear's Captive Air tires to get them to their destination. The Goodyear Captive Air claimed it would "last as far as a tank of gas will take you." The Firesweep would make its appearance only in the United States, Chrysler Canada was building only the Firedome and Fireflite. Adding the Firesweep gave DeSoto price penetration into 91 percent of

the market. It was claimed that DeSoto models covered everything except the low-price market (which held the lion's share of the industry).

The previous year's low-priced line, the Firedome (S25), moved up to the middle rung on the sales ladder. A true DeSoto, it rode the same 126-inch wheelbase as before. Both it and the upscale Fireflite (S26) were powered by 341-ci V-8, the Firedome version pumping out 270 horses, and the Fireflite producing 295. Firedome models included the Sportsman hardtop with two- or four-doors, a four-door sedan, and convertible.

As the top-of-the-line, the Fireflite series offered every model offered by the other two, including the Shopper and Explorer station wagons, four-door sedan, and both Sportsman hardtops.

Making its debut in December was the Adventurer, first in hardtop form and later joined by a convertible. A high-performance luxury automobile, both Adventurers came in white or black with gold trim and most every option as standard equipment. Built on the 126-inch-wheelbase chassis, the Adventurer was powered by a dual four-barrel 345-ci Hemi V-8 pumping out 345 horsepower.

Producing 345 horses from 345 cubes was an engineer's dream—one horsepower per cubic inch—but it was Chevrolet, with its optional Rochester fuel-injected 283 Corvette V-8, that got

DeSoto station wagons were rarely seen, even when new. This 1954 Powermaster wagon is one of just 500

built for the year, and it is in original condition. *Jim Benjaminson*

While convertibles are the most desirable collector cars, sedans like this 1954 Firedome are more plentiful. *John Jung*

the credit and publicity, not DeSoto! The 283-hp Chevrolet was rarely seen (it was also offered as an option in the full-size Bel Air convertible as well as the Corvette), but neither marque sold enough of either engine to be noticeable. The 345-horsepower Adventurer saw just 1,650 hardtops and 300 convertibles built.

Regardless, DeSoto had been the first to make such an engine as the standard power-plant for the series. Adventurers also sported dual headlamps as standard equipment, while Firesweeps, Firedomes, and Fireflites were designed to accommodate either single or dual lamps, depending on where the vehicle was to be sold. (Eight of the 48 states had not yet made them legal went the 1957 DeSotos went on the market.)

TorqueFlite, Chrysler's new three-speed automatic transmission, was made optional on both the Firesweep and Firedome, but buyers could still choose PowerFlite on Firesweep models. Joining the option list this year was a six-way power front seat. Nineteen fifty-seven DeSotos were available in any of 14 solid colors or 32

The Exner-designed 1955 Firedome Special helped lead the way for Chrysler to be crowned king in the styling department. *John Jung*

Buttoned up for an inclement day is this 1954 Firedome droptop. *John Jung*

DeSoto entered the world of high-performance personal luxury cars with the 1956 Adventurer. Buyers were given the choice of white and gold or black and gold trim. *National DeSoto Club*

reversible two-tone combinations. (Firesweeps pared the reversible two-tone combinations to 25.)

Fleet sales continued to offer industrial ambulance and hearse conversions, as well as special seven-passenger sedans. Also available was a line of DeSoto police specials and special taxi models (the taxis having been dropped two years earlier).

Nineteen fifty-seven would prove to be DeSoto's third-best year. With the addition of the Firesweep, it was the only medium-priced car to enjoy a sales gain over the previous year. DeSoto still placed 11th with calendar-year sales of 117,747 units. Nineteen fifty-seven had been a pivotal year for DeSoto, unfortunately it would be all downhill from here.

DeSoto 1958

Sportsman two-and four-door hardtop, convertible, Adventurer ★★★★★
Nine-passenger station wagon ★★★
Four-door and six-passenger wagon ★★

DeSoto for 1958

In the second year of its body cycle, the 1958 DeSoto received only a mild facelift.

Chosen to pace the 1956 Indianapolis 500, DeSoto put together a special Pacesetter convertible. Both the Pacesetter and Adventurer shared high-performance V-8 engines along with special gold trim. *National DeSoto Club*

A new front grille-bumper, with round parking lamps added below the main bar and a revised medallion, were the only noticeable changes except for the dual headlamps, which were now standard on all models. Trim changes included moving the color sweep higher up on the body side, sweeping upward as it reached the rear of the car.

Model and body style choices remained the same as for 1957 except for the addition of a convertible to the Firesweep line (again Canadian buyers were deprived of the Firesweep series).

It was under the hood where major changes had taken place. The Hemi, although among the most efficient and powerful engines ever built, was expensive to build, and it was heavier than desirable, much like carrying an anchor over the front wheels of the car. Hot rodders nicknamed it "The Elephant." Eighteen months prior to the introduction of the 1958 models, Chrysler engineers began work on a "clean sheet of paper" design to replace the Hemi. It would be another classic design, one that most MoPar fans instantly recognize. It was the engine that became the 383, 400, 413, and 440 of later years. In the Firesweep (still on its 122-inch wheelbase Dodge chassis) it was 350-ci producing 280 horsepower in standard form, with 295 horses optional.

In the Firedome and Fireflite, it was 361 ci, with Firedomes running with 295 horses, the Fireflite having 305. The Adventurer, too, received the 361 developing 345 horsepower from dual-four-barrel carburetors.

Optional for the Adventurer was the short-lived Bendix Electrojector fuel injection, which promised 355 horsepower. Trouble-prone and unreliable, the Bendix system proved unworkable, and the few cars built with the option were later recalled to have the unit replaced by the standard dual-four-barrel carburetor system. No accurate production figures for the Bendix system have been found, and although it is rumored that at least a dozen DeSotos were sold with the system, none are known to exist today. Externally the only clue to the car's powerplant was a fuel injection medallion on the front fender.

The 1956 Golden Adventurer is shown in white and gold. *Jim Benjaminson*

The engine compartment of the Golden Adventurer was filled with a dual four-barrel carburetor Hemi-head V-8. *Jim Benjaminson*

Beginning with the 1958 models, Chrysler Corporation began a new series of engineering codes for its cars, using letters of the alphabet to designate model years. Under the new system, the Firesweep became an LS1-L. (The first L indicating 1958, the S indicating DeSoto, the numeral 1 indicating the low-line series, and the second L designating the low-price line. Cars would be designated as L for low-price, M for medium-price, H for high-price, and S for specialty models such as the Adventurer.) The Firedome was now an LS2-M, the Fireflite was an LS3-H, and the Adventurer was an LS3-S.

DeSoto again gave buyers 14 solid colors or 86 two-tone combinations to choose from (Firesweeps pared the two-tones to just 80 combinations).

DeSoto built its two-millionth car during the year, which happened to be its 30th Anniversary as well. Nineteen fifty-eight was a recession year for the industry and automobile sales fell accordingly. Some were hit harder than others, but it was the medium-price cars that were hit the hardest, and there was new competition on the block, as Ford Motor Company unveiled the Edsel. DeSoto sales had fallen like a rock:

Swept wing styling in its purest form, the 1957 Fireflite Sportsman two-door hardtop. *National DeSoto Club*

calendar-year sales managed to climb to just 36,556 units. Despite the drop, DeSoto still managed to cling to 13th place for the year. Regardless, the corporation decided to move DeSoto production out of its own factory and into Chrysler's Jefferson Avenue plant. To many industry observers, DeSoto was in deep trouble.

DeSoto 1959
Sportsman two and four-door hardtop, convertible, Adventurer ★★★★★
Nine-passenger station wagon ★★★
Four-door and six-passenger wagon ★★

DeSoto for 1959
Now in the third and final year of its styling cycle, Chrysler Corporation found itself again at a disadvantage against its rivals. Both Ford and GM were fielding new cars for the year. The GM cars among the wildest creations ever to hit the highways. Realizing the need for change, $150 million were appropriated to redesign Chrysler's

The 1958 Fireflite convertible displays its "signal tower" taillamps and recessed license plate. It was a view seen by many motorists who tried unsuccessfully to catch up! *H. DeSoto, M.D.*

The 1958 Fireflite Sportsman Spring Special. *National DeSoto Club*

products lines, and most of the money went to restyle Plymouth. DeSoto, whose sales had fallen by 75 percent in 1958, would have to be content with a minor facelift of front and side trim.

DeSoto's familiar wide-oval mouth became busier: two air scoops adorned with small raised ribs rode above a larger lower "mouth," and the bumper overriders were capped with rubber tips. A conventional rectangular-mesh grille rode above these gaping holes, running between the headlamps. Letters spelling out DeSoto ran across the hood, which was now shorn of medallions.

Side trim again featured a sweep spear. Looking like an elongated check mark, the spear dipped behind the rear wheelwell before sweeping up to the crest of the tailfin. Around back, the familiar triple-tower taillamps again appeared. A busier rear bumper incorporated the license plate holder (it had nestled in its own cove on the deck lid of the 1957-1958 DeSotos). Two overriders, also capped by rubber, completed the package.

The 1959 model line-up included the Firesweep (MS1-L) on its own unique 122-inch wheelbase, the Firedome (MS2-M), the Fireflite (MS3-H), and the Adventurer (also MS3-H) retaining the 126-inch wheelbase of years past.

The standard powerplant for the Firesweep was the 295-horsepower, 361-ci V-8, but buyers could specify an optional engine: the same 350-horsepower, 383 found under the hood of the Adventurer.

Raising the hood of the senior cars revealed a 383-ci big-block V-8, the Firedome running a 305-horse version compared to the Fireflite's 325-horse version. Like the Firesweep, either series could be fitted with the optional 350-horsepower Adventurer 383.

Adventurer engines continued to utilize dual-four-barrel carburetors and hotter cams to achieve its 350-horsepower rating, and all 383s demanded the use of premium fuel. TorqueFlite transmissions were included as standard equipment on all series.

Firesweep body styles included the Sportsman hardtops, in two- or four-doors, a regular four-door sedan, convertible, six-passenger

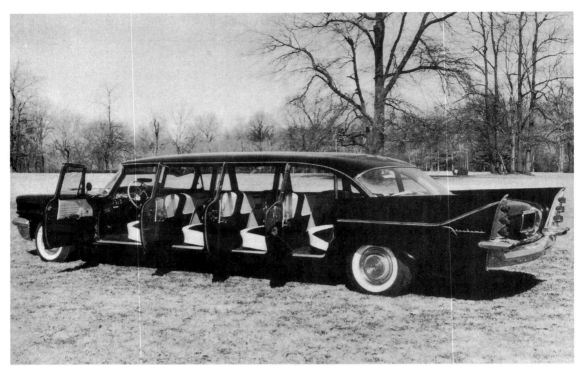

Built to special order through DeSoto fleet sales, this 1958 Firedome eight-door sedan was built as an airport limousine. *National DeSoto Club*

Shopper, or nine-passenger Explorer station wagon. Canadian buyers continued to find the Firesweep missing from their sales catalogs.

These same models were available in Firedome trim with the exception of the two wagon models, which reappeared in the Fireflite line along with the Sportsman hardtops and sedan.

The Adventurer coupe and convertible retained its two distinctive color schemes of white or black with gold anodized trim. As the high-performance personal luxury offering, the Adventurer had whitewall tires, dual exhausts, power steering, and power brakes as standard equipment.

Also standard was the novel "Sports Swivel Seat." Designed to provide semi-bucket-type seating with a fold-down center armrest, the Sport Swivel Seat could seat three abreast if desired, but its main feature was that the outer driver and passenger seats could be unlatched to swivel outward. The idea was to make entry and exit into the vehicle easier. Sport Swivel Seats were available manually or, as an option, power-operated. In later years, the seats would be designed to automatically swivel out when the

door was opened. Swivel seats never really caught on, although they were cataloged for the next few years. The seats were optional on all Fireflites except station wagons, although some sources disagree on whether they were available on the Fireflite four-door sedan.

Sales rose only slightly for the year, to 41,423 units. Rumors began to circulate that DeSoto's days were numbered, a rumor Chrysler continued to deny. Industry insiders, predicting Chrysler Corporation would switch to unibody construction in the near future, assumed DeSoto would not live to make the switch—despite a 13th place showing for 1959, DeSoto still had a little life left to it.

DeSoto 1960
Two- and four-door hardtop ★★★★
Four-door ★★

DeSoto for 1960
Things were changing rapidly at DeSoto but at least it was still part of the family. DeSoto made the switch to unibody construction, utilizing

The 1959 Adventurer continued to be DeSoto's high-performance luxury car. White and gold trim helped distinguish the Adventurer from lesser models. *Brent Walker*

what was (and had been in the past) a Chrysler body reskinned to give DeSoto its own identity, at least until 1960. Now it took a good, long look to differentiate between the two marques.

A flat, drop-center grille dominated the front view of the DeSoto. (Could the design have been pirated from Exner's 1954 Adventurer I dream car?) And there were dual headlamps nestled into the upper corners of the grille. Parking lamps rode in the far corners of the grille cavity while the front bumper dipped in a vee at the center of the car. The familiar sweep-spear side trim was narrowed to a straight band running from front to rear. Now called "Stabilizers," the fins began at the center of the front door and swept upward, canting as they rose to the rear of the car. Gone were the triple-tower taillamps, replaced by a full lens cut into the rear of the tailfin. The rear bumper featured upswept "windwings," which were repeated in lesser form around the license plate opening, which rode under the deck lid opening.

Model offerings were paired to just two series. What had been the top-line Fireflite (PS1-L) now became the bottom of the line. The high-performance Adventurer had gone by the wayside, replaced by a three-body line-up (all Adventurers coded PS3-M) that matched those in the Fireflite line: four-door sedan, two-door hardtop, and four-door hardtop sedan. Convertibles and station wagons had been relegated to the history books at DeSoto.

Both the Fireflite and Adventurer now rode a 122-inch wheelbase shared with the Chrysler Windsor and Dodge Matador/Polara. Fireflites' standard engine was the 295-horsepower 361 with the 325-horse 383 as an option. Standard in the Adventurer was the 305-horse 383 with choice of optional 383s rated at 325 or 330 horses, and the 330 featuring ram-induction manifolds. TorqueFlite was now an option on all Fireflite models, although it is doubtful many left the factory with "standard" manual-shift transmissions. TorqueFlite was standard on all Adventurers.

As sales continued their dizzying slide, rumors of DeSoto's demise continued to appear in the trade press. *Motor Trend* magazine, in its February 1960 issue, answered the question as to whether Chrysler would drop DeSoto claiming "...officials say they

The 1960 Fireflite grille looked similar to that of the 1954 Adventurer show car. *National DeSoto Club*

have no intention of pulling the plug, claiming they have plans for DeSoto cars up through 1962. There are those who say, however, that any new DeSotos planned will be luxury versions of the Valiant."

That rumor seemed plausible. The Plymouth and DeSoto divisions had been merged into one division on July 1, 1959, and 39 days later, on August 8, a second realignment brought forth the Plymouth-Valiant-DeSoto division.

With just 19,411 sales for calendar year 1960, *Motor Trend*, in its November 1960 issue, reported that "many observers seriously doubted whether DeSoto would introduce any car, let alone a new car for 1961."

For DeSoto, suddenly it *was* 1960, but there would at least be a last gasp for 1961.

1961 DeSoto
Two- and four-door hardtop ★★★★

DeSoto for 1961
The first of the last DeSotos began coming off the Jefferson Avenue assembly line in August of 1960 with

Canted tail fins beginning at the front door gave the 1960 four-door hardtop a massive appearance. *National DeSoto Club*

Canted headlamps leading to canted rear fenders gave the 1961 DeSoto a distinctive appearance, as did the unusual "air scoop" above the grille, a feature more people disliked. *Robert and Gail Kruse*

the new-model announcement date set for October 14.

Again based on the 122-inch-wheelbase Chrysler body, the car was changed enough to make identification over the previous model easy. Canted dual headlamps (shared with Chrysler) slid into a grille cavity featuring rectangular crate work. Matching the angle of the headlamps, bumper tips protected angled parking lamp lenses nestled into the corner of the fenders. It was the protruding air scoop above the normal grille that gave the DeSoto its distinctive (most said odd) appearance. Around back, new taillamps filled the notch at the end of the canted tailfins. The ribbed deck lid (four embossed ribs and a chrome-trimmed center rib) with the letters "DeSoto" widely spaced across the deck lid broke up the expanses of sheet metal. Back-up lamp lenses were fitted into the cove under the deck lid, with the license plate centered above a plain rear bumper.

Coded the RS1-L series, there were no longer any model names associated with the marque— no more Adventurer, Fireflite, Firedome, or Firesweep. It was now known simply as DeSoto.

Only two body styles were cataloged, a two-door hardtop and four-door hardtop. Power brakes, power steering, and TorqueFlite were all optional, as was the Hiway Hi-Fi introduced back in 1956. The only engine was the 265-horsepower 361.

Most observers wondered why anyone had even bothered with a 1961 model—including corporate brass. Notification of the decision to discontinue DeSoto came on November 18, 1960, when dealers received a telegram reading: "Chrysler Corporation is discontinuing production of the 1961 DeSoto. Your factory dealer council has been informed of the decision. Sound business judgment dictates concentrating selling effort in the low priced segment of the market where volume potential has been steadily improving. With two highly acceptable entries, Plymouth and Valiant, your profit and volume forecast is excellent. Public reception of these fine cars has been gratifying and confirms that another high volume year is ahead for all of us. Letter follows."

It was signed by E. C. Quinn, General Manager, Sales Division, Chrysler Motors Corporation.

In its last year, the 1961 DeSotos were available only as a two-door or four-door hardtop sedan. From this angle, one has to wonder why more weren't sold. Just 911 two-door hardtops were built. *Robert and Gail Kruse*

The final DeSoto rolled out of Jefferson Avenue November 30, 1960. The final count was dismal, just 911 two-door hardtops and 2,123 four-door hardtops.

What killed DeSoto? The blame has been laid on many factors, including Chrysler Corporation's lack of interest in the car; a realignment of divisions resulting in competition from the Chrysler Windsor and upscale Dodges, which invaded DeSoto's marketplace; as well as an overcrowded medium-price car market and the economic recession of 1958.

Although DeSoto had claimed its 1957 models penetrated 91 percent of the market in "all but the low-priced field," it must be remembered Chevrolet and Ford sold over half the new cars in the United States. The remainder of the market had to be divided too many ways. DeSoto joined a list of ten U.S. auto makers who went out of business in the period between 1950 and 1960, all of them competing in the same middle-price market. It was a sad ending to a once-grand and glorious marque. Chrysler Canada's 1958 DeSoto sales catalog had read "DeSoto for 1958 Bids Farewell To The Past." Now it could read simply DeSoto Bids Farewell.

Had there been a 1962 DeSoto, this is most likely what it would have looked like. Prototype models that were photographed indicated DeSoto was planning a convertible along with other models.

This was the proposed 1962 DeSoto Adventurer sedan.

Chapter 5

Export DeSoto Vehicles

From 1937 through 1961, Chrysler Corporation built and sold a series of "junior" DeSotos for sale only in export markets. Virtually unknown to most collectors in the United States, these "junior" DeSotos were based on the smaller Plymouth body shell and used, in most cases, look-alike grilles, with real DeSoto nameplates, hubcaps, and other trim.

The practice of disguising Plymouth bodies as other makes was not a new idea to the corporation. The first such conversion took place during the depression year of 1932, when the Plymouth PB series was converted to become the export-only Dodge DM. The reason behind the conversions was simple enough—to provide overseas dealers with a less-expensive product to sell. Dodge had a well-established reputation overseas and the conversion of the PB Plymouth gave Dodge a less-expensive four-cylinder car to sell, opening up markets where either Plymouth dealers did not exist, or where the Plymouth name was not as well known.

In its infancy, Chrysler thought it best to hide the Plymouth mechanicals—frame, four cylinder engine, etc.—underneath a Dodge body. By 1933 the conversions took on a new twist; realizing it would be less costly to use the Plymouth body as well as chassis and drivetrain, the only changes necessary would be to the front sheet metal, fitting a grille that looked like the full-size Dodge to the Plymouth sheet metal. This in many cases required tooling a similar but not altogether identical grille different from the "senior" cars because of the size differences between the smaller Plymouths and larger Dodges.

DeSoto conversions didn't become part of the corporation offerings until model year 1937. Under the corporate structure, all car lines were assigned engineering codes for identification. Plymouths were all "P" series, Chryslers were "C" series, and

The 1947 DeSoto Diplomat was based on the P15 Plymouth. In DeSoto trim the car was known as the SP15 series. Over 9,000 conversions took place between 1946 and 1948. *Carlos Heiligmann*

Dodges were "D" series. Because of the duplication of the first letter in the car name, DeSotos became the "S" series. In the case of the conversion cars, the "junior" DeSotos were coded "SP."

Early DeSoto SP Models

For 1937 and 1938, the DeSoto conversions were built only on the price-leader Plymouth P3 "Business" and P5 "Roadking" chassis. It would appear all regular Plymouth body styles were offered as SP DeSoto conversions. SP DeSoto serial numbers were not altered from those used by Plymouth. (For reasons unknown, Dodge conversions were assigned their own serial number sequences, however.) By 1939, both the P7 Roadking and P8 Deluxe Plymouths were converted to DeSotos, and were

All Plymouth models were offered as DeSoto conversions, even the convertible coupe. Conversions called for a special DeSoto-like grille, which often was not the same as regular production DeSotos. *Roadmaster*

labeled as the SP7 and SP8. Catalog illustrations show even the four-door convertible sedan available. Whether any were actually built remains a mystery.

Conversions continued up to World War II and resumed again after the war, when 9,612 P15 Plymouths were converted to SP15 DeSotos in both Deluxe and Special Deluxe trim, the only early years for which actual conversion production figures are known.

From 1949 through 1954 conversion production figures were combined with Dodge conversions, and all cars, whether sold as Dodge or DeSoto, were counted as Plymouths in the corporation's year-end figures.

With introduction of the "second series" '49 Plymouths, the SP DeSoto was offered in three distinct series: SP17 Diplomat on the 111-inch wheelbase chassis; SP18 Diplomat Deluxe; and SP18 Diplomat Custom on the 118-1/2-inch wheelbase chassis, offering all of the same body styles as the parent Plymouth. The Diplomat nameplate would be used on conversions through the 1961 model year, and even later by Dodge on a domestic series of cars.

Little is known about the pricing structure of these "junior" DeSotos except for model year 1952. U.S. Government Office of Price Stabilization records authorized Chrysler Corporation to price the DeSoto conversion $35.23 above the price of the Plymouth model on which it was based. (Dodge conversions were priced $20.28 higher.) Unlike the senior cars, SP DeSotos did not get V-8 power until Plymouth began offering V-8s in 1955, nor did they offer automatic transmissions, or overdrive, any sooner than did Plymouth, although these items were offered earlier on the "senior" DeSotos.

SP DeSotos began to look more like real DeSotos with the 1957 models. This became a reality, not to make it easier for the corporation to convert Plymouths to DeSotos, but because of another corporate decision that all station wagons would share the same body, whether it be DeSoto, Chrysler, Plymouth, or Dodge. Although each would carry its own make's identifying front clip, all would have to mate readily to the same body. With this accomplished, it was now possible to mate "real"

Similar yet different describes the 1951 DeSoto Diplomat when compared to a regular 1951 Plymouth Cranbrook. *John Goldsmith*

DeSoto sheet metal to the Plymouth body shell. Such would not be the case, however, as the SP DeSoto used front sheet metal from the Firesweep series, which in reality was a Dodge front clip modified to resemble the senior Firedome and Fireflites!

Production figures for the 1957 SP DeSoto show a total of 4,572 conversions built. This total dropped to 3,250 for 1958, the majority of both years being sold as six-cylinder cars. Nineteen fifty-nine production figures dropped to 2,364 conversions with the six edging out V-8s by about 250 units.

Nineteen fifty-nine marked the last year Plymouth would provide bodies for the SP series DeSotos, this time using actual DeSoto sheet metal.

Nineteen fifty-nine would also be the only year a DeSoto Diplomat Adventurer would be offered as well.

Nineteen sixty DeSoto Diplomats would be based on the new Dodge Dart. In this case, the corporation made no attempt to disguise the Dodge to look like a DeSoto. Outside of DeSoto nameplates and DeSoto-like swept-spear body side chrome, the car was pure Dodge.

Even though the senior DeSotos disappeared in the fall of 1960 after only a few '61 models had

been built, the DeSoto Diplomat lived on, again as a name change-only Dodge Dart. While no production figures have been found for the 1961 conversions, it is altogether possible "fake" DeSotos outnumbered the real things.

With the demise of the real DeSoto came an end to the DeSoto conversions as well. Plymouth got to play a unique role as the source for most of these unique conversions. During its lifetime Plymouths were sold not only as Dodges and DeSotos, in England they were sold as Chryslers, too!

The name game didn't stop here, however. The 1934 DeSoto SE and 1935 SG were sold in England as the Chrysler Croydon, and the '36 and '37 DeSotos were sold as the Chrysler Richmond. In an even stranger turn of events, the real 1939 Chrysler was sold as a Dodge!

DeSoto Trucks

Relatively unknown was Chrysler Corporation's use of the DeSoto name on commercial vehicles in export markets around the world. Reasoning behind this move can only be surmised at this point, considering the corporation also built and sold a line of commercial vehicles under the Fargo

The DeSoto Diplomat convertible for 1956 featured a fine mesh grille. *David Allen*

By 1960, Plymouth would be replaced as the source for DeSoto conversions by Dodge. Little effort outside of nameplates and side trim would be made to disguise the Dodge body. *Collectible Automobile Magazine*

Never seen in the United States was the DeSoto truck. Built only for export markets, the DeSoto (like the Canadian Fargo) was based on Dodge trucks. Only the grille and nameplates differed. *Don Bunn*

nameplate. Fargos were commonly seen in Canada and in fact, Chrysler's Windsor, Ontario, factories built them in ranges from half-ton pickups to three-, four-, and five-ton models. Fargos were also built in the United States, but all were shipped overseas. Why a third line of trucks under the DeSoto banner is a mystery.

Export records show the DeSoto name first being used on commercial vehicles beginning in September of 1938, presumably as 1939 models. Models ranged from the DC1 116-inch wheelbase half-ton pickup, up to the DC6-20 205-inch wheelbase two-ton truck. By the next year, the line had been expanded to include trucks with a three-ton rating. In all, the '39 DeSoto truck came in 17 different ratings, climbing to 25 ratings for 1940.

Like the Fargo, DeSoto trucks used Dodge sheet metal and differed only in nameplates and ornamentation. DeSoto trucks were assigned the same serial number sequences as the parent Dodge trucks. (Fargo trucks, at least in the early years, had their own serial number sequences.) DeSoto truck production came to a halt during the war years, although a few models are recorded as having been built in 1944 and 1945.

After the war, a simplified method was devised to identify the trucks. All would carry the same serial number, whether they were badged Dodge, DeSoto, or Fargo, and each would be separately identified by the prefix code.

For example, a Dodge B series pickup was officially a B-1-B; the same truck in Fargo trim would be an F-1-B; and a DeSoto would be an S-1-B. No doubt this made things a lot easier for corporate record-keepers and the parts department. Exactly when the practice of converting Dodge trucks to DeSoto trucks is unclear. The Fargo line was continued after 1972 in Canada. Existing photographs show DeSoto trucks still being built as late as 1959.

Chapter 6

Plymouth Commercial Vehicles

Plymouth's first successful commercial vehicle was the PJ Commercial Sedan of 1935. Based on the flat-back sedan, the commercial sedan carried a third door at the rear of the body, with removable window blanks covering the rear side windows. *Jim Benjaminson*

1930-1931 30U
Commercial Sedan ★★★★★
1935-1941
Commerical Sedan ★★★★★
1939-1942
Roadking utility sedan ★★★★★

Between the years 1930 and 1942, Plymouth built a confusing array of commercial vehicles, utilizing both passenger car and truck chassis. Regardless of the platform on which they were built, their production figures were never large and these commercial offerings, due to their low initial production, have gone virtually unnoticed in the hobby today. Throughout their production runs, Plymouth Commercial Cars, like the Canadian-based and for-export Fargo, would be a companion marque based on the mechanicals and sheet metal of the Dodge truck line.

Plymouth's first "Commercial Car" arrived in 1937 in Express (pickup) or cab and chassis form. This would be its best sales year. *Jim Benjaminson*

Also built on the truck chassis for 1937 was the panel delivery. *Don Hermany*

Passenger Car Chassis

For the sake of clarity, we will examine the passenger car-based commercial offerings first. Plymouth's first entry into this market came with the 30U models, built in 1930-31. Called the "Commercial Sedan," it was little more than a two-door sedan with a third door added at the rear of the body. The rear quarter-windows were blanked out with removable panels (these panels usually carried the name of the business).

The idea behind the Commercial Sedan was to serve two purposes for the small businessman who could afford only one vehicle. During the week, it could serve as his delivery truck, but on the weekend, with the window panels removed, and the optional rear seat in place, it could serve as the family car. As a passenger car-styled vehicle, even while in the commercial mode, it could travel in restricted areas where true commercial vehicles were prohibited. Despite the obvious advantages, it met with little sales success as only 80 were built. At $750 (later reduced to $675) it was considerably more expensive than the $565 two-door sedan on which it was based, which may account for its low sales volume.

The Commercial Sedan did not reappear until 1935. Again it was based on the lowest priced two-door sedan, with a third door cut into the rear of the body. Although 1935 bodies were of all-steel construction, the framing for the rear door was done with wood. Again, the rear seat was optional for those wanting to convert from commercial to personal use, with snap-in window blanks used to advertise the name of the business. With the window blanks removed, the rear quarter-windows could be rolled down like those on regular sedans.

Built by Briggs, the $635 Commercial Sedan (body code number 651-B), was priced $100 higher than the regular PJ Business two-door sedan (body code 651) on which it was based. Sales of 1,142 such models no doubt reflected this modest price difference.

For 1936 Plymouth saw fit to build the Commercial Sedan with its own special body rather than from convert two-door sedans. Based on the P1 "Business" passenger car chassis, prices were reduced $20 over the previous year as sales climbed to a record 3,527 vehicles.

The quarter-window panels were now permanent and no rear seats were offered to even attempt converting this delivery sedan to passenger-car use. Like the 1935 version, there was a single door at the rear of the body with the spare tire carried in the right front fender.

A major change occurred with the 1937 Commercial Sedans (and will be covered more in depth

The wood body Westchester Suburban station wagon was built on the Plymouth commercial car chassis for only one year, 1937. *Paul Swett*

in the Commercial Car section of this chapter) when it was decided to build this model, as well as the wood body station wagon on the truck chassis. The only "commercial" vehicles on the passenger-car chassis in 1937 were the ambulance/hearse conversion and pickup-box options. (Although based on passenger-car chassis in previous years, station wagons had always been considered by the factory as "commercial" vehicles.)

For 1938 the sedan delivery, or panel delivery as Plymouth preferred to call it, remained on the commercial chassis, with the wood body station wagon returning to the passenger-car chassis.

Plymouth Commercial Cars for 1939 were built on a new, truck-type 116-inch-wheelbase chassis, which may explain why the panel delivery was once again reverted to the passenger-car chassis. Designed to match the passenger car, the panel delivery, utility sedan, and station wagon carried the spare tire in a side-mount fenderwell.

The panel delivery still had its own special body, only now with two rear doors. Split vertically, each door contained a retractable window, with flush-mounted inside handles. Joining the line-up this year was a new "Utility Sedan," which, like the commercial sedans of 1930 and 1935, was a converted two-door passenger car built without a rear seat. The partition between the passenger compartment and truck was eliminated, as was done for the ambulance conversions. Below the windows, paneling replaced upholstery while the floor was

Hit by the recession of 1938, Plymouth pickup sales fell to their lowest level. While pickups looked like the passenger cars, no sheet metal or trim interchanged between the two. *Jim Benjaminson*

covered with full-length rubber mat. Unlike the panel delivery, which came with only a driver's bucket seat (passenger side optional), the Utility Sedan was shipped with two bucket seats. An optional screened partition with locking gate was offered to separate the driver from the load compartment of the Utility Sedan. Only 341 of the $685 Utility Sedans were sold, in comparison to 2,270 panel deliveries, which commanded a $715 price tag.

Plymouth's 1940 passenger-based "commercial" offerings included the Utility Sedan and panel delivery on the P9 Roadking chassis. Styling followed that of the passenger cars, with the Utility Sedan being a stripped two-door sedan, while the panel delivery again had its own special body. The panel delivery's most obvious change from 1939 was placement of the spare tire in a special well on the right side of the body, in front of the rear fender. Utility Sedan production was up slightly, to 589 units at a price of $699, while 2,889 panel deliveries were built despite a $5 price increase to $720.

These same two passenger-based body styles were offered again in 1941. At $739 production of the

Utility Sedan fell to 468 units. Sedan delivery production rose slightly, to 3,200 units, as did the price to $745. The panel delivery was discontinued for 1942, although the limited-production Utility Sedan was still available. Also missing from the 1942 line-up was the ambulance conversion. Nineteen forty-two would prove to be the last year for any passenger-based Plymouth commercial vehicles. Only 82 1942 Utility Sedan units were built. At $842, the Utility Sedan was now priced $8 under the price of the P14S Deluxe two-door sedan on which it was based.

1937 PT50
pickup and station wagon ★★★★★

The Commercial Car Chassis—1937 PT50

Production of the new Plymouth Commercial Car line began in December of 1936. Plymouth's first truck-chassis pickup was little more than a disguised Dodge pickup. All new for 1936, the Dodge was "updated" for 1937—it and the "new" '37 Plymouth pickups were virtually identical except for minor trim differences such as the grille and tailgate. Mechanically, the

Panel delivery bodies returned to the passenger car chassis in 1939. Only the station wagon, panel delivery, and utility sedan carried the spare tire in the front fender. *Joe Eberle*

Plymouth pickup used a Plymouth engine, coded series PT50 by the factory. (Dodge trucks were coded "T" series, and Plymouths thus became "PT," for Plymouth truck, to indicate their heritage.)

Built on a 116-inch wheelbase, ladder-type frame with five cross-members, the new Plymouth "Commercial Car" bore a strong family resemblance to the passenger cars. The resemblance was in looks only, as no sheet metal or trim interchanged between the 1937 passenger car and 1937 truck with the exception of front bumper, hubcaps, and dash knobs. Unlike Dodge, which offered a complete range of models, Plymouth commercial cars were built in just four versions: the Express (pickup), cab and chassis (which included full-length running boards and rear fenders), panel delivery, and station wagon. A "flat face cowl" could also be ordered for those wanting to mount their own special body.

Attractively styled, the PT50 series included safety glass in all windows, chrome front bumper (rear bumper optional; panel deliveries had a rear bumper as standard equipment), and spare tire mounted in the right front fender. A left fender well was available at extra cost. The box was 6 feet long and 47 1/2-inches wide, of all-steel construction, including the floors.

Under the hood sat a familiar valve-in-block six displacing 201 ci, the same as all Plymouth passenger cars from 1934 through 1941. The truck engine was rated at 70 horsepower at 3,000 rpm, while 1937 passenger cars were rated at 82 horsepower.

The panel delivery, which up to this time had been on the passenger-car chassis, was now part of the commercial chassis line. Priced $50 higher than 1936, the panel delivery found 3,256 buyers.

Some 10,709 pickups, 158 cab and chassis, 602 station wagons, and 3,256 panel deliveries found buyers, making 1937 the best sales year Plymouth Commercial Cars would see.

1938 PT57
pickup ★★★★★

Plymouth pickups received all new bodies for 1939. The wheelbase remained the same although the cab and box were enlarged. *Pete Brophy*

1938 PT57

Plymouth's 1938 commercial cars were so little changed, except for minor appearance items, that production lines were shut down for less than a day for model-year changeover. The grille was shorter and wider, matching changes made to the passenger car line for 1938. Again, there was no interchange of either trim or sheet metal pieces between the passenger and commercial car lines. The Suburban Westchester wagon was reverted back to the passenger-car chassis.

No mechanical changes were made with the exception of an optional four-speed transmission with power take-off capability.

Assembly of the PT57 models came to a halt August 17, 1938, with only 4,620 pickups and 95 cab and chassis having been assembled.

1939 PT81
pickup ★★★★★

1939 PT81

When Plymouth unveiled its new commercial car models for 1939, things had definitely changed. Gone was the "passenger car" look. The new pickups had a decidedly truck-like appearance to them. Literally all new from the ground up, the Plymouth commercial car was still a clone of the Dodge; the frame was still of the ladder type, the wheelbase remained at 116-inches but from there, similarities ended.

The new cab was moved forward, as was the engine, to provide for a 6 1/2-inch longer cargo bed without drastically increasing the outward dimensions of the vehicle. The cab had a more modern look, with a ship's prow front end, headlamps mounted on the fender catwalks, and a two-piece vee'd windshield among the more noticeable changes. The cab was claimed to be the biggest offered by the "Big Three" and was advertised as a true "three man cab."

The box was increased in size, measuring 78-1/8 inches long by 48-1/4 inches wide. Departing from the all-steel boxes used in 1937-1938, the new box had a wooden floor, made up of 13/16-inch-thick planking protected by steel skid strips.

Other exterior changes included more massive fenders, each featuring four prominent "speed lines," and the elimination of fender-mounted spare tires; the spare now rode in a special carrier under the box at the rear of the frame. (Some 1940 PT105 trucks are known to have the spare tire mounted above the running board forward of the right rear fender. These trucks have a special indent in the rear fender to allow this type of mount, with the mounting arm attached to the frame passing through an opening in the running board splash aprons. These trucks also have the gasoline tank mounted at the rear of the frame, instead of under the seat. The filler neck on these trucks is located on the left rear fender instead of the cab sidewall. It is believed trucks equipped this way may have been military issue.)

The 1940 Plymouth pickup gained sealed-beam headlamps like the passenger car. Three chrome strips on the radiator shell and small parking lamps atop the headlamps distinguished the 1940 from the 1939. An unusual feature of this pickup is the rear-mounted spare tire, indicating this truck was originally shipped to the military. *Jim Benjaminson*

Plymouth's last sedan delivery was built in 1941 on the P11 passenger car chassis. *Elwood Hummer*

Outside of the sailing ship hood ornament, headlamp rings, and hubcaps, no bright metal trim appeared on the new models. Even the front bumpers, which had been chrome-plated on the 1937-38 pickups, were painted black or aluminum. The windshield frame, headlamps, and entire radiator shell was available chrome-plated at additional cost, but few were so equipped.

Mechanically, the PT81 series differed little from its predecessors. The engine remained a 70-horsepower, 201-ci six, with three-speed manual transmission standard and four-speed optional.

1940 PT105
pickup ★★★★★

1940 PT105

The 1940 series PT105 saw only minor appearance changes. New for the year was the addition of sealed-beam headlamps. With the addition of the sealed-beam it was no longer possible to mount the parking lamp in the headlamp itself, so a rather odd-looking "pod" was added to the top of the headlamp bucket. The upper grille shell was livened up by the addition of three horizontal stainless strips. Horsepower was increased from 70 to 79, although bore and stroke figures remained the same as previous years. Despite a $10 price hike, sales of the PT105 series increased slightly with sales of 6,879 pickups and 174 cab and chassis units.

1941 PT125
pickup ★★★★★

1941 PT125

Minor changes marked the 1941 Plymouth commercial cars, most for the better, although the most obvious change—moving the headlamps from the catwalk to the crown of the fender—was a change for the worst in the opinion of many.

Without making any changes to the basic radiator sheet metal, designers fashioned a chrome overlay patterned after the 1941 passenger-car grille. Starting at the leading edge where the hood meets the radiator shell, a stainless strip ran forward to converge at the front of the radiator, from there plunging down in two vertical strips to the bottom of the grille shell. In the center was a large Plymouth sailing ship emblem. On either side of this, on the left and right outer grille panels, were five horizontal stainless strips, similar to the strips used on the 1939 and 1940 Plymouth passenger cars. Paint stripes accented the bars between the stainless strips. The front bumper, while still painted, had a pronounced vee in the center.

"Plymouth" nameplates, which had graced the sides of the upper radiator shell on the PT81 and PT105, were centered on the hood panels. The awkward pod-shaped parking lamps atop the headlamp shells were replaced by attractive bullet-shaped lamps mounted on the cowl, but it was the outward movement of the headlamps that gave the truck its startling new appearance.

Under the hood, engine horsepower increased to 82 (as opposed to 79 in 1940), with the engine mated to a new three-speed synchro-shift

The last Plymouth pickups were built in 1941. Noticeable changes included a fancier grille, headlamps moved to the crown of the fenders, and a vee'd front bumper. *Willard Stein*

transmission. Also new for the year were "stepped" brake cylinders with different-size pistons in the same cylinder. The front pistons measured 1 1/4-inches, actuating the front brake shoes, with 1 3/8-inch pistons actuating the rear shoes. This difference in size—or stepping—was claimed to exert equal pressure of both shoes against the brake drum.

PT125 sales decreased to the lowest level since recession year of 1938 (this at a time when industry sales were up), caused perhaps by the $40 price increase for 1941. Sales of 6,073 pickups and 196 cab and chassis units mattered little. As production wound down on the PT125 models, so too did an era at Plymouth. With the dawn of the 1942 models, the commercial car line was quietly dropped. The reasons why were never publicly discussed. No doubt, lower-than-expected sales volume was a factor. A plausible explanation probably lies in commitments made to the military in supplying vehicles for our allies leading up to our involvement in the war effort. Plymouth truck production halted prior to our entry into the war, but within months, all civilian truck production came to a halt

(on April 30, 1942) as Chrysler Corporation helped turn Detroit into the "Arsenal of Democracy."

Historically, it is interesting to question whether the addition of a Plymouth commercial line helped or hurt corporate truck sales. Studying sales figures provided by the Automobile Manufacturers Association, Dodge garnered only 4.5 percent of new truck sales in 1932. The dominant truck manufacturers then, as now, were Ford and Chevrolet. For 1933 and 1934, Dodge took 11.6 percent of the market, climbing slightly, to 11.7 percent in 1935. The all-new Dodge line for 1936 raised the sales figures to 13.4 percent of the market.

With the introduction of the Plymouth truck in 1937, Dodge sales fell to 11.1 percent of the market, with Plymouth picking up 2.1 percent for a corporate total of 13.2 percent. (No figures are given for Fargo, although it is assumed they were counted as Dodges.)

During the recession year of 1938, as other sales fell dramatically, Dodge maintained a 9.4 percent market penetration while Plymouth fell to just .9 percent for a corporate total of 10.3 percent. Nineteen thirty-nine sales for Dodge came to 10.6 percent, plus 1.4 percent for Plymouth. While the 1940 Dodge trucks posted a gain to 13 percent, Plymouth remained nearly static at 1.7 percent, for a 14.7 percent corporate total, the best prewar performance Dodge would see, although the 1941 corporate total slipped only .1 percent to 14.6 percent. This gain came solely through Dodge sales, as Plymouth captured only .5 percent of the market, its poorest showing ever.

It should be remembered that Plymouth offered only a single line of light-duty trucks while Dodge and all the others offered a full line of light-, medium-, and heavy-duty trucks. All in all, the addition of Plymouth as a companion did little to increase corporate penetration of the new-truck market. Although built and marketed at little cost, the results may not have been worth the effort.

Top Ten List

Given the opportunity to pick your favorite Plymouth or DeSoto, what would your choices be? This was the question asked by Lanny Knutson, editor of the *Plymouth Bulletin*, published by the Plymouth Owners Club on the occasion of the club's 30th Anniversary in 1987.

Knutson asked Bulletin readers to vote—and comment—on the Plymouths they felt were the best-looking Plymouths ever built. Expanding on the subject, Knutson also asked readers to vote for the "Worst Five" cars as well.

D. David Duricy, Jr., co-editor of the National DeSoto Club's *DeSoto Adventures* asked that club's membership the same question in 1996. Duricy's survey, in addition to asking for the best and worst cars, asked readers to vote for the DeSoto that contributed most to the advancement of the automobile—and for the most underrated DeSoto. Ironically, the car voted number one in contributing to the advancement of the automobile—the 1934 Airflow DeSoto—was also the number one underrated DeSoto!

DeSoto Club members were also asked if they thought Chrysler Corporation should revive the DeSoto nameplate, a subject that was voted down by the narrowest of margins, 51 percent to 49 percent. Perhaps most interesting of the entire survey was the reader loyalty poll, asking what type of car, 1985 or later, they currently drive. Even though the last DeSoto came off the assembly line 36 years ago, fully 50 percent indicated they still drove a Chrysler product.

Here are the Top Ten Plymouths and DeSotos as voted by members of both organizations. It is interesting to note the top six spots in the DeSoto survey covered the final six years of DeSoto's life, where only three Plymouths of this era made the top ten list, none with a ranking higher than fifth.

Ranking	Plymouth	DeSoto
1.	1934	1957
2.	1946-48 (*)	1956
3.	1932 (***)	1955
4.	1941	1959
5.	1955	1960
6.	1956	1958
7.	1949	1942
8.	1933	1937
9.	1957	1946 (**)
10.	1964	1941

(*) All three years were combined in the Plymouth Club survey
(**) 1946, 1947, and 1948 were counted separately in the DeSoto Club survey
(***) PB series only

And here are the "Worst Five," as voted by members of these organizations.

Ranking	Plymouth	DeSoto
1.	1961	1961
2.	1960	1934
3.	1962	1951
4.	1938	1953
5.	1939	1949

In both surveys, the 1961 models ran away with top honors for the ugliest cars built by both marques. In the case of Plymouth, the cars of the early 1960s slid solidly into second and third spots. Perhaps it's just as well there was no 1962 DeSoto.

Club Directory

Readers wanting information about various Plymouth, DeSoto, and Chrysler organizations can write to them at the following addresses.

Plymouth Owners Club, Inc.
PO Box 416
Cavalier, ND 58220-0416
Phone: 701-549-3746
FAX: 701-549-3744

National DeSoto Club, Inc.
1521 Van Cleave Road NW
Albuquerque, NM 87107

Barracuda-Cuda Owners Club
RD 2, 26 Strathmore Road
Freehold, NJ 07728

National Chrysler Products Club, Inc.
14 Princeton Drive
New Providence, NJ 07974-1220

Slant Six Club of America
PO Box 4414
Salem, OR 97302

W P C Club, Inc.
PO Box 3504
Kalamazoo, MI 49003-3504

Dodge Brothers Club
259 East Main Street
Bath, PA 18014
215-837-7742

Index